TOP STOCKS 2005

11th YEAR of PUBLICATION

Martin Roth

Wrightbooks

The author and publisher would like to thank Aspect Huntley for permission to include the five-year shareholder return figures, and Alan Hull (author of *Active Investing*) for supplying the five-year share price graphs (www.alanhull.com).

This 11th edition first published 2004 by Wrightbooks
an imprint of John Wiley & Sons Australia, Ltd
33 Park Road, Milton, Qld 4064

Offices also in Sydney and Melbourne

First edition published as *Top Stocks* by Wrightbooks in 1995.
New edition published annually.

Typeset in 11/12 pt Berkeley LT

ISBN: 0 731402057

Cover design by Rob Cowpe

Printed in Australia by McPherson's Printing Group

10 9 8 7 6 5 4 3 2 1

Disclaimer

The material in this publication is of the nature of general comment only, and neither purports nor intends to be advice. Readers should not act on the basis of any matter in this publication without considering (and if appropriate taking) professional advice with due regard to their own particular circumstances. The author and publisher expressly disclaim all and any liability to any person, whether a purchaser of this publication or not, in respect of anything and of the consequences of anything done or omitted to be done by any such person in reliance, whether in whole or part, upon the whole or any part of the contents of this publication.

Contents

CONTENTS (CONT'D)

PART II THE TABLES

APPENDIX

PREFACE

This 11th edition of *Top Stocks* offers more to sharemarket investors than ever before:

- Fully 115 companies have met the tough criteria for entry to the book, the most ever. The previous highest was *Top Stocks 2000*, with 113 companies. The last edition of the book, *Top Stocks 2004*, had just 91.
- At a time when the resources sector is booming, there are more resource stocks in the book than ever before. Traditionally, *Top Stocks* has never included many resources companies, as so few are able to make a profit and pay a dividend for five consecutive years, and these are requirements for inclusion in the book. Admittedly, there are only nine resource companies in *Top Stocks 2005*, but that's the highest number ever.
- For the first time, there is a cluster of high-tech companies — only four of them, but in most editions of the book there have been none. I used to think it a weakness of *Top Stocks* that it seldom contained high-tech companies — because so few could make a profit and pay a dividend for five consecutive years — but after the dot-com 'meltdown' of 2000 I realised it was a strength.
- For the first time, this edition of *Top Stocks* contains an appendix, 'Top of the stocks', listing those superior companies in the book that have achieved five-year records of an average return on equity figure of more than 15% and annual average growth in earnings per share of at least 15%.

WHO IS TOP STOCKS WRITTEN FOR?

Top Stocks is written for every investor who has ever wondered:

There are 1,500 companies on the stock exchange — where do I start?

These investors know that there are many excellent companies out there — companies that seem to prosper through good times and bad — but they are just not sure which ones they are, apart from some obvious names.

For whatever may be happening in the market, the fact remains that there are plenty of good, solid companies with excellent long-term records of regular dividends and capital growth. They may not double or triple in price within the space of months. But so long as a company's business continues to flourish its shares should certainly come to represent good value.

This book is for investors seeking out these stocks.

It is not a how-to book. It does not give step-by-step instructions to 'winning' on the stock market. Rather, it is an independent and objective evaluation of leading companies, based on rigid criteria, with the intention of yielding a large selection of stocks that can become the starting point for investors wishing to do their own research.

A large amount of information is presented on each company, and another key feature of the book is that the data is presented in a common format, to allow readers to make easy comparisons between companies.

It is necessarily a conservative book. All stocks must have been listed for five years even to be considered for inclusion (which is why earlier editions missed the dot-com boom entirely). It is especially suited for those seeking out value stocks for longer term investment.

Yet, perhaps ironically, the book is also increasingly being used by short-term traders seeking a good selection of financially sound and reliable companies whose shares they can trade.

In addition, there are many regular readers who buy the book each year, and to them in particular I express my thanks.

What are the entry criteria?

The criteria for inclusion in *Top Stocks* are strict:

- All companies must be included in the All Ordinaries Index, which comprises Australia's 500 largest stocks (out of approximately 1,500). The reason for excluding smaller companies is that there is often little investor information available on many of them and some are so thinly traded as to be almost illiquid. In fact, the 500 All Ordinaries companies comprise, by market capitalisation, around 98% of the entire market.
- It was necessary that all companies be publicly listed since at least the end of 1999, and have a five-year record of profits and dividend payouts. An exception is companies de-merged from another company in the All Ordinaries Index. These require just a two-year record of profits and dividend payouts. The only such company in this edition is Origin Energy, formerly part of Boral.
- All companies were required to post a return-on-equity ratio of at least 9% in their latest financial year.
- No company should have a debt-to-equity ratio of more than 75%.
- It must be stressed that share price performance is NOT one of the criteria for inclusion in this book. The purpose is to select companies with good profits and a strong balance sheet. These may not offer the spectacular share-price returns of a biotech start-up, but they should also present far less risk. To use an Olympics analogy, the stocks in this book

are more like marathon runners than sprinters. They should last the distance, providing solid — if un-flashy — performance over the long term.

- There are several notable exclusions. Investment trusts like Australian Foundation Investment Company are out, as these mainly buy other shares or investments. Also omitted are property trusts.
- A further exclusion is the foreign stocks listed on the Australian Stock Exchange. There is sometimes a lack of information available about such companies. In addition, their stock prices tend to move on events and trends in their home countries, making it difficult at times for local investors to follow them.

Changes to this edition

Such has been the strength of the Australian economy that most of the corporations in this book recorded rising profits in their latest financial reporting, and only 13 companies from *Top Stocks 2004* have been excluded from the present edition. Three of these — Casinos Austria, Freedom Group and Peter Lehmann Wines — are being privatised, and one — Westfield Holdings — has merged with its sister companies and is now essentially a property trust.

Three companies from *Top Stocks 2004* were excluded because they had debt-to-equity ratios that rose higher than 75%. They were:

- CMI
- Tabcorp Holdings
- Telstra

And the following six companies had return-on-equity figures that fell below 9%:

- Australian Pharmaceutical Industries
- Coal & Allied Industries
- OPSM Group
- PaperlinX
- Ridley Corporation
- Spotless Group

There are 37 new companies in this book (though some of them have appeared in earlier editions of the book, but were not in *Top Stocks 2004*), which is far more than in any previous edition. These companies are:

- Adcorp Australia
- AJ Lucas Group
- Auspine
- Brazin
- Cabcharge Australia
- Candle Australia

- Cedar Woods Properties
- Cellnet Group
- Coffey International
- Colorado Group
- Computershare
- Corporate Express
- Coventry Group
- Equigold
- Fantastic Holdings
- Foodland Associated
- Great Southern Plantations
- Gunns
- Housewares International
- Integrated Group
- ION
- John Fairfax Holdings
- Macquarie Goodman Management
- Orica
- OrotonGroup
- Plaspak Group
- Portman
- Primary Health Care
- Programmed Maintenance Services
- Publishing & Broadcasting
- Schaffer Corporation
- Sigma Company
- Tasmanian Perpetual Trustees
- Technology One
- Troy Resources
- Volante Group
- West Australian Newspapers Holdings.

Companies in every edition of Top Stocks

The 13 companies listed below have appeared in every edition of *Top Stocks*:

- ANZ
- Commonwealth Bank of Australia
- CSR
- Harvey Norman
- Hills Industries
- Incitec Pivot (formerly just Incitec)
- National Australia Bank
- QBE Insurance
- Santos
- Suncorp-Metway
- Wesfarmers
- Westpac Banking
- Woolworths.

Changes in Australian Accounting Standards

From 2005, all companies will have to prepare their financial reports in accordance with new international financial reporting standards, as adopted by the Australian Accounting Standards Board (AASB).

Among the changes, companies will have to alter the manner in which they account for property values, intangibles, goodwill and some other elements of their finances. It is still unclear — even at this late stage — exactly how this will affect the final accounts. But it is generally agreed that it could make company accounts more volatile than at present, with the possibility of some one-off profit shocks.

However, that is an issue to be confronted by *Top Stocks 2006*. In the meantime, please enjoy *Top Stocks 2005*. I hope it will serve you well.

Martin Roth
Melbourne
September 2004

INTRODUCTION

The 115 companies in this book have been placed as much as possible into a common format, for ease of comparison. Please study the following explanations in order to get as much as possible from the large amount of data. Each page begins with a brief introduction to the company and its activities. Then follow the highlights of its latest business results. For the majority of the companies these are their June 2004 results, which were issued during July and August 2004. Finally there is a section on the outlook for the company, sometimes including comment on the performance of the shares.

TABLES

The tables have been made as concise as possible, though they repay careful study, as they contain large amounts of information. Note that the tables for the banks have been arranged a little differently from the others; details of these are later in this Introduction.

At the top of each page is a small table with the following data.

SHARE PRICE

This is the closing price on 18 August 2004. Also included are the 12-month high and low prices, as of the same date.

MARKET CAPITLISATION

This is the size of the company, as determined by the stock market. It is the share price (again, as of 18 August 2004) multiplied by the number of shares in issue. All companies in this book must be in the All Ordinaries Index, which comprises Australia's 500 largest stocks, as measured by market capitalisation.

PRICE-TO NET-TANGIBLE-ASSETS-PER-SHARE RATIO

The NTA-per-share figure expresses the worth of a company's net tangible assets — that is, its assets minus its liabilities and intangible assets — for each share of the company. The price-to-NTA-per-share ratio relates this figure to the share price.

A ratio of one means that the company is valued exactly according to the value of its assets. A ratio below one suggests that the shares are a bargain, though usually there is a good reason for this. Profits are more important than assets.

Three companies in this book, Computershare, John Fairfax Holdings and McPherson's, have a negative NTA-per-share figure — as a result of having intangible assets valued at more than their remaining net assets — and a price-to-NTA-per-share ratio cannot be calculated.

See Table M, in the second part of this book, for a little more detail on this ratio.

FIVE-YEAR SHARE PRICE RETURN

This is the total return you could have received from the stock in the five years to September 2004. It includes reinvested dividends, bonus stock, rights issues and capital gain from the stock's appreciation. It is expressed as a compounded annual rate of return. These figures have been supplied by Aspect Huntley.

PRICE-EARNING RATIO (PER)

The PER is one of the most popular measures of whether a share is cheap or expensive. It is calculated by dividing the share price — in this case the closing price for 18 August 2004 — by the EPS figure. Obviously the share price is continually changing, so the PER figures in this book are for guidance only. Many newspapers publish each morning the latest PER for every stock.

DIVIDEND YIELD

This is the latest full-year dividend expressed as a percentage of the share price. Like the PER, it changes as the share price moves. It is a useful figure, especially for investors who are buying shares for income, as it allows you to compare this income with alternative investments, such as a bank term deposit or a bond fund.

SECTOR COMPARISONS

It is often useful to compare a company's price-earnings ratio and its dividend yield with those of its sector. Often the stocks in a sector move together. Thus, if a particular stock is lagging the averages, this may — depending on the reasons — be a buying opportunity.

Figures used in this book are those of the S&P/ASX sectors, again as of 18 August, 2004.

SHARE PRICE CHART

Also at the top of each page is a five-year share price chart, provided by Alan Hull. Please note that the charts show the share price to 7 September 2004, whereas the share price listed in the adjacent table is for 18 August 2004.

Website

Most public companies now have websites, and the website addresses of companies in this book are placed under the share-price chart.

Be aware that some sites are little more than corporate brochures for the company, with glossy photos and beat-up prose. A few are wildly out of date. But increasingly, public companies are using the internet as a means of providing timely data to shareholders.

Thus, you may now find all the latest ASX company announcements — often placed on the site simultaneously to their ASX release — along with media releases and even, sometimes, speeches and presentations to stock market analysts.

If you are following a particular company it is highly recommended that you become familiar with that company's website.

Main tables

In the main tables you will find the following.

Revenues

These are the company's revenues from its business activities, generally the sale of products or services. It does not usually include additional income from such sources as investments, bank interest or the sale of assets. If the information is available, the revenues figure has been broken down into the major product areas.

Earnings before interest and taxation

Earnings before interest and taxation (EBIT) is the firm's profit from its operations before the payment of interest and tax. This figure is often used by analysts examining a company. The reason is that some companies have borrowed extensively to finance their activities, while others have opted for alternative means. By expressing profits before interest payments it is possible to compare more precisely the performance of these companies. The net interest figure — interest payments minus interest receipts — has been used for this calculation.

EBIT margin

This is the company's EBIT expressed as a percentage of its revenues. It is a gauge of a company's efficiency. A high EBIT margin suggests that a company is achieving success in keeping its costs low.

Gross margin

The gross margin is the company's gross profit as a percentage of its sales. The gross profit is the amount left over after deducting from a company's sales figure its cost of sales: that is, its manufacturing costs or, for a retailer, the cost of purchasing the goods it sells. The cost of goods sold figure does not usually include marketing or administration costs. As there are different ways of calculating the cost of goods sold figure, this ratio is best used for year-to-year comparisons of a single company's efficiency, rather than in comparing one company with another. Not all companies present a cost of goods sold figure, so a gross margin ratio is not given for every stock in this book. The revenues for some companies include a mix of sales and services. Where a breakdown is possible, the gross profit figure will reflect sales only.

Operating profit before tax/profit after tax

The operating profit before tax figure is simply the EBIT figure minus net interest payments. The profit after tax figure is, of course, the company's profit after the payment of tax, and also after the deduction of minority interests. Minority interests are that part of a company's profit that is claimed by outside interests, usually the other shareholders in a subsidiary which is not fully owned by the company. Many companies do not have any minority interests, and for those that do it is generally a tiny figure.As much as possible, I have adjusted the profit figures to exclude non-recurring profits and losses, which are called significant items. It is for this reason that the profit figures in *Top Stocks* sometimes differ from those in the financial media or on financial websites, where profit figures normally include significant items.

The Significance of significant items

Significant items are those that have an abnormal impact on profits, even though they happen in the normal course of the company's operations. Examples are the profit from the sale of a business, or losses from a business restructuring, the write-down of property, an inventory write-down, a bad-debt loss or a write-off for research and development expenditure.

They were formerly called abnormals, and were part of the statement of financial performance. Now they are simply included among the notes to the statement.

Significant items are controversial. It is often a matter of subjective judgment as to what is included and what excluded. The relevant reporting standard states:

> *When a revenue or an expense from ordinary activities is of such a size, nature or incidence that its disclosure is relevant in explaining the financial performance of the entity for the reporting period, its nature and amount must be disclosed separately in the notes in the financial report.*

But, after analysing the accounts of hundreds of companies, while writing this book, it is clear that different companies use quite widely varying interpretations of what is significant.

Further, when they do report a significant item there is no consistency as to whether they use pre-tax figures or after-tax figures. Some report both, making it easy to adjust the profit figures in the tables in this book. But difficulties arise when only one figure — generally pre-tax — is given for significant items. A telephone call to the company usually elicits the other figure, but not always.

Fortunately, most companies do not report significant items. But investors should be aware of this issue.

Earnings per share

Earnings per share (EPS) is the after-tax profit divided by the number of shares. Because the profit figure is for a 12-month period the number of shares used is a weighted average of those on issue during the year. This number is provided by the company in its annual report and its results announcements.

Cash flow per share

The cash flow per share ratio tells — in theory — how much actual cash the company has generated from its operations.

In fact, the ratio in this book is not exactly a true measure of cash flow. It is simply the company's depreciation and amortisation figures for the year added to the after-tax profit, and then divided by a weighted average of the number of shares. Depreciation and amortisation are expenses that do not actually utilise cash, so can be added back to after-tax profit to give a kind of indication of the company's cash flow.

By contrast, a true cash flow — including such items as newly raised capital and money received from the sale of assets — would require quite complex calculations based on the company's statement of cash flows.

However, many analysts use the ratio as I present it, because it is easy to calculate, and it is certainly a useful guide to how much funding the company has available from its operations.

Dividend

The dividend figure is the total for the year, interim and final. It does not include special dividends. The level of franking is also provided.

Net tangible assets per share

The NTA per share figure tells the theoretical value of the company — per share — if all assets were sold and then all liabilities paid. It is very much a theoretical figure, as there is no guarantee that corporate assets are really worth the price put on them in the balance sheet. Intangible assets such as goodwill, newspaper mastheads and patent rights are excluded because of the difficulty in putting a sales price on them, and also because they may in fact not have much value if separated from the company.

As already noted, three companies in this book — Computershare, John Fairfax Holdings and McPherson's — have a negative NTA, due to the fact that their intangible assets are so great, and no figure can be listed for them.

Where a company's most recent financial results are the half-year figures, these are used to calculate this ratio.

Interest cover

The interest cover ratio indicates how many times a company could make its interest payments from its pre-tax profit. A rough rule of thumb says a ratio of at least three times is desirable. Below that and fast-rising interest rates could imperil profits. The ratio is derived by dividing the EBIT figure by net interest payments. Some fortunate companies have interest receipts that are higher than their interest payments, which turns the interest cover into a negative figure, and so it is not listed.

Return on equity

Return on equity (ROE) is the after-tax profit expressed as a percentage of the shareholders' equity. In theory, it is the amount that the company's managers have made for you — the shareholder — on your money. The shareholders' equity figure used is an average for the year.

Debt-to-equity ratio

This ratio is one of the best-known measures of a company's debt levels. It is total borrowings minus the company's cash holdings, expressed as a percentage of the shareholders' equity. Some companies have no debt at all, or their cash position is greater than their level of debt, which results in a negative ratio, so no figure is listed for them. Where a company's most recent financial results are the half-year figures, these are used to calculate this ratio.

Current ratio

The current ratio is simply the company's current assets divided by its current liabilities. Current assets are cash or assets that can, in theory, be converted quickly into cash. Current liabilities are normally those payable within a year. Thus, the current ratio measures the ability of a company to repay in a hurry its short-term debt, should the need arise. The surplus of current assets over current liabilities is referred to as the company's working capital.

Where a company's most recent financial results are the half-year figures, these are used to calculate this ratio.

Banks

The tables for the banks are somewhat different from those for most other companies. EBIT and debt-to-equity ratios have little relevance for them, as they have such high interest payments (to their customers). Other differences are examined below.

Operating income

Operating income is used instead of sales revenues. Operating income is the bank's net interest income — that is, its total interest income minus its interest expense — plus other income, such as bank fees, fund management fees and income from businesses such as corporate finance and insurance.

Net interest income

Banks borrow money — that is, they accept deposits from savers — and they lend it to businesses, home buyers and other borrowers. They charge the borrowers more than they pay those who deposit money with them, and the difference is known as net interest income.

Operating expenses

These are all the costs of running the bank. Banks have high operating expenses, and one of the keys to profit growth is cutting these expenses. Add the provision for doubtful debts to operating expenses, then deduct the total from operating income, and you get the pre-tax profit.

Non-interest income to total income

Banks have traditionally made most of their income from savers and from lending out money. But increasingly this is becoming a commodity business, with a growing number of entrants offering higher interest rates to savers and lower rates to borrowers. In response the big banks are working to diversify into new fields, and this ratio is an indication of their success.

Cost-to-income ratio

As noted, the banks have high costs — numerous branches, expensive computer systems, many staff, and so on — and they are all striving to reduce these. The cost-to-income ratio expresses their expenses as a percentage of their operating income, and is one of the ratios most often used as a gauge of efficiency. The lower the ratio drops the better.

Return on assets

Banks have enormous assets, in sharp contrast to, say, a high-tech start-up whose main physical assets may be little more than a set of computers. So the return on assets — the after-tax profit expressed as a percentage of the year's average total assets — is another measure of efficiency.

PART I

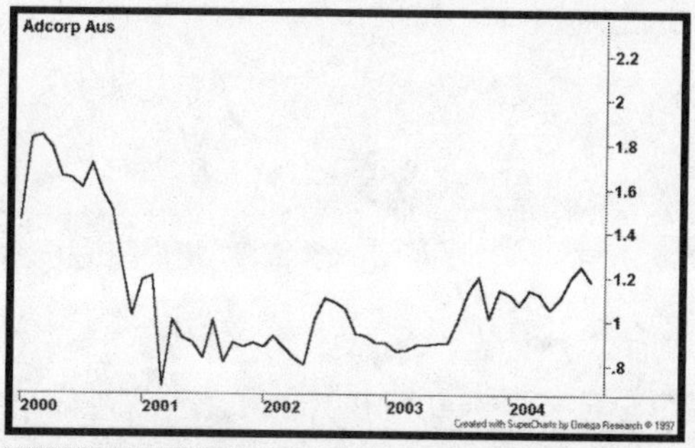

www.adcorp.com.au

Adcorp Australia Limited

Share price ($)	1.17	
12-month high ($)	1.22	
12-month low ($)	0.92	
Market capitalisation ($mn)	70.8	
Price-to-NTA-per-share ratio	7.8	
5-year share price return (% p.a.)	15.5	
Sector: Consumer discretionary	**Company**	**Sector**
Price-earnings ratio (times)	14.4	23.8
Dividend yield (%)	5.6	1.5

Sydney-based advertising agency services provider Adcorp has its origins in recruitment advertising. It has since grown by acquisition into a leading provider of a wide range of advertising and communications services. Recent acquisitions include Raisin & Lines Advertising, Green Advertising and Donald & Donald Advertising, and, in New Zealand, Lewis Advertising and Brema Advertising. The company's technology division is involved in website and database development services. Adcorp — which operates from 10 offices throughout Australia and New Zealand — has joined with News Corporation in the development of the CareerOne job recruitment website.

Latest business results (June 2004, full year)

The company experienced solid growth in revenues and profits, thanks in particular to its New Zealand operations. Domestic sales rose 15%, but domestic EBIT actually edged down. By contrast, New Zealand achieved a 32% revenues gain, with EBIT soaring to 42%. New Zealand business represents just 17% of company revenues, but 30% of profit. Domestically, Queensland was strong, and the company realised good growth for its real estate and motor vehicle advertising activities.

Outlook

Adcorp is working to restructure its operations with a management shake-out that includes redundancies and the hiring of new senior executives, particularly in the key markets of NSW and Victoria. It believes it can achieve restored margins and profit growth of at least 10% in the June 2005 year. It is also striving to diversify away from its dependence on recruitment advertising, which represents half of company revenues, with increasing emphasis on real estate (23% of total sales) and motor vehicle advertising (15%) as new streams of revenue. It has achieved good growth in the commercial real estate sector, and sees this as providing support in the event of a significant real estate downturn. It does, however, see continued growth in recruitment advertising, with early signs of staff shortages in some specialities, forcing employers to increase their advertising spending. Adcorp's recent growth has been organic. However, it is has little debt, and net cash holdings of nearly $10 million, and has expressed interest in further acquisitions that will add additional profitable revenue streams or provide competitive advantage.

AAU Year to 30 June	2003	2004
Revenues ($mn)	155.8	183.2
EBIT ($mn)	6.7	7.2
EBIT margin (%)	4.3	3.9
Gross margin (%)	20.5	18.4
Operating profit before tax ($mn)	6.9	7.5
Profit after tax ($mn)	4.4	4.9
Earnings per share (¢)	7.5	8.1
Cash flow per share (¢)	12.0	12.6
Dividend (¢)	6	6.5
Percentage franked	100	100
Net tangible assets per share ($)	0.10	0.15
Interest cover (times)	~	~
Return on equity (%)	20.7	20.3
Debt-to-equity ratio (%)	~	~
Current ratio	1.1	1.2

Adelaide Bank Limited

Share price ($)	8.69	
12-month high ($)	8.90	
12-month low ($)	7.24	
Market capitalisation ($mn)	831.1	
Price-to-NTA-per-share ratio	1.6	
5-year share price return (% p.a.)	17.8	
Sector: Financials	**Company**	**Sector**
Price-earnings ratio (times)	11.7	12.9
Dividend yield (%)	5.1	5.2

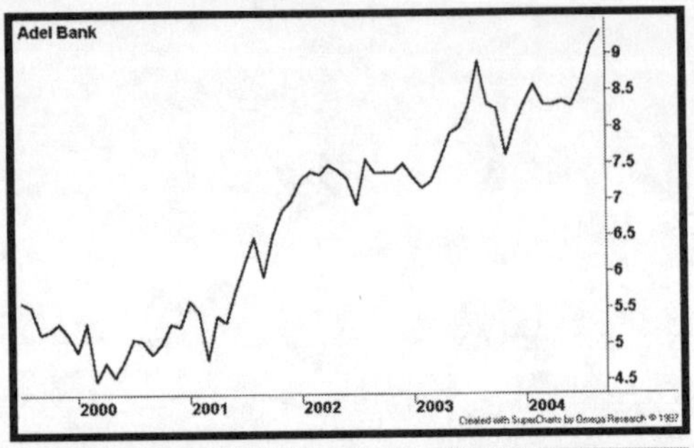

www.adelaidebank.com.au

Adelaide Bank dates back to its establishment as the Cooperative Building Society of South Australia in 1900. It achieved bank status in 1994. It occupies a strong position within South Australia, and is also a prominent home lender in other states. Its Leveraged Equities subsidiary specialises in margin lending.

Latest business results (June 2004, full year)

Record lending and reduced cost ratios powered Adelaide Bank to another record profit. Loans under management rose 28% to $14.2 billion, on the back of a 52% surge in loan approvals. The main growth came from home lending, and the bank claimed that during the year its share of national home loan approvals rose from 2.1% to 3.5%. The business lending portfolio grew 9% to $1.2 billion. Total assets under management stood at $15.6 billion in June 2004, compared with $12.3 billion a year earlier. The Leveraged Equities subsidiary saw its margin-lending book grow 18% to $1.4 billion, generating $8.6 million in pre-tax profit, up 13% from the previous year.

Outlook

Its strong base in its home state, its ability to contain costs and its emphasis on the national mortgage market have handed Adelaide Bank some impressive growth, as well as making it one of the most efficient of the regional banks. It is striving to boost its relationship with the leading national mortgage brokers, and around 70% of its lending business is now sourced from outside South Australia. It is also working to boost its margin-lending business, with Leveraged Equities increasing its market share to become Australia's fourth-largest margin-lending business. However, the bank's emphasis on using mortgage brokers for its growth means it must pay high commissions, and also prevents it from developing ongoing business relationships with its customers. In addition, with some 80% of its assets in housing, the bank is highly vulnerable to any sharp housing downturn. Bank management insist that they engage in prudent risk management practices, with, for example, very little exposure to the inner-city apartment market. The bank is working to streamline its operations through the progressive introduction of new high-tech systems, and it might reduce even further its already small branch network.

ADB Year to 30 June	2003	2004
Operating income ($mn)	201.1	234.9
Net interest income ($mn)	167.5	216.5
Operating expenses ($mn)	120.1	133.0
Operating profit before tax ($mn)	74.3	94.0
Profit after tax ($mn)	51.2	65.1
Earnings per share (¢)	58.3	74.1
Dividend (¢)	37	44
Percentage franked	100	100
Non-interest income to total income (%)	16.7	7.9
Net tangible assets per share ($)	4.63	5.49
Cost-to-income ratio (%)	59.7	56.6
Return on equity (%)	14.2	14.0
Return on assets (%)	0.7	0.7

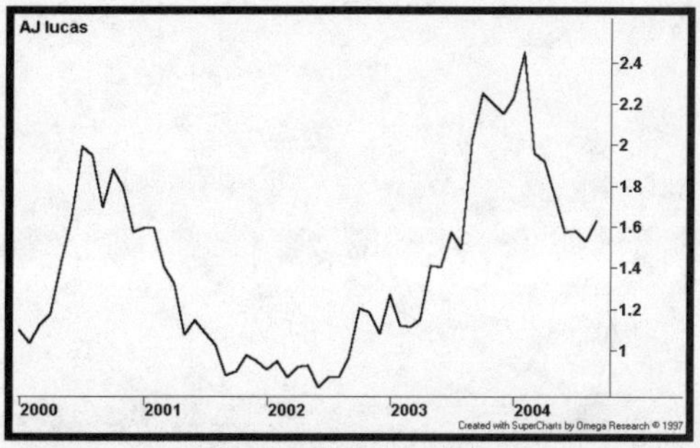

www.lucas.com.au

AJ Lucas Group Limited

Share price ($)	1.53	
12-month high ($)	2.55	
12-month low ($)	1.35	
Market capitalisation ($mn)	77.4	
Price-to-NTA-per-share ratio	1.7	
5-year share price return (% p.a.)	20.0	
Sector: Industrials	**Company**	**Sector**
Price-earnings ratio (times)	7.4	14.8
Dividend yield (%)	5.2	4.2

Sydney-based AJ Lucas, founded in the 1950s, is one of Australia's pre-eminent infrastructure technology companies, providing outsourced services to the energy, water and telecommunications industries in Australia and the Asia-Pacific. It is a leader in the engineering and construction of utility infrastructure, including gas, oil and electricity distribution, water and sewerage systems and telecommunications networks. It is also the largest directional drilling company in the Asia-Pacific, and has become a world leader in horizontal drilling technology. Its Lucas Coal Technologies division is a leader in drilling for coal seam gas. It acquired long-established construction and project management company Stuart Pty in November 2003.

Latest business results (June 2004, full year)

Revenues fell sharply, due to the completion of the SEA Gas pipeline from Port Campbell in Victoria to Adelaide. As a result, pipeline division profits also dropped. Revenues for the horizontal directional drilling division were down, reflecting the long lead time between projects. However, division profits rose, thanks to improved margins from projects in Asia. Gas management revenues soared 59%, and this business moved out of the red and into profit. There was a maiden contribution from the Stuart acquisition, classified as specialist infrastructure services. The company paid little tax, due to research and development tax concessions and to changes in the tax treatment of overseas income.

Outlook

AJ Lucas occupies a key position in the resources and energy industries in both Australia and the Asia-Pacific, and it is a beneficiary of prevailing buoyant conditions. It is a leader of most of the sectors in which it operates, and with high barriers to entry, margins can be high. It is working to reduce the volatile nature of its mainstay pipeline business by building up the infrastructure services division, through organic growth and selective acquisitions, with Stuart Pty the first of these. It is also striving to secure a selected number of large, long-term projects with strategic clients in each of its businesses, in order to provide more balance to its operations. Its business of extracting coal seam gas has grown 450% in two years, and is expected to double again in the June 2005 year.

AJL Year to 30 June	2003	2004
Revenues ($mn)	151.2	116.8
Pipelines (%)	82	48
Specialist infrastructure (%)	0	29
Gas management (%)	5	12
Horizontal directional drilling (%)	13	11
EBIT ($mn)	10.4	10.1
EBIT margin (%)	6.9	8.6
Operating profit before tax ($mn)	10.8	10.2
Profit after tax ($mn)	7.7	10.0
Earnings per share (¢)	18.9	20.8
Cash flow per share (¢)	31.6	29.5
Dividend (¢)	8	8
Percentage franked	0	28
Net tangible assets per share ($)	0.68	0.91
Interest cover (times)	~	~
Return on equity (%)	34.7	25.6
Debt-to-equity ratio (%)	~	~
Current ratio	1.3	2.0

ALESCO CORPORATION LTD

	Company	Sector
Share price ($)	7.20	
12-month high ($)	7.29	
12-month low ($)	5.05	
Market capitalisation ($mn)	499.7	
Price-to-NTA-per-share ratio	3.7	
5-year share price return (% p.a.)	22.4	
Sector: Industrials	**Company**	**Sector**
Price-earnings ratio (times)	17.8	14.8
Dividend yield (%)	4.6	4.2

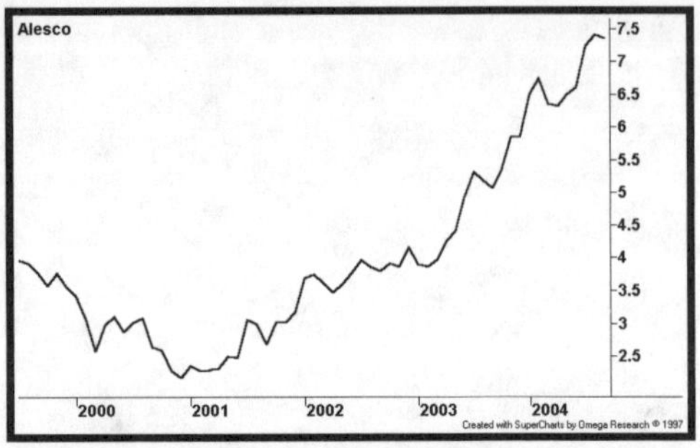

www.alesco.com.au

Alesco has its roots in a general merchant business established in Fremantle in 1896. Today, based in Sydney, it invests in and develops leading industrial brands operating in niche markets. The largest of its four business units is the building and renovations division, centred on Parbury, which distributes branded building products, and also includes the Robinhood kitchen rangehood business. The construction and mining division incorporates Marathon Tyres, which distributes heavy-duty tyres, and Parchem, which supplies chemical products to the construction industry. The automotive division markets car and motorcycle parts and accessories. The scientific and testing division comprises Biolab, the largest distributor of scientific and testing equipment in Australia and New Zealand. In mid-2004, Alesco acquired B&D Doors and Openers, Australia's largest manufacturer of garage doors.

LATEST BUSINESS RESULTS (MAY 2004, FULL YEAR)

Profits and revenues rose strongly. The buoyant home renovations market, productivity gains and the strong Australian dollar meant record results for both Parbury and Robinhood, and a doubling of profits for the building and renovations division. The new scientific and testing division achieved excellent growth, with productivity initiatives contributing to a significant enhancement of margins. The automotive division experienced flat sales and profits, with a strong performance by the Ingram auto-parts business offset by weakness at the McLeod motorcycle accessories business. But profits edged down in the construction and mining division, with the Marathon Tyres business suffering a slump in demand.

ALS Year to 31 May	2003	2004
Revenues ($mn)	392.1	481.5
Building & renovations (%)	30	32
Construction & mining (%)	39	30
Automotive (%)	26	21
Scientific & testing (%)	5	16
EBIT ($mn)	23.0	33.5
EBIT margin (%)	5.9	7.0
Gross margin (%)	33.2	33.1
Operating profit before tax ($mn)	18.7	29.8
Profit after tax ($mn)	12.7	19.8
Earnings per share (¢)	32.4	40.4
Cash flow per share (¢)	64.0	72.6
Dividend (¢)	26	33
Percentage franked	100	100
Net tangible assets per share ($)	1.00	1.96
Interest cover (times)	5.4	9.0
Return on equity (%)	10.0	11.0
Debt-to-equity ratio (%)	53.4	2.0
Current ratio	1.3	2.1

OUTLOOK

Its exposure to the booming home renovations business seems set to provide further growth for Alesco, and the company is forecasting an EPS gain of approximately 15% in May 2005. The B&D acquisition is intended as a prime driver for expansion, and is set to provide more than a third of total company profits in the May 2005 year, with significant scope for productivity gains. The construction and mining unit is also expected to show higher profits, following a significant restructuring of the Marathon Tyre business — including the closure of non-profitable branches and a greater focus on customer service — and a series of supply contracts won by Parchem for major infrastructure projects in NSW.

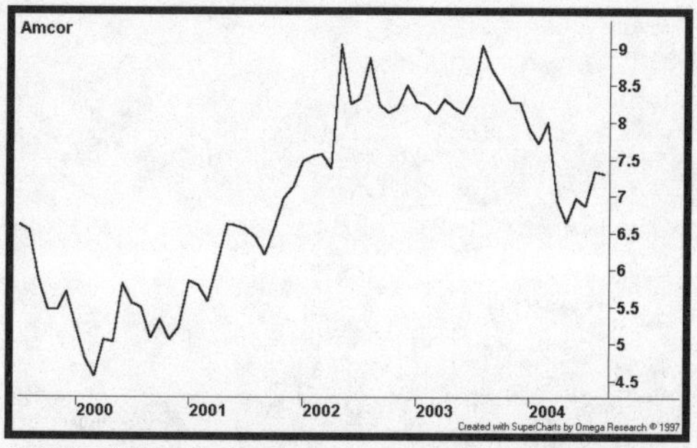

www.amcor.com.au

AMCOR LIMITED

Share price ($)	6.80	
12-month high ($)	9.16	
12-month low ($)	6.51	
Market capitalisation ($mn)	6,181.1	
Price-to-NTA-per-share ratio	2.3	
5-year share price return (% p.a.)	9.3	
Sector: Materials	**Company**	**Sector**
Price-earnings ratio (times)	13.4	14.3
Dividend yield (%)	4.7	2.6

Melbourne-based Amcor, started in the 1860s as a paper maker, is today one of the world's three largest manufacturers of packaging. It has manufacturing sites in 42 countries, and around 80% of its revenues come from abroad. It is the world's biggest producer of PET (polyethylene terephthalate) plastic bottles and jars, and this business comprises about a third of total company sales. It is also a global force in three other areas: closures (lids) for the food and beverages markets, flexible plastic packaging for the food and beverage industries, and specialty printed cartons for the tobacco, confectionary and health and beauty markets.

LATEST BUSINESS RESULTS (JUNE 2004, FULL YEAR)

Revenues edged down and profits were essentially flat, hurt by the strength of the dollar. In local currencies, after-tax profit actually rose 11%. The big Amcor PET business saw sales revenues just edge down, but EBIT fell 9%, with strength in Europe offset by difficult conditions in North America and the appreciation of the dollar. The Amcor Australasia division saw sales up 3% and EBIT up 13%, with solid growth in glass containers, fibre packaging, folding cartons and food cans, as well as cost reduction initiatives. The Amcor Flexibles division achieved a sales gain, but EBIT dipped, hurt by low productivity at some key plants. The best result came from the Amcor Rentsch/Amcor Closures division, with sales down 23%, but EBIT up 26%, thanks to booming profits from Amcor Rentsch, which manufactures cigarette cartons.

OUTLOOK

After six years spent building and shaping the company, management now say they will concentrate on streamlining the entire operation, with the goal of lifting earnings by 20% within two years. In pursuit of this aim, the company has launched a $160 million program to lower the cost base of its PET and Flexibles operations, involving the closure of eight plants and the cutting of 900 jobs, and a target of $65 million in annual cost savings. The company is also working to raise its selling prices in North America. It is expecting a cyclical recovery from the underperforming Amcor Sunclipse operation, which manufactures and distributes specialised packaging materials in North America.

AMC Year to 30 June	2003	2004
Revenues ($mn)	10,709.9	10,405.9
Amcor PET Packaging (%)	30	31
Amcor Australasia (%)	23	24
Amcor Flexibles (%)	20	22
Amcor Sunclipse (%)	12	11
Amcor Rentsch & Closures (%)	12	10
EBIT ($mn)	730.5	703.5
EBIT margin (%)	6.8	6.8
Operating profit before tax ($mn)	575.3	571.3
Profit after tax ($mn)	431.4	440.3
Earnings per share (¢)	51.7	50.8
Cash flow per share (¢)	124.4	120.4
Dividend (¢)	30	32
Percentage franked	45	40
Net tangible assets per share ($)	2.93	2.91
Interest cover (times)	4.7	5.3
Return on equity (%)	9.8	9.7
Debt-to-equity ratio (%)	40.4	50.4
Current ratio	1.0	1.0

Angus & Coote (Holdings) Limited

Share price ($)	7.96	
12-month high ($)	8.75	
12-month low ($)	6.00	
Market capitalisation ($mn)	95.0	
Price-to-NTA-per-share ratio	1.7	
5-year share price return (% p.a.)	23.0	
Sector: Consumer discretionary	**Company**	**Sector**
Price-earnings ratio (times)	11.7	23.8
Dividend yield (%)	5.0	1.5

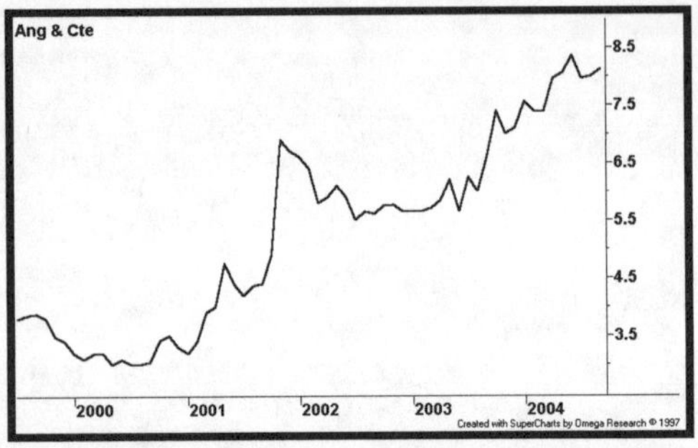

www.anguscoote.com.au

Sydney-based Angus & Coote, founded in 1895, is Australia's dominant specialist jewellery retailer, with a 15% market share. It operates through two main divisions: the A&C division markets jewellery, watches, clocks, silverware, crystal and related products from 143 jewellery stores throughout Australia, under the names Angus & Coote, Dunklings the Jewellers, Amies the Family Jewellers and Edments. The division also operates tax-free stores at Sydney and Melbourne airports. The Goldmark division operates 120 jewellery stores throughout Australia, and is the country's largest national jewellery brand.

Latest business results (July 2004, full year)

Continued strength in consumer spending, new marketing initiatives and the company's cost-cutting efforts all combined to hand Angus & Coote a handsome profit increase. However, official interest rate rises in November and December had a noticeable dampening effect on sales, and the company noted a continuing trend towards shoppers waiting for the post-Christmas sales for their purchases. One of the strongest drivers of sales was high-turnover, lower-priced silver accessories, said by the company to be favoured by young women. The result was aided by a sharp reduction in net debt, down from $24.4 million to $8.1 million.

Outlook

Angus & Coote's business is quite dependent on trends in consumer discretionary spending. This has remained strong, although the company could be hurt by any economic slowdown, and especially by further rises in interest rates. It has now positioned its two divisions to entice different age groups. The A&C Division is targeted at the 25- to 49-year-old market, with the company's sales strategies aimed particularly at appealing to women customers. The Goldmark business focuses on the fashion-conscious 14- to 29-year-old market. The company has been experimenting with innovative new store designs, and believes the success of these has in part been responsible for the big jump in profits in the latest results. Angus & Coote now plans to open a further 15 new stores in the July 2005 year. A trial US operation, comprising four stores, has ended, following the American partner's withdrawal from the venture. However, the company expresses optimism about its prospects overseas, and hopes to find a new US partner.

ANC Year to 25 July*	2003	2004
Revenues ($mn)	217.9	239.0
EBIT ($mn)	10.4	12.9
EBIT margin (%)	4.8	5.4
Gross margin (%)	59.6	58.0
Operating profit before tax ($mn)	8.7	11.6
Profit after tax ($mn)	5.7	8.1
Earnings per share (¢)	47.5	68.2
Cash flow per share (¢)	110.7	135.2
Dividend (¢)	36	40
Percentage franked	100	100
Net tangible assets per share ($)	4.41	4.72
Interest cover (times)	5.9	10.3
Return on equity (%)	11.0	14.8
Debt-to-equity ratio (%)	45.9	14.3
Current ratio	1.6	1.8

* 27 July 2003

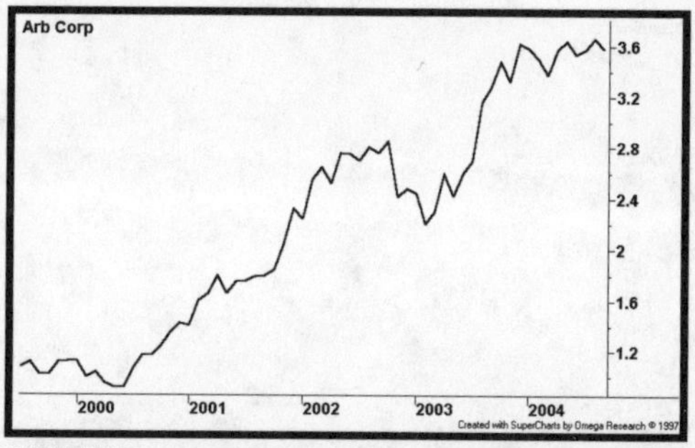

www.arb.com.au

ARB CORPORATION LIMITED

Share price ($)	3.52	
12-month high ($)	3.70	
12-month low ($)	2.80	
Market capitalisation ($mn)	224.4	
Price-to-NTA-per-share ratio	5.5	
5-year share price return (% p.a.)	32.6	
Sector: Consumer discretionary	**Company**	**Sector**
Price-earnings ratio (times)	18.4	23.8
Dividend yield (%)	2.7	1.5

Melbourne-based ARB is a small manufacturer of specialty automotive accessories, and an international leader in the design and production of equipment for four-wheel-drive (4WD) vehicles. Its products are divided into broad groupings: mechanical products, notably the prize-winning 'air locker' air-operated locking differential system; fabricated metal products, such as bull bars, roof racks and tow bars; the Old Man Emu range of suspension products; ARB canopies; and imported and locally produced 4WD accessories for which ARB acts as local distributor. In December 2003, it acquired Kingsley Enterprises, a leading manufacturer and supplier of products for 4WD and light commercial vehicles. ARB maintains a significant export business.

LATEST BUSINESS RESULTS (JUNE 2004, FULL YEAR)

Strong domestic consumer spending and a buoyant auto market pushed ARB to its 13th straight profit rise, overcoming sales declines in most export markets, which were adversely affected by exchange-rate movements. In the US — responsible for about 15% of total company revenues — sales growth of 11% in US dollar terms translated to a 9% decline in sales in Australian dollars, and profits plunged. A new state office and warehouse in Queensland led to very strong sales in the state. The company realised a maiden contribution from Kingsley Enterprises.

OUTLOOK

ARB has become a major beneficiary of the growing popularity of 4WD vehicles in Australia, America and many other countries, and the result has been continuing strong increases in sales and profits and, for some years, a surging share price. Despite uncertainties about the direction of the currency, it continues to expand. It is building a new $6 million factory and warehouse specifically for Kingsley — to be completed in 2005 — and expects to achieve significant operational efficiencies. It has commissioned the construction of a new warehouse in Seattle for its US sales, and expects this to enable it to expand its business there. It is also spending $4.5 million to expand by 40% its Melbourne factory/warehouse premises. It sees the establishment of ARB retail sites — both company-owned and franchised — as an important new growth opportunity, and has bought land in Morphett Vale, South Australia and Wentworthville, NSW for new stores.

ARP Year to 30 June	2003	2004
Revenues ($mn)	88.0	100.7
EBIT ($mn)	14.7	17.3
EBIT margin (%)	16.7	17.2
Gross margin (%)	31.9	32.9
Operating profit before tax ($mn)	14.5	17.1
Profit after tax ($mn)	10.3	12.1
Earnings per share (¢)	16.3	19.2
Cash flow per share (¢)	21.1	24.9
Dividend (¢)	8	9.5
Percentage franked	100	100
Net tangible assets per share ($)	0.56	0.64
Interest cover (times)	62.1	87.9
Return on equity (%)	29.5	29.3
Debt-to-equity ratio (%)	10.5	7.9
Current ratio	1.6	1.6

AUSPINE LIMITED

Share price ($)	3.75	
12-month high ($)	3.95	
12-month low ($)	2.72	
Market capitalisation ($mn)	203.4	
Price-to-NTA-per-share ratio	0.8	
5-year share price return (% p.a.)	22.7	
Sector: Materials	**Company**	**Sector**
Price-earnings ratio (times)	7.0	14.3
Dividend yield (%)	5.5	2.6

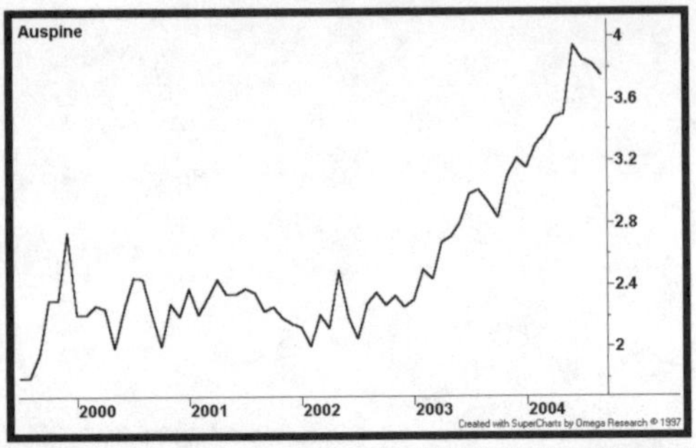

www.auspine.com.au

Based in South Australia, Auspine was founded in 1978 as a timber industry consultancy. It has since grown through acquisition to become an important owner and manager of timber plantations, and producer of a range of timber products. Its 46,500 hectares of land encompass 67 separate planting areas, spread throughout south-western Victoria (approximately 60%), south-eastern South Australia (nearly 40%) and a small amount in Tasmania. Auspine also operates two of the largest sawmills in Australia, at Tarpeena in South Australia and at Scottsdale in Tasmania, as well as several smaller timber processing facilities in other locations, and it is one of Australia's largest wholesale distributors of timber products. In addition, it operates a major woodchip facility in Portland, Victoria, and has become one of the world's largest plantation softwood woodchip exporters.

LATEST BUSINESS RESULTS (JUNE 2004, FULL YEAR)

Sales fell as the company reduced its exposure to some low-profit areas of its markets. However, the pre-tax profit rose solidly, and a large tax benefit led to a big increase in the after-tax profit. There was a record harvest volume from company plantations. Woodchip export volumes rose 7% to 616,000 tonnes, reflecting the restoring of shortfalls in purchases in the previous year. But a 10% improvement in the US-dollar price was dented by the strengthening of the Australian dollar.

OUTLOOK

Auspine is benefiting from growing demand for timber products and from its own efforts to achieve higher returns. Thanks to its substantial land and plantation base, its own manufacturing facilities, and its own sales and logistics infrastructure, Auspine is one of the few industry participants with full control of an integrated supply chain. The company hopes to take advantage of this strength to boost its value-added operations and to develop new sources of revenue. The market has been placing a greater emphasis on timber suppliers being able to offer a range of premium treated and engineered products, and Auspine is particularly well placed to capitalise on this opportunity. It expects the Australian timber industry to enter a period of rationalisation, which it believes could offer growth opportunities by way of acquisition.

ANE Year to 30 June	2003	2004
Revenues ($mn)	227.0	203.7
EBIT ($mn)	25.4	28.5
EBIT margin (%)	11.2	14.0
Gross margin (%)	17.5	15.7
Operating profit before tax ($mn)	21.5	24.5
Profit after tax ($mn)	14.9	28.9
Earnings per share (¢)	27.6	53.6
Cash flow per share (¢)	44.1	70.4
Dividend (¢)	17	20.5
Percentage franked	100	100
Net tangible assets per share ($)	3.61	4.80
Interest cover (times)	6.4	7.1
Return on equity (%)	7.6	12.7
Debt-to-equity ratio (%)	35.9	28.7
Current ratio	1.9	1.7

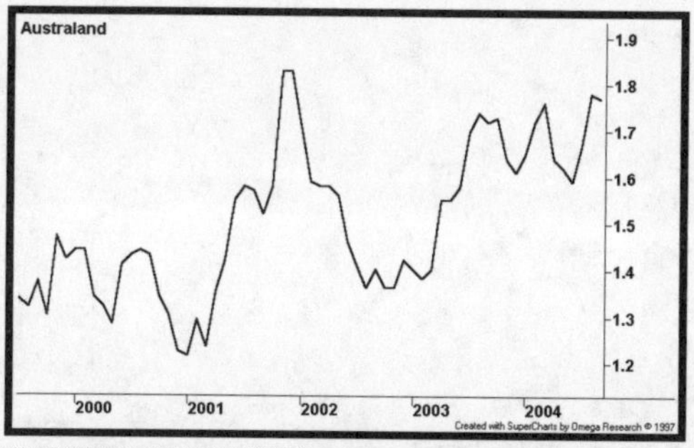

www.australand.com.au

Australand Holdings Limited

Share price ($)	1.67	
12-month high ($)	1.82	
12-month low ($)	1.56	
Market capitalisation ($mn)	1,378.9	
Price-to-NTA-per-share ratio	1.2	
5-year share price return (% p.a.)	18.5	
Sector: Financials	**Company**	**Sector**
Price-earnings ratio (times)	9.3	12.9
Dividend yield (%)	8.0	5.2

Sydney-based Australand is one of Australia's largest property development companies with operations covering: large-scale land development projects; medium density and detached housing projects in Sydney, Melbourne, Brisbane and Perth; apartment buildings; commercial office buildings; and purpose-built industrial facilities. In addition, it manages property trusts. Australand is also listed on the Singapore Stock Exchange.

Latest business results (June 2004, half-year)

Revenues fell sharply, as Australand reduced its exposure to the volatile apartments market, and the pre-tax profit also edged down. However, the after-tax profit jumped, thanks to a substantially lower tax bill and a big contribution from the company's burgeoning property trust business. Continuing strength in the homes market led to a healthy 10% jump in profit for the land and housing division, due mainly to an increase in margins. However, apartments division profits slumped, down 73%, with sales falling 59%. The commercial and industrial division fell into the red, on a 21% decline in sales, due to unanticipated costs incurred in finishing some pre-committed buildings on time for key clients and the write-down of the carrying value of two projects. The company's property investment business provided a handsome $27.7 million pre-tax profit.

Outlook

The company has announced that it expects a full-year after-tax profit of around $144 million, suggesting a powerful second half. Much of the gain will come from the investment property division, which in May 2004 acquired its third wholesale property trust. The division now manages a $600 million portfolio of 26 office and industrial properties generating recurrent income of approximately $50 million annually. The company also expects a healthy recovery in its commercial and industrial division. The apartments business appears likely to remain muted, though the company has noted early signs of a reduction in the cost pressures that have been a recent concern in the industry.

ALZ Year to 31 December	2002	2003
Revenues ($mn)	1,138.5	1,405.4
EBIT ($mn)	132.1	156.7
EBIT margin (%)	11.6	11.1
Gross margin (%)	17.9	20.9
Operating profit before tax ($mn)	131.2	146.4
Profit after tax ($mn)	90.4	95.2
Earnings per share (¢)	17.4	17.9
Cash flow per share (¢)	19.4	19.4
Dividend (¢)	12	13.36
Percentage franked	88	90
Interest cover (times)	138.9	15.2
Return on equity (%)	12.4	10.8

Half-year to 30 June	2003	2004
Revenues ($mn)	615.1	472.1
Land & housing (%)	38	49
Commercial & industrial (%)	26	27
Apartments (%)	36	19
Operating profit before tax ($mn)	66.3	63.4
Profit after tax ($mn)	41.2	51.7
Earnings per share (¢)	7.4	7.1
Dividend (¢)	6	8
Percentage franked	100	100
Net tangible assets per share ($)	1.31	1.39
Debt-to-equity ratio (%)	55.0	66.7
Current ratio	2.8	3.0

Australia & New Zealand Banking Group Limited

Share price ($)	17.73	
12-month high ($)	19.44	
12-month low ($)	15.94	
Market capitalisation ($mn)	32,533.1	
Price-to-NTA-per-share ratio	2.4	
5-year share price return (% p.a.)	19.2	
Sector: Financials	**Company**	**Sector**
Price-earnings ratio (times)	11.4	12.9
Dividend yield (%)	5.4	5.2

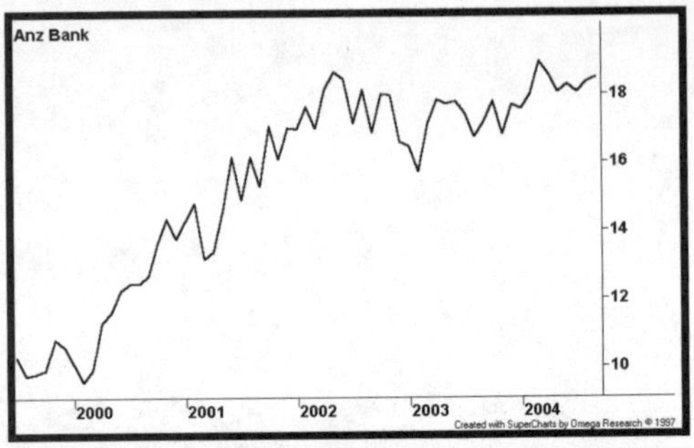

www.anz.com.au

ANZ is one of Australia's four banking giants, with significant interests in numerous areas of finance. It has a stake in online stockbroker E*Trade Australia, and operates a funds management joint venture with Dutch giant ING. Its December 2003 acquisition of National Bank of New Zealand (NBNZ), for $4.9 billion, has made ANZ the market leader in NZ banking.

Latest business results (March 2004, half-year)

Profits rose again, thanks in part to a four-month contribution from the NBNZ acquisition, though most traditional businesses were also strong. Excluding NBNZ, profits were up about 9%. Average lending grew 28% from the March 2003 half year, with NBNZ responsible for more than half this growth. However, competitive pressures forced the net interest margin down, putting a dent in mortgage earnings growth. Small business and corporate banking performed well, and personal banking benefited from an environment of rising interest rates. There was an excellent result from the ING joint venture. The cost-to-income ratio declined further to 45.1%, confirming ANZ as Australia's most efficient bank.

Outlook

ANZ is working to integrate NBNZ into its operations. It believes this will be completed by the end of 2005, with synergies from the acquisition delivering cost savings of $110 million annually by 2007. ANZ now has 93% of its assets in Australia and New Zealand, part of a deliberate policy to reduce risk by limiting exposure to offshore markets. Only 12% of company profit now derives from outside Australia or New Zealand, compared to 32% in 1997. It is working to use skills developed through its strong corporate banking businesses to revitalise its personal banking activities, where it lags its three large rivals. It has invested heavily in this business, with the aim of boosting market share. However, like all the banks, it remains vulnerable to any sharp housing downturn. And because it is already highly efficient — it claims its productivity is among the top 5% of banks worldwide — there is just limited scope for further efficiency gains.

ANZ Year to 30 September	2002	2003
Operating income ($mn)	6,988.0	7,013.0
Net interest income ($mn)	4,018.0	4,311.0
Operating expenses ($mn)	2,905.0	3,228.0
Operating profit before tax ($mn)	3,223.0	3,277.0
Profit after tax ($mn)	2,322.0	2,348.0
Earnings per share (¢)	155.1	155.1
Dividend (¢)	85	95
Percentage franked	100	100
Non-interest income to total income (%)	42.5	38.5
Cost-to-income ratio (%)	41.6	46.0
Return on equity (%)	21.1	18.6
Return on assets (%)	1.3	1.2
Half-year to 31 March	**2003**	**2004**
Operating income ($mn)	3,492.0	4,192.0
Operating profit before tax ($mn)	1,587.0	1,977.0
Profit after tax ($mn)	1,141.0	1,312.0
Earnings per share (¢)	72.0	78.9
Dividend (¢)	44	47
Percentage franked	100	100
Net tangible assets per share ($)	8.13	7.48

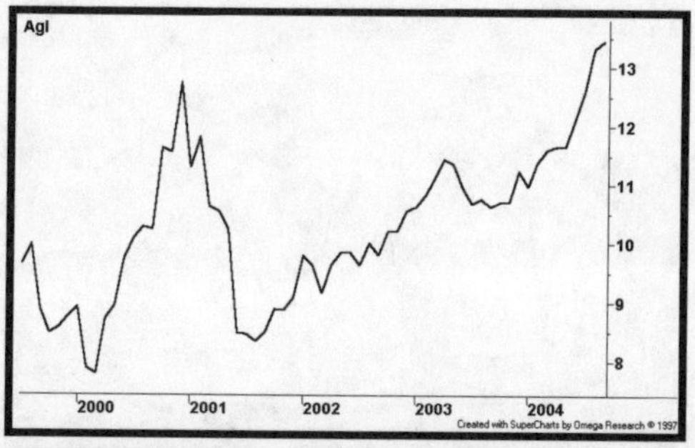

www.agl.com.au

THE AUSTRALIAN GAS LIGHT COMPANY

Share price ($)	12.65	
12-month high ($)	12.85	
12-month low ($)	10.41	
Market capitalisation ($mn)	5,780.3	
Price-to-NTA-per-share ratio	4.0	
5-year share price return (% p.a.)	13.9	
Sector: Utilities	**Company**	**Sector**
Price-earnings ratio (times)	16.5	17.1
Dividend yield (%)	4.7	4.9

AGL, established in 1837 to light the streets of Sydney, is one of the nation's oldest business enterprises. It now owns power generation facilities and operates a major supply network for gas and electricity, with more than three million customers in Australia and New Zealand. It owns 30% of the listed Australian Pipeline Trust, and 50% of Elgas, Australia's largest liquefied petroleum gas distributor. It also operates energy assets in Chile.

LATEST BUSINESS RESULTS (JUNE 2004, FULL YEAR)

AGL enjoyed another year of solid profit growth, with most businesses performing well. The core energy sales and marketing business saw EBIT up 11%, thanks to an additional month's contribution from the Pulse Energy business and strong weather-related gas sales in Victoria and NSW. The gas network business — which transports gas to 924,600 customers across NSW — achieved an 8% rise in EBIT, due to a tariff increase and higher customer demand. Electricity network activities — centred on the north-west suburbs of Melbourne — saw EBIT up 9.5%, due mainly to increased demand. AGL's Agility business, which operates and develops energy infrastructure assets, saw EBIT up 10%, and there was a 25% rise from the company's investments in the Australian Pipeline Trust, Elgas and others. However, New Zealand business was down 35% from the previous year, which had been boosted by asset sales and by several businesses which have since been sold.

OUTLOOK

AGL occupies a key position in Australia's energy infrastructure. It has built up an enviable collection of assets, and is now working to develop these further and achieve additonal synergies. It has expressed its belief that it can further boost profits in the June 2005 year. However, in the short term it could be hurt by sharply heightened competition among gas and electricity retailers, following deregulation of energy retail sales in states where AGL is active, and it has reported that customer churn rates are on the increase. It is expanding its Agility infrastructure business, which has moved into Tasmania and is making inroads into the water industry. It hopes to augment its power generation assets, through acquisition or new developments. It has made a decision to sell its New Zealand power generation interests.

AGL Year to 30 June	2003	2004
Revenues ($mn)	3,872.4	4,153.8
EBIT ($mn)	679.9	691.6
EBIT margin (%)	17.6	16.6
Gross margin (%)	32.1	31.3
Operating profit before tax ($mn)	514.0	567.0
Profit after tax ($mn)	320.8	349.5
Earnings per share (¢)	73.2	76.8
Cash flow per share (¢)	130.1	130.5
Dividend (¢)	55	60
Percentage franked	62	100
Net tangible assets per share ($)	2.77	3.13
Interest cover (times)	4.1	5.6
Return on equity (%)	12.8	11.8
Debt-to-equity ratio (%)	63.1	68.8
Current ratio	1.1	0.8

Australian Stock Exchange Limited

Share price ($)	14.75	
12-month high ($)	17.35	
12-month low ($)	13.00	
Market capitalisation ($mn)	1,510.7	
Price-to-NTA-per-share ratio	7.0	
5-year share price return (% p.a.)	13.9	
Sector: Financials	**Company**	**Sector**
Price-earnings ratio (times)	18.2	12.9
Dividend yield (%)	3.8	5.2

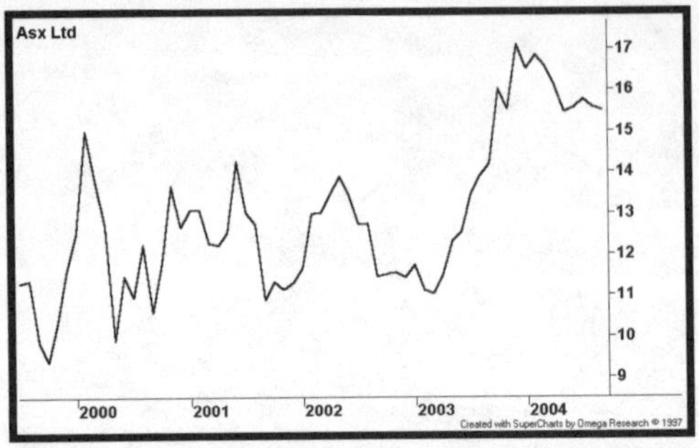

www.asx.com.au

The Australian Stock Exchange (ASX) was formed in 1987 through the amalgamation of six independent stock exchanges that formerly operated in the state capital cities. Each of those exchanges had a history of share trading dating back to the 19th century. Though originally a mutual organisation of stockbrokers, in 1998 the ASX become a listed company, with its shares traded on its own market. As well as operating Australia's primary national stock exchange for equities, derivatives and fixed-interest securities, it also provides a comprehensive market data service.

Latest business results (June 2004, full year)

A robust stock market sent the ASX's profits soaring. Revenues from its core equities trading operations increased by 17%, with an average of 69,700 trades per day, compared to 56,100 daily trades in the June 2003 year. The listings business recorded a 39% surge in revenues, thanks to 180 new listings, up from just 81 in the previous year. Derivatives revenues were virtually unchanged. The options market enjoyed firm growth, but this was offset by difficult market conditions for the warrants business. Revenues from the company's supply of market data rose nearly 6%, as a result of new products and a streamlining of services. Strong market conditions helped the 50%-owned ASX Perpetual Registrars move out of the red and into profit.

Outlook

The ASX's profits are highly geared to the levels of stock market activity — powering its shares to impressive gains during 2003 — and the June 2004 period was an exceptional year that will not easily be repeated. A particular concern is the plan of News Corporation to move its domicile to the US, which could mean a sharp decline in the trading of its shares on the ASX. Trading in News Corporation shares is responsible for up to 2.5% of ASX revenues. But new listings remain firm, and a third Telstra listing would provide a boost to market activity. The company continues to introduce new products, and it is working to develop relationships with foreign exchanges to enhance investor access to global markets. Possible future ASX acquisitions or merger partners include the Sydney Futures Exchange and the New Zealand Stock Exchange.

ASX Year to 30 June	2003	2004
Revenues ($mn)	206.8	241.2
Equities trading (%)	46	44
Listings (%)	20	22
Derivatives trading (%)	20	16
Market data (%)	14	12
EBIT ($mn)	79.2	109.4
EBIT margin (%)	38.3	45.3
Operating profit before tax ($mn)	85.6	116.6
Profit after tax ($mn)	61.3	82.7
Earnings per share (¢)	60.1	81.1
Cash flow per share (¢)	77.0	97.1
Dividend (¢)	39.6	56.6
Percentage franked	100	100
Net tangible assets per share ($)	2.06	2.11
Interest cover (times)	~	~
Return on equity (%)	29.9	38.3
Debt-to-equity ratio (%)	~	~
Current ratio	2.6	2.5

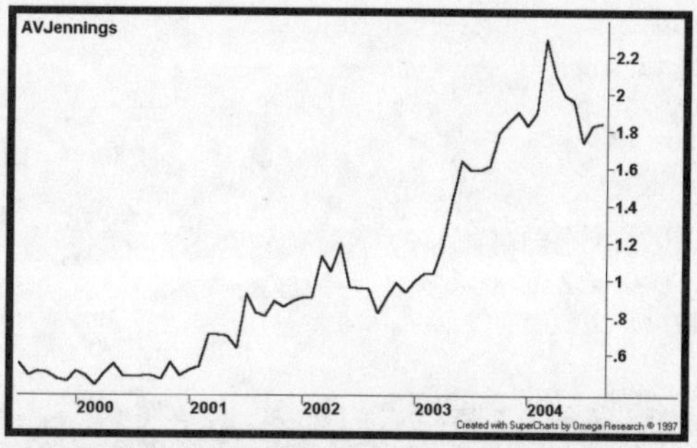

www.avjennings.com.au

AV Jennings Homes Limited

Share price ($)	1.76	
12-month high ($)	2.32	
12-month low ($)	1.50	
Market capitalisation ($mn)	381.0	
Price-to-NTA-per-share ratio	1.4	
5-year share price return (% p.a.)	42.6	
Sector: Financials	**Company**	**Sector**
Price-earnings ratio (times)	5.5	12.9
Dividend yield (%)	6.3	5.2

Melbourne-based AV Jennings, one of Australia's best-known names in housing development, was founded in Victoria in 1932. Today, it is one of Australia's largest home builders and creators of residential communities, selling over 3,000 properties each year. It operates in four states: New South Wales, Victoria, Queensland and South Australia. More than 40% of its equity is held by a Singapore public company, SG Global Developments.

Latest business results (March 2004, full year)

The housing boom delivered another excellent profit to AV Jennings, its ninth successive earnings rise. The company sold 1,200 developed lots as land-only sales, 650 lots with housing (including strata-titled units) and 1,250 contract houses constructed on the customers' own land. The big boost to profits came from a 71% surge in its land-only business, with sales of $147 million and margins rising. By contrast, revenues from housing development fell 13% to $231 million, and contract housing sales dipped 2% to $172 million. Despite an appreciable increase in developed lot sales, the company still boosted its developable land inventory to more than 8,000 developable lots, up from around 6,600 a year earlier.

Outlook

AV Jennings has transformed itself from a builder of cheap contract housing into a developer of 'urban infill' projects, generally for existing home owners who want to move into a bigger and/or newer dwelling in their own suburbs. This involves finding suitable suburban land sites, and then developing them. It also creates new residential communities, and then sells plots of land. Its land holdings are currently spread across some 50 development sites, with a particular emphasis on Melbourne and Brisbane. Though it will almost certainly feel the impact of a housing downturn, the company is largely unaffected by changes in first-home owner and investor activity. Nor does it have any exposure to CBD high-rise developments. The company itself has reported that though sales now come later in the building cycle, it has been holding just negligible quantities of unsold developed land or completed houses, and it expects March 2005 profits to be comparable with those of March 2004.

AVJ Year to 31 March	2003	2004
Revenues ($mn)	525.8	550.0
Developments (%)	66	69
Project housing (%)	34	31
EBIT ($mn)	80.8	98.1
EBIT margin (%)	15.4	17.8
Operating profit before tax ($mn)	80.7	97.7
Profit after tax ($mn)	56.8	68.5
Earnings per share (¢)	26.4	31.8
Cash flow per share (¢)	27.6	34.2
Dividend (¢)	10	11
Percentage franked	100	100
Net tangible assets per share ($)	1.00	1.22
Interest cover (times)	598.6	228.7
Return on equity (%)	28.8	27.9
Debt-to-equity ratio (%)	35.4	40.4
Current ratio	2.6	2.6

AXA Asia Pacific Holdings Limited

Share price ($)	3.91	
12-month high ($)	3.94	
12-month low ($)	2.52	
Market capitalisation ($mn)	6,785.5	
Price-to-NTA-per-share ratio	1.9	
5-year share price return (% p.a.)	16.8	
Sector: Financials	**Company**	**Sector**
Price-earnings ratio (times)	12.4	12.9
Dividend yield (%)	2.6	5.2

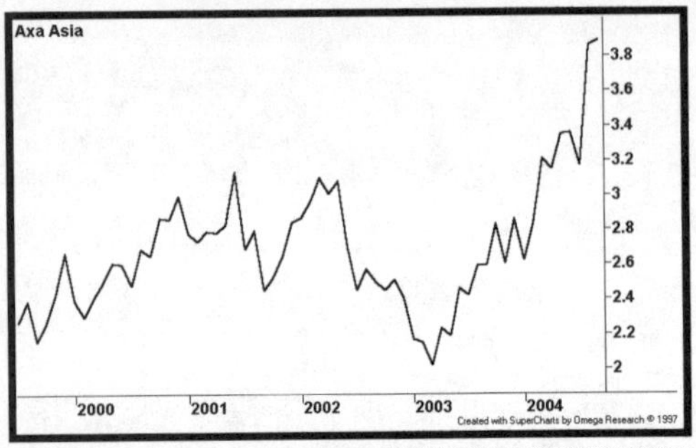

www.axa.com.au

AXA Asia Pacific is one of Australia's insurance giants. Established in 1869 as the National Mutual Life Association of Australasia, it is now a 52%-owned subsidiary of the French insurance and financial services giant AXA SA. It is a leading supplier of life insurance and superannuation products in Australia and New Zealand, with a big funds-management operation and a growing financial planning business. It has a major insurance business in China, and is also active in Indonesia, the Philippines, Singapore and Thailand. In August 2004, AXA's French parent announced its desire to acquire the remaining 48% of AXA's shares it did not already own.

Latest business results (June 2004, half-year)

After-tax operating earnings for the company actually rose to $163 million, from $146 million in the June 2003 half. This reflected a favourable claims experience and the rebound in the Australian equity market, which drove funds under management and under administration higher, and generated additional fee revenue. The increased profitability of Hong Kong business was offset by the strength of the Australian dollar against the Hong Kong currency. However, after-tax investment earnings of $66 million were substantially down from $189 million in the June 2003 half, largely due to a reduction in the value of fixed-interest securities, following the previous year's significant rise.

Outlook

The future of AXA Asia Pacific as an independent entity listed on the ASX, now depends on the outcome of the French parent's attempt to fully acquire the company. AXA SA has stated that, although the Australian company's underlying business is fundamentally sound and performing well, it is not growing as rapidly as it could due to financial constraints arising from the fact that it is a publicly listed company. There has been speculation that AXA SA sees enormous potential in AXA Asia Pacific's China business. AXA SA has said it will offer $3.75 per AXA share, and desires to acquire the shares by way of an amicable arrangement, rather than through a takeover bid.

AXA Year to 31 December	2002	2003
Revenues ($mn)	2,723.0	4,761.0
Operating profit before tax ($mn)	253.0	898.0
Profit after tax ($mn)	316.0	547.0
Earnings per share (¢)	18.0	31.4
Dividend (¢)	9.75	10.25
Percentage franked	60	39
Return on equity (%)	10.4	16.2
Half-year to 30 June	**2003**	**2004**
Revenues ($mn)	2,486.0	1,928.0
Operating profit before tax ($mn)	293.0	226.0
Profit after tax ($mn)	287.0	194.0
Earnings per share (¢)	16.5	11.2
Dividend (¢)	4.75	5.25
Percentage franked	60	15
Net tangible assets per share ($)	2.05	2.20
Debt-to-equity ratio (%)	~	~

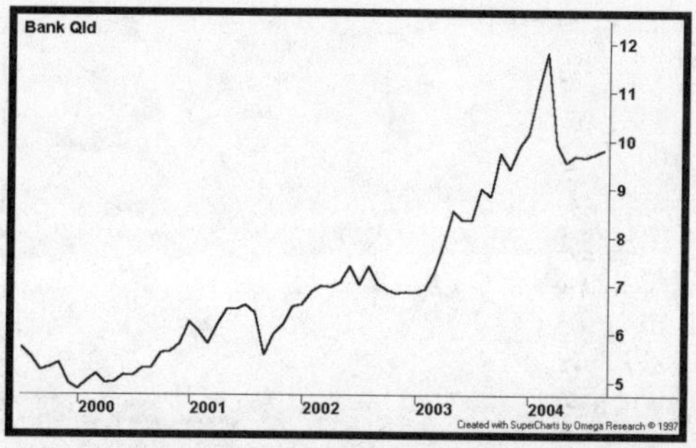

www.boq.com.au

Bank of Queensland Limited

Share price ($)	9.47	
12-month high ($)	12.20	
12-month low ($)	8.70	
Market capitalisation ($mn)	870.9	
Price-to-NTA-per-share ratio	1.6	
5-year share price return (% p.a.)	18.7	
Sector: Financials	**Company**	**Sector**
Price-earnings ratio (times)	14.8	12.9
Dividend yield (%)	3.9	5.2

The Bank of Queensland was established in 1874 as the Brisbane Permanent Benefit Building and Investment Society, later gaining a banking licence. It has an estimated 6% share of the banking market in Queensland, with some 133 branches.

Latest business results (February 2004, half-year)

An aggressive expansion program helped the bank to a healthy rise in profits. It has now doubled its first-half profit in two years. The result was achieved from a 75% increase in home loan approvals, to $2.7 billion, from the February 2003 half, a doubling in business loan approvals, to $1.3 billion, and a 35% jump in deposits, to $4.6 billion. At February 2004 the bank had $9.7 billion of loans under management. It also had $11.3 billion in assets under management, a 55% rise from the February 2003 half. The bank opened 12 new branches during the period.

Outlook

Bank of Queensland has become one of the fastest-growing banks in Australia, thanks in part to its buoyant home mortgage business and its high exposure to the booming south-east Queensland housing market. However, this makes it very vulnerable to any sharp housing downturn. In response, in June 2004 the bank withdrew from the mortgage broker market, which was responsible for sourcing 22% of the bank's home loans in the February 2004 half. Though this will likely have a short-term impact on lending volumes, it should boost the profitability of this business. The bank is also striving to diversify its activities, including the acquisition of the equipment finance company UFJ Finance Australia and the third-party ATM provider ATM Solutions Australasia. It has also launched an interstate expansion program, with a target of 100 branches in Victoria and NSW by August 2006, and aims at doubling its national home-loan market share to 5% within three to five years. It also aims at lowering its cost-to-income ratio to 64%. Takeover speculation has provided good support for the share price, though in May 2004 the Commonwealth Bank sold its 12% stake.

BOQ Year to 31 August	2002	2003
Operating income ($mn)	173.9	214.3
Net interest income ($mn)	109.1	132.7
Operating expenses ($mn)	124.0	139.0
Operating profit before tax ($mn)	40.6	63.6
Profit after tax ($mn)	28.7	44.7
Earnings per share (¢)	45.8	64.1
Dividend (¢)	29	37
Percentage franked	100	100
Non-interest income to total income (%)	37.2	38.1
Cost-to-income ratio (%)	71.3	64.9
Return on equity (%)	12.3	14.0
Return on assets (%)	0.6	0.7
Half-year to 29 February*	**2003**	**2004**
Operating income ($mn)	101.1	136.1
Operating profit before tax ($mn)	30.7	40.5
Profit after tax ($mn)	21.3	28.1
Earnings per share (¢)	27.2	29.8
Dividend (¢)	17	21
Percentage franked	100	100
Net tangible assets per share ($)	4.42	5.88

* 28 February 2003

Bendigo Bank Limited

Share price ($)	9.79	
12-month high ($)	11.00	
12-month low ($)	8.11	
Market capitalisation ($mn)	1,309.5	
Price-to-NTA-per-share ratio	2.2	
5-year share price return (% p.a.)	16.1	
Sector: Financials	**Company**	**Sector**
Price-earnings ratio (times)	17.7	12.9
Dividend yield (%)	4.1	5.2

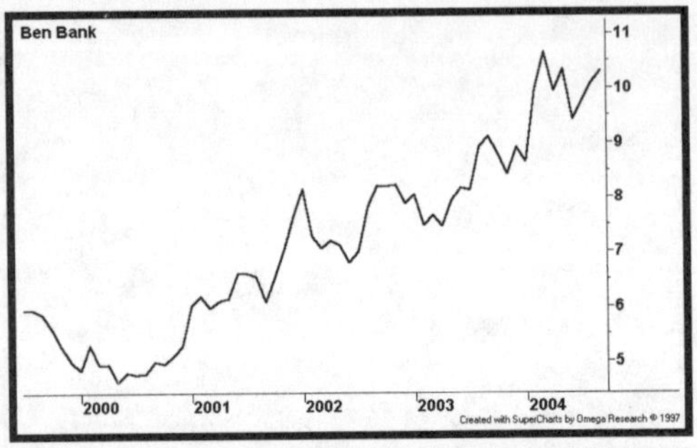

www.benbank.com.au

Established as a building society in 1858, Victoria's Bendigo Bank is today Australia's only remaining regionally based bank, and is also one of the smallest of all the listed banks. It has a network of 276 branches — including 132 community bank branches — concentrated in Victoria, southern NSW and Queensland. It has moved into various niche businesses, including the establishment of Elders Rural Bank in a joint venture with Futuris Corporation, to provide banking services to rural Australia. Its Sandhurst Trustees subsidiary, founded in 1888, provides a wide range of wealth management services. Its flourishing community bank model launches new bank branches together with local communities.

Latest business results (June 2004, full year)

Bendigo Bank reported its fourth consecutive year of strong profit growth, along with an improvement in most efficiency ratios. Retail deposits grew 20% to $9.1 billion, with total group deposits up 23% to $10.2 billion. Lending approvals grew 26% to $6.1 billion. Funds managed by Sandhurst Trustees grew 24% to $2.2 billion, underpinning an 80% surge in profits from the bank's wealth solutions division. Community bank profits jumped 62%, and there was a 15% rise in the earnings contribution from the Elders joint venture. A $6.6 after-tax profit — mainly from the sale of shares in Cashcard Australia — was reported as a significant item.

Outlook

Bendigo Bank continues its impressive expansion. It will open a further 30 new community banks in the June 2005 year, along with three new company-owned branches. However, despite recent improvements, the bank's costs remain high, and among the highest of all the banks. In addition, its strong gearing to housing makes Bendigo vulnerable to any sharp downturn in that sector. Nevertheless, bank management forecasts 15% to 18% profit growth in the June 2005 year. The company is working to boost its business banking and wealth management operations. It is also striving to reduce its dependence on Victoria, which now represents less than 60% of total business. It has launched a new Community Telco Australia initiative, modelled on its community bank venture, intended to help communities start their own locally owned telecommunications businesses. A new strategic alliance with E*Trade Australia is intended to provide Bendigo customers with a full suite of online share trading services.

BEN Year to 30 June	2003	2004
Operating income ($mn)	346.6	411.1
Net interest income ($mn)	222.3	253.6
Operating expenses ($mn)	241.9	282.0
Operating profit before tax ($mn)	89.3	106.6
Profit after tax ($mn)	59.0	73.2
Earnings per share (¢)	46.8	55.2
Dividend (¢)	33.5	40
Percentage franked	100	100
Non-interest income to total income (%)	35.9	38.3
Net tangible assets per share ($)	3.80	4.40
Cost-to-income ratio (%)	69.8	68.6
Return on equity (%)	11.3	11.9
Return on assets (%)	0.7	0.7

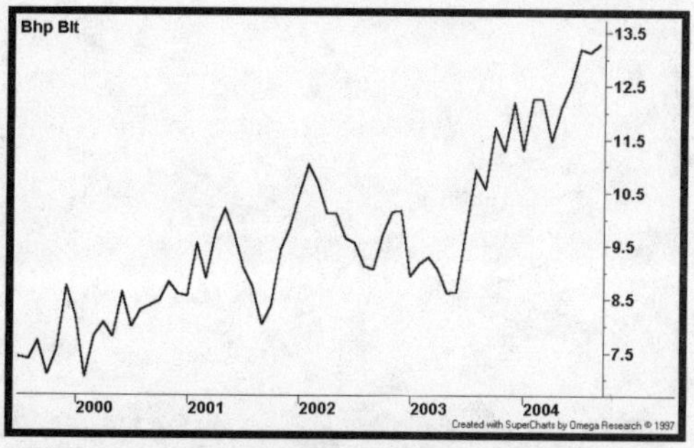

www.bhpbilliton.com

BHP Billiton Limited

Share price ($)	13.15	
12-month high ($)	13.39	
12-month low ($)	10.23	
Market capitalisation ($mn)	49,430.2	
Price-to-NTA-per-share ratio	4.7	
5-year share price return (% p.a.)	13.4	
Sector: Materials	**Company**	**Sector**
Price-earnings ratio (times)	17.5	14.3
Dividend yield (%)	2.8	2.6

BHP Billiton — formed from the 2001 merger of Australian resources giant BHP and British-based mining major Billiton — is the world's largest diversified resources company. It has more than 100 operations in approximately 20 countries, and occupies industry leader or near industry leader positions in major commodity businesses, including aluminium, energy coal and metallurgical coal, copper, ferro-alloys, iron ore and titanium minerals. It also has substantial interests in oil, gas, liquefied natural gas, nickel, diamonds and silver.

Latest business results (June 2004, full year)

Rising commodities prices and the boom in Chinese demand helped BHP to a stunning jump in its annual profit result. All divisions were strong, with the best performance coming from the base metals division — revenues up 75% and EBIT rocketing 304% — thanks to the surging copper price. The petroleum business also enjoyed a strong year, with revenues up 70%, though the EBIT rise was a more subdued 18%. Aluminium revenues were up 31%, with a 34% increase in EBIT. For carbon steel materials the figures were 31% and 9%, for diamonds and specialty products 15% and 37%, for energy coal 23% and 18%, and for stainless-steel materials a superb 58% and 281%. Note that BHP Billiton reports its financial results in US dollars. For the purposes of this book, these have been converted into Australian dollars at the rates of A$1 = US$0.667 for the June 2003 results and A$1 = US$0.718 for the June 2004 results. Thus, figures in this book should be used for general guidance only.

Outlook

BHP Billiton is one of the great beneficiaries of the global boom in resources that has in large part been ignited by the spectacular growth of the Chinese economy. Many observers expect a continuing period of growth over many years. At the same time, the company is finding rising demand from both Europe and the US for many products. In response, it is working to boost production capacity for commodities in short supply. It also has 14 major projects, costing US$5 billion, under development and intended to deliver sustainable long-term growth.

BHP Year to 30 June*	2003	2004
Revenues ($mn)	23,400.3	31,876.0
Petroleum (%)	18	21
Carbon steel materials (%)	21	19
Aluminium (%)	19	17
Base metals (%)	11	13
Energy coal (%)	12	10
Diamonds & specialty products (%)	8	7
Stainless steel materials (%)	6	7
EBIT ($mn)	4,841.1	7,310.6
EBIT margin (%)	31.0	31.9
Operating profit before tax ($mn)	4,172.4	6,736.8
Profit after tax ($mn)	2,788.6	4,682.5
Earnings per share (¢)	44.9	75.3
Cash flow per share (¢)	85.7	115.5
Dividend (¢)	21.74	36.21
Percentage franked	100	100
Net tangible assets per share ($)	2.80	3.07
Interest cover (times)	10.9	17.7
Return on equity (%)	15.4	26.4
Debt-to-equity ratio (%)	47.6	33.0
Current ratio	1.6	1.7

* BHP Billiton reports its financial results in US dollars. For this book they have been converted to Australian dollars.

Blackmores Limited

Share price ($)	10.54	
12-month high ($)	11.00	
12-month low ($)	6.60	
Market capitalisation ($mn)	170.4	
Price-to-NTA-per-share ratio	6.1	
5-year share price return (% p.a.)	26.7	
Sector: Health care	**Company**	**Sector**
Price-earnings ratio (times)	17.7	35.8
Dividend yield (%)	4.4	1.8

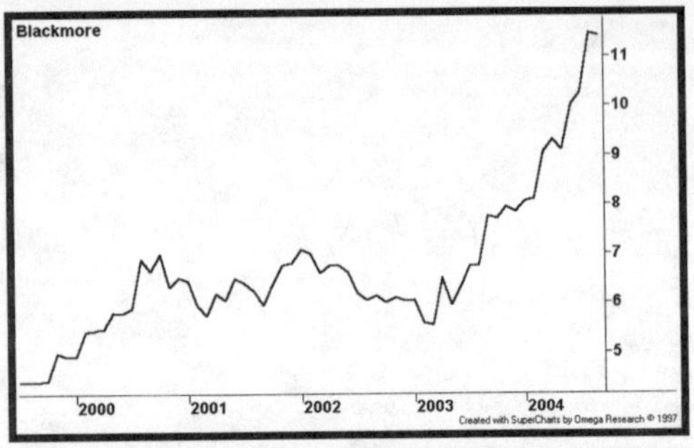

www.blackmores.com.au

Founded in the 1930s, Sydney-based Blackmores is a leading manufacturer and distributor of a wide range of natural health care products, nutritional supplements and cosmetics. Its brands include Vitaglow and BioACE. It exports to South East Asia and New Zealand.

Latest business results (June 2004, full year)

The company enjoyed a booming year of record sales and profits. This was due in particular to the problems experienced by rivals, who often found their products in short supply — having previously been supplied by Pan Pharmaceuticals — and who had been forced to struggle to put in place alternative manufacturing arrangements. Pan Pharmameuticals was the company whose products were subject to a mass recall in April 2003. Blackmores also enjoyed a noticeable lift in its market shares, reflecting a consumer-driven flight to quality and trust, following the Pan recall. Asian sales continued to grow, particularly in the company's two key markets of Malaysia, where sales were up 40% from the previous year, and Thailand, where they grew 20%. New Zealand sales fell as the company shifted its marketing strategies, but profits rose.

Outlook

The company has reported that total nationwide sales of natural health products have risen to a level higher than that which prevailed before the Pan recall, indicating that consumer confidence in the industry has fully returned. Blackmores, which continues to emphasise its adherence to strict ethical principles in all its business dealings, is the prime beneficiary of this, and it has moved quickly to take advantage of fresh market opportunities with new products, new pack sizes, new labels and other enhancements. It is also boosting its focus on research and development, including a greater investment in clinical trial programs and the development of key strategic research relationships. In addition, it is increasing its levels of investment in new product development and support. It continues to view Asia as offering great growth potential, and expects profitability there to continue to grow. New Zealand profitability has been enhanced by moving from a wholly-owned and managed organisation in that market to a royalty-based arrangement with a prominent third-party distributor. Blackmores provides a shareholders card that gives a 25% discount on its products, and this has become a further incentive for the share price.

BKL Year to 30 June	2003	2004
Revenues ($mn)	94.7	115.7
EBIT ($mn)	10.1	14.1
EBIT margin (%)	10.7	12.2
Gross margin (%)	63.0	60.0
Operating profit before tax ($mn)	8.9	13.2
Profit after tax ($mn)	6.2	9.3
Earnings per share (¢)	41.1	59.5
Cash flow per share (¢)	53.5	73.5
Dividend (¢)	35	46
Percentage franked	100	100
Net tangible assets per share ($)	1.50	1.72
Interest cover (times)	8.4	16.7
Return on equity (%)	29.9	37.0
Debt-to-equity ratio (%)	36.2	21.8
Current ratio	1.2	1.6

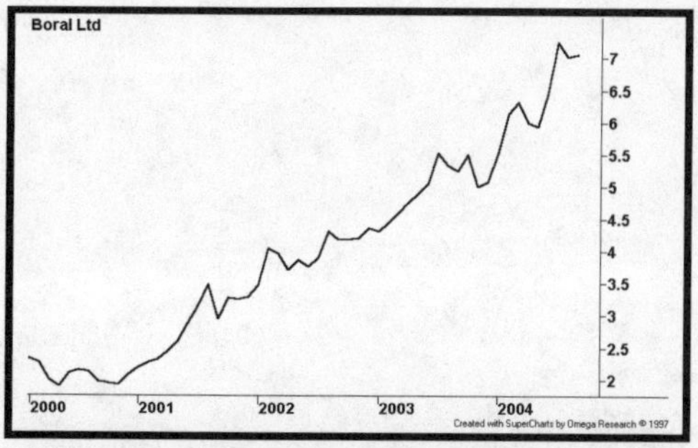

www.boral.com.au

Boral Limited

Share price ($)	6.98	
12-month high ($)	7.43	
12-month low ($)	4.92	
Market capitalisation ($mn)	4,007.6	
Price-to-NTA-per-share ratio	1.9	
5-year share price return (% p.a.)	24.7	
Sector: Materials	**Company**	**Sector**
Price-earnings ratio (times)	10.9	14.3
Dividend yield (%)	4.3	2.6

Sydney-based Boral is one of Australia's largest producers of building and construction materials, and it has operations in several countries. It is this country's biggest brick, clay paver and concrete masonry producer, and is also one of the largest in America. It owns half of a large plasterboard joint venture in Asia. The Australian housing market accounts for 36% of total revenues, the Australian non-dwelling building market for 14%, and the Australian roads, highways, subdivisions and bridges construction market for 22%. More than a quarter of total sales revenues — including exports and overseas production — comes from abroad.

Latest business results (June 2004, full year)

The continuing domestic housing boom, coupled with cost-cutting initiatives of previous years, gave Boral another big earnings rise. Sales rose just 8% but the after-tax profit jumped 31%. Virtually all the company's domestic markets were flourishing, enabling it to raise many of its prices and boost operational efficiencies. Of the company's four operating divisions, construction materials saw sales up 14% and EBIT surge 29%, and building product sales were up 5% with EBIT jumping 33%. American sales revenues edged down, with profits flat, while Asian sales rose 17%, with EBIT up 21%.

Outlook

Boral's after-tax profit has almost tripled in three years, thanks to the power of the domestic housing boom and the company's drive to cut costs. Now the company itself says a slowdown is looming, especially in the housing market, although it expects this to be counter-balanced by continuing strength in the non-dwelling market. Its early forecast is for just 5% growth in profits in the June 2005 year. Efficiency moves continue, with an extensive program of plant upgrades. The mid-2004 acquisition of Hanson's quarry and concrete business in Thailand expands the company's construction materials position in Asia. Though Asian business is relatively small, it is very profitable, with excellent growth prospects. In particular, the company is planning significant moves into China. Boral has abandoned its attempts to acquire cement producer Adelaide Brighton, but is believed to be seeking some major new US acquisitions.

BLD Year to 30 June	2003	2004
Revenues ($mn)	3,831.0	4,149.8
EBIT ($mn)	477.7	599.6
EBIT margin (%)	12.5	14.4
Gross margin (%)	36.9	38.4
Operating profit before tax ($mn)	409.9	534.0
Profit after tax ($mn)	283.2	369.8
Earnings per share (¢)	49.1	63.8
Cash flow per share (¢)	82.8	97.4
Dividend (¢)	23	30
Percentage franked	88	100
Net tangible assets per share ($)	3.27	3.65
Interest cover (times)	7.0	9.1
Return on equity (%)	13.9	16.5
Debt-to-equity ratio (%)	35.7	39.8
Current ratio	1.4	1.3

Brazin Limited

Share price ($)	1.78	
12-month high ($)	1.90	
12-month low ($)	0.91	
Market capitalisation ($mn)	214.0	
Price-to-NTA-per-share ratio	3.8	
5-year share price return (% p.a.)	–6.6	
Sector: Consumer discretionary	**Company**	**Sector**
Price-earnings ratio (times)	12.5	23.8
Dividend yield (%)	3.4	1.5

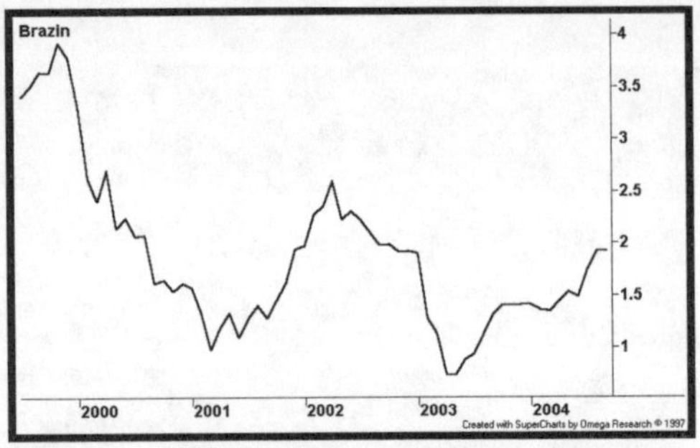

www.brazin.com.au

Sydney-based music and apparel chain Brazin was founded in 1980 with the opening of a music store in Victoria. It now operates stores under several divisions. Its Entertainment Australia unit has 234 stores, mainly under the Sanity banner. Its women's apparel division operates 140 BNT (formerly Bras N Things) stores. Its Dome Exchange business designs and distributes women's beachwear under the Aztec Rose and Cheetah labels, and the company has also moved into footwear, with 39 Ghetto stores. It has sold its British music store business.

Latest business results (June 2004, full year)

A strong retail environment and restructuring initiatives helped Brazin achieve a good result. Revenues were down, reflecting the sale of its British music business, though on a same-store basis they rose 4%. The high-margin BNT stores made a strong $14.9 million contribution to EBIT, though down from $17.5 million a year earlier, with the division hurt by labour and inventory control problems. The Entertainment Australia business moved from a $7.7 million EBIT loss in June 2003 to a $7.4 million profit, due to lower labour costs, tighter inventory control and growing consumer demand for DVDs. The footwear and beachwear design businesses were in the red, and the company also recorded a loss on its now-sold British music store business.

Outlook

After a period of mixed results, Brazin is working to restructure its businesses, and believes a strong June 2004 second half indicates that it is achieving success. In particular, it is streamlining its inventory control systems in order to cut costs, and it is introducing new marketing promotions. The Entertainment Australia division has been hurt by sluggish CD sales, a result of the growing trend towards downloading music from the internet. In response, the company has been successfully repositioning itself as a DVD retailer. Brazin's 50%-owned EzyDVD business expects to have 50 to 60 stores by December 2004, and the company has also announced an alliance with Myer to establish a series of Virgin home entertainment outlets inside Myer stores. The Dome Exchange beachwear business is developing new lines with the aim of restoring profitability. It also plans a lingerie line, Ruby Rose.

BRZ Year to 26 June*	2003	2004
Revenues ($mn)	539.2	421.3
Entertainment Australia (%)	50	63
Women's apparel (%)	18	24
Entertainment UK (%)	30	7
EBIT ($mn)	12.4	20.0
EBIT margin (%)	2.3	4.8
Gross margin (%)	37.3	41.0
Operating profit before tax ($mn)	12.1	19.8
Profit after tax ($mn)	10.9	16.7
Earnings per share (¢)	9.4	14.3
Cash flow per share (¢)	18.4	23.2
Dividend (¢)	10	6
Percentage franked	100	100
Net tangible assets per share ($)	0.46	0.47
Interest cover (times)	42.9	81.5
Return on equity (%)	15.0	23.3
Debt-to-equity ratio (%)	~	~
Current ratio	1.3	1.6

* June 28, 2003

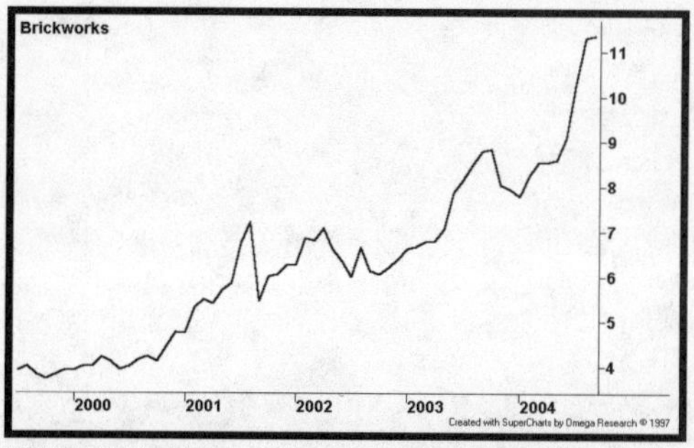

www.brickworks.com.au

Brickworks Limited

Share price ($)	10.35	
12-month high ($)	10.40	
12-month low ($)	7.70	
Market capitalisation ($mn)	1,369.9	
Price-to-NTA-per-share ratio	2.1	
5-year share price return (% p.a.)	27.3	
Sector: Materials	**Company**	**Sector**
Price-earnings ratio (times)	8.7	14.3
Dividend yield (%)	2.3	2.6

Sydney-based Brickworks, founded in 1934, has become Australia's largest brick producer, following its acquisition of rival Bristile. It was already the country's largest producer of floor tiles and, in addition, is one of the largest roof tile manufacturers. It also manages an extensive land portfolio. It has spun off its extensive equity portfolio into a new listed entity, Brickworks Investment Company. In a cross-shareholding arrangement designed to prevent takeovers, it owns 41% of the equity of Washington H. Soul Pattinson, while Soul Pattinson owns nearly 50% of the equity in Brickworks.

Latest business results (June 2004, full year)

The Bristile acquisition and the ongoing housing boom handed Brickworks a massive increase in sales and profits, with sales prices and profit margins higher for most products. However, second-half sales volumes were 7% below those of the first half. There were stronger returns from the company's property portfolio and from its holding in Washington H. Soul Pattinson. Export sales rose 137%, including unprecedented growth in New Zealand, where demand outstretched supply.

Outlook

Thanks to the Bristile acquisition, Brickworks has transformed itself from a state-based clay products manufacturer to a leading national building products company, with national branding and a presence in all Australian states. The company has said that it expects a modest building slowdown but that this would, in some cases, simply allow supply to catch up with demand. All the company's plants remain at full capacity. However, with many of these having operated continually since 2000 or longer, major overhauls are planned for the Christmas/New Year period, which will affect unit production costs and total output in 2005. It is also considering new brick plants in Victoria and Western Australia. Demand from New Zealand continues at high levels, and the company also exports to Japan, Hong Kong and South Korea. It sees China and the Middle East as offering good prospects as export markets. Property development is becoming another area of great potential for Brickworks, with active developments in NSW, Victoria, South Australia and Western Australia. It expects its development at Horsley Park, west of Sydney, to deliver $150 million in revenues over 10 to 12 years.

BKW Year to 30 June	2003	2004
Revenues ($mn)	179.6	485.7
EBIT ($mn)	78.7	214.5
EBIT margin (%)	43.8	44.2
Gross margin (%)	40.2	38.6
Operating profit before tax ($mn)	75.3	190.3
Profit after tax ($mn)	72.7	157.4
Earnings per share (¢)	55.2	119.5
Cash flow per share (¢)	63.8	147.8
Dividend (¢)	20	24
Percentage franked	100	100
Net tangible assets per share ($)	4.61	4.91
Interest cover (times)	23.0	8.9
Return on equity (%)	12.6	21.0
Debt-to-equity ratio (%)	5.0	30.1
Current ratio	1.0	1.1

Cabcharge Australia Limited

Share price ($)	3.67	
12-month high ($)	3.73	
12-month low ($)	2.73	
Market capitalisation ($mn)	411.9	
Price-to-NTA-per-share ratio	3.5	
5-year share price return (% p.a.)	8.5	
Sector: Industrials	**Company**	**Sector**
Price-earnings ratio (times)	17.8	14.8
Dividend yield (%)	3.7	4.2

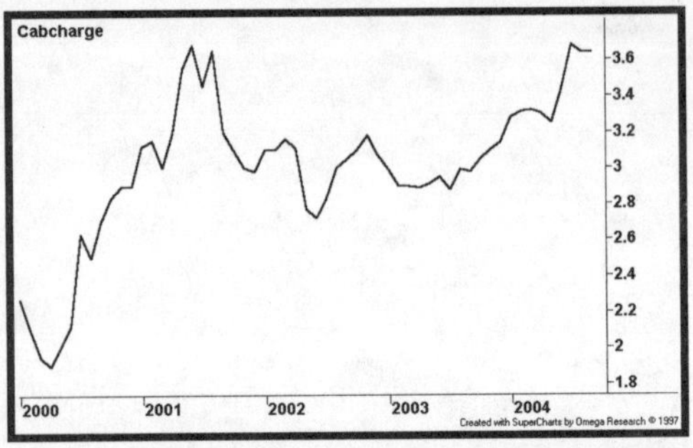

www.cabcharge.com.au

Sydney-based Cabcharge, founded in 1976, manages a charge-card system that allows taxi users to pay fares without requiring cash. The system, which is now online, is used by more than 95% of Australian taxis, and also by other companies, such as limousine services. Cabcharge has more than 44,000 account customers, ranging from large corporations and government departments to small businesses and individuals. Cabcharge also owns Australia's largest taxi company, Sydney-based Combined Communications Network. In August 2003 it acquired Melbourne-based Black Cabs Combined and in April 2004 it acquired ABC Radio Taxi Cooperative in Sydney. It has established a small presence in the UK, with a joint venture operation in several cities.

Latest business results (June 2004, full year)

Cabcharge continued its solid record of growth, with 7% growth in revenues from its taxi charge operation translating into 16% profit growth, thanks to cost controls and economies of scale. Electronic transactions represented 52% of all business, up from 48% in the previous year. Cabcharge's much smaller taxi service operation — about 7% of total company turnover — saw sales revenues up nearly 19%, thanks to the Black Cabs and ABC Radio Taxi Cooperative acquisitions and the closure of loss-making operations, with profits up 18%.

Outlook

Thanks to its overwhelming penetration of the domestic taxi charge business, Cabcharge will enjoy strong profits while the economy and the taxi industry remain buoyant. It continues to enhance its technology, with new systems that are aimed at reducing costs, and it is seeing a steady move to its online systems. The acquisition of taxi companies hands Cabcharge a new stream of earnings, and the company also reaps higher profits when its charge cards are used on its own taxis. It hopes to launch its business in Europe as a means for further growth, and sees its new operations in the UK as providing a base for further expansion. It is also seeking further acquisitions domestically, both within and outside the taxi industry. However, the company also faces a review of its near-monopoly status from the Australian Competition and Consumer Commission (ACCC), and this has the potential to hurt its business.

CAB Year to 30 June	2003	2004
Revenues ($mn)	633.6	681.1
EBIT ($mn)	26.3	30.6
EBIT margin (%)	4.1	4.5
Operating profit before tax ($mn)	27.9	32.5
Profit after tax ($mn)	20.3	23.1
Earnings per share (¢)	18.0	20.6
Cash flow per share (¢)	23.8	28.5
Dividend (¢)	12	13.75
Percentage franked	100	100
Net tangible assets per share ($)	1.04	1.05
Interest cover (times)	~	~
Return on equity (%)	18.0	18.7
Debt-to-equity ratio (%)	~	~
Current ratio	4.1	3.3

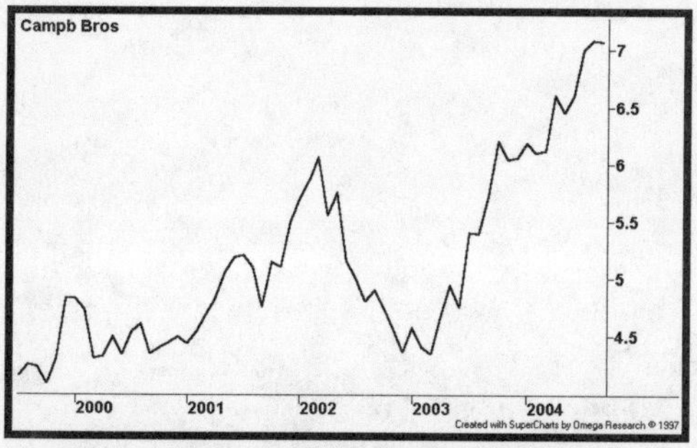

www.campbell.com.au

Campbell Brothers Limited

Share price ($)	7.00	
12-month high ($)	7.16	
12-month low ($)	5.28	
Market capitalisation ($mn)	284.4	
Price-to-NTA-per-share ratio	4.6	
5-year share price return (% p.a.)	17.3	
Sector: Materials	**Company**	**Sector**
Price-earnings ratio (times)	19.0	14.3
Dividend yield (%)	4.7	2.6

Established in 1863, Brisbane-based Campbell Brothers is one of the world's largest providers of laboratory analysis services to the minerals industry, with operations in 17 countries. It is also a leading manufacturer and distributor of household laundry and cleansing products, it offers sales and marketing systems to grocery manufacturers and retailers and it distributes consumer and industrial goods throughout the South Pacific. As well, it is an Australian leader in the importation, manufacture and distribution of chemicals and associated products, and in the provision of engineering system services and water treatment technologies.

Latest business results (March 2004, full year)

Campbell's booming laboratory operations were largely responsible for another solid boost to earnings. Laboratory services profits surged 32% and industrial division profits were up 18%. By contrast, consumer product earnings fell 12%. The laboratories business benefited from a consolidation of expansion initiatives of previous years, leading to higher market share in Australia, Asia and the Americas, and increased margins. Though representing less than a third of company revenues, laboratory services now contribute some 60% of profits. Acquisitions, along with new products and services, boosted the industrial division's three business units.

Outlook

Campbell's under-performing consumer products business faces continuing competitive pressures from both domestic and multinational suppliers of household laundry and detergent products. In response, the company is attempting to boost its exposure to higher-margin servicing businesses, such as pest control and contract washroom hygiene, and it is selling several laundry and detergent brands to Colgate-Palmolive, in order to concentrate on its laboratory operations, which continue to expand. Campbell is opening new laboratories in China and South Africa, giving it access to the sizable minerals market in Africa, as well as to the emerging environmental and chemical testing markets in China. It is also pursuing a number of opportunities in 'green testing' for environmental contaminants in the electrical and electronic equipment markets. It views this business as offering great potential. It is seeking further acquisitions for its industrial division, and it plans to expand this division's distribution network in Australia and New Zealand.

CPB Year to 31 March	2003	2004
Revenues ($mn)	359.3	390.3
Industrial (%)	31	36
Consumer (%)	37	33
Laboratory services (%)	32	31
EBIT ($mn)	25.0	30.2
EBIT margin (%)	7.0	7.7
Gross margin (%)	26.0	30.1
Operating profit before tax ($mn)	19.9	24.4
Profit after tax ($mn)	11.9	14.6
Earnings per share (¢)	30.5	36.8
Cash flow per share (¢)	70.1	76.5
Dividend (¢)	30	33
Percentage franked	100	100
Net tangible assets per share ($)	1.53	1.53
Interest cover (times)	4.9	5.2
Return on equity (%)	9.4	11.2
Debt-to-equity ratio (%)	67.8	69.3
Current ratio	2.0	2.3

Candle Australia Limited

Share price ($)	1.75	
12-month high ($)	1.77	
12-month low ($)	1.20	
Market capitalisation ($mn)	69.2	
Price-to-NTA-per-share ratio	5.6	
5-year share price return (% p.a.)	–6.7	
Sector: Industrials	**Company**	**Sector**
Price-earnings ratio (times)	14.8	14.8
Dividend yield (%)	5.1	4.2

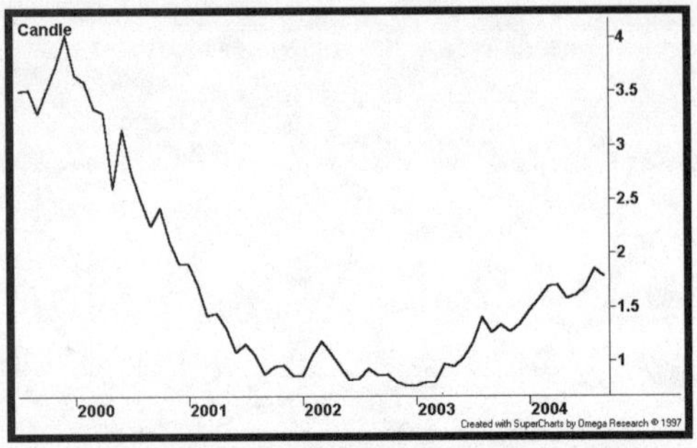

www.candle.com.au

Sydney-based Candle Australia, founded in 1984, has grown through a series of mergers and acquisitions to become a leading nationwide specialist provider of recruitment services to the information communications technology, banking, finance, insurance and government sectors. Its divisions include Candle Information and Communications Technology (Candle ICT), Alliance Recruitment, Freeman Adams, Technology Co-Sourcing Solutions, Workskills Professionals and Premier Personnel. It also provides payroll services, and it operates in New Zealand.

Latest business results (June 2004, full year)

A solid gain in revenues generated further strong growth in profits. There was a particularly strong performance from the company's core Candle ICT business, both in Australia and New Zealand. There was also a good result from the banking and finance recruitment business Freeman Adams, and maiden contributions from two acquisitions made during the year, Workskills Professionals and Premier Personnel, both of which performed above expectations.

Outlook

Candle is a key participant in the highly competitive white-collar recruitment industry. Virtually debt-free, it is seeking to continue to grow by acquisition. It has put in place a solid portfolio of businesses and it believes that these offer the scope for cross-selling and for a stream of productivity benefits. As long as the economy remains firm and the white-collar job market stays tight, the company expects to continue its impressive long-term record of boosting profits. It is a leader in IT recruitment, and sees growing evidence of a rise in demand for IT professionals. Its banking and finance business Freeman Adams has moved into Melbourne, and is performing well. The acquisition of Perth-based Workskills Professionals has strengthened the company's position in Western Australia. The company is realising good growth in its permanent- placement business and is launching a renewed marketing focus on this sector, including the addition of a new specialist division, Executive Search and Selection. It is seeking new acquisitions to support this business. Candle Australia is one of several listed companies in the recruitment business whose shares have attracted support on the potential for a big shake-out in the sector, which is seen as particularly likely if the economy should start to falter and unemployment rises.

CND Year to 30 June	2003	2004
Revenues ($mn)	161.9	179.2
EBIT ($mn)	5.5	7.0
EBIT margin (%)	3.4	3.9
Operating profit before tax ($mn)	5.2	6.8
Profit after tax ($mn)	3.5	4.6
Earnings per share (¢)	9.5	11.8
Cash flow per share (¢)	14.7	16.2
Dividend (¢)	6	9
Percentage franked	100	100
Net tangible assets per share ($)	0.34	0.31
Interest cover (times)	21.5	38.7
Return on equity (%)	8.6	10.2
Debt-to-equity ratio (%)	1.5	0.5
Current ratio	1.7	1.4

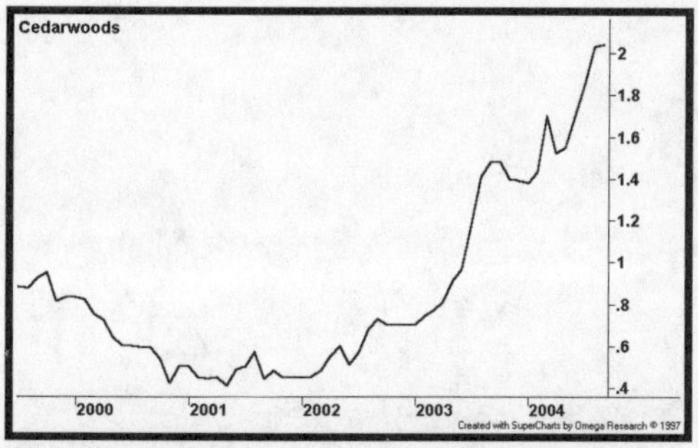

www.cedarwoods.com.au

Cedar Woods Properties Limited

Share price ($)	2.05	
12-month high ($)	2.05	
12-month low ($)	1.29	
Market capitalisation ($mn)	109.1	
Price-to-NTA-per-share ratio	2.3	
5-year share price return (% p.a.)	27.6	
Sector: Financials	**Company**	**Sector**
Price-earnings ratio (times)	10.1	12.9
Dividend yield (%)	4.9	5.2

Perth-based Cedar Woods, founded in 1987, is a prominent property developer in Western Australia. Its main interests are in urban land subdivision for residential, commercial and industrial purposes. It is also active in Melbourne.

Latest business results (June 2004, full year)

Cedar Woods rode the housing boom to a strong surge in revenues and profits. Much of the growth came from new projects that were brought to account during the period. Revenue at the Mariners' Cove waterfront development at the Port Mandurah coastal community increased during the year, following the successful launch of the first canal island. There was a particular boost to company sales and profits during the second half, with the successful launch of the first stage of The Kestrels, a major new residential development at Tapping, and the start of construction of the Aria apartments at Rockingham, both projects on the outskirts of Perth. All stage one lots at Tapping have been sold, as have all the Aria apartments.

Outlook

Though Cedar Woods will struggle to escape the impact of a housing downturn, company management note that the Western Australian economy is predicted to outpace the national economy, and housing affordability is less of an issue in Perth than in Sydney and Melbourne. The company's own target is for medium-term EPS growth of 10% per year, and based on pre-sales to date it believes it can achieve this goal in the June 2005 year. Among the projects to contribute will be the second island at Mariners' Cove, the Kestrels residential development at Tapping, the Rivergums estate at Baldivis, a new waterfront townhouse development at Port Mandurah, the Garden Village estate at Canning Vale and the Axis commercial site at Balcatta. Following the success of the Aria apartments in Rockingham, the company plans another nearby development, Nautilus Apartments. Cedar Woods also plans a major 275-hectare development on the former Laverton airfield, in West Melbourne, with a significant contribution to company revenues and profits expected over an eight-year period from around 2005 or 2006. In addition, the company is actively seeking other sites in Melbourne that will contribute to continued growth.

CWP Year to 30 June	2003	2004
Revenues ($mn)	36.9	57.0
EBIT ($mn)	11.1	15.9
EBIT margin (%)	30.1	27.9
Gross margin (%)	47.2	45.4
Operating profit before tax ($mn)	10.9	14.7
Profit after tax ($mn)	7.1	10.3
Earnings per share (¢)	14.5	20.2
Cash flow per share (¢)	14.6	20.4
Dividend (¢)	7	10
Percentage franked	100	100
Net tangible assets per share ($)	0.75	0.90
Interest cover (times)	58.9	12.8
Return on equity (%)	21.7	24.2
Debt-to-equity ratio (%)	15.8	48.4
Current ratio	0.9	1.2

Cellnet Group Limited

Share price ($)	1.34	
12-month high ($)	1.49	
12-month low ($)	0.63	
Market capitalisation ($mn)	67.7	
Price-to-NTA-per-share ratio	1.4	
5-year share price return (% p.a.)	23.3	
Sector: Information technology	**Company**	**Sector**
Price-earnings ratio (times)	7.3	28.7
Dividend yield (%)	8.5	2.5

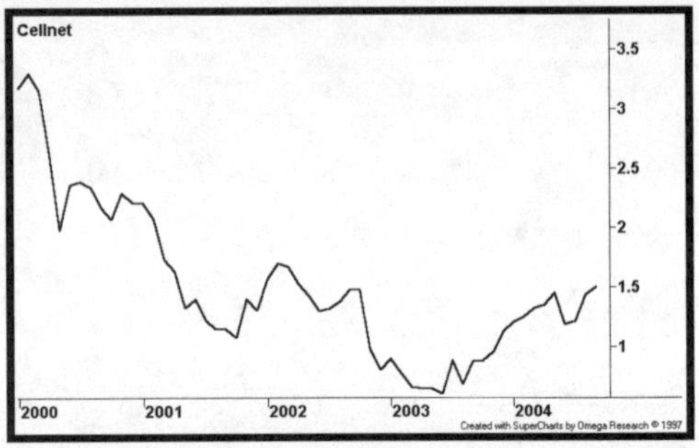

www.cellnetgroup.com.au

Brisbane-based Cellnet, established in 1992, is a prominent wholesale distributor in Australia and New Zealand of mobile phones and accessories and of IT products and related consumables. With warehouse facilities and offices in Brisbane, Sydney, Melbourne, Perth, Adelaide and Auckland, the company distributes a wide range of products. It is a leading distributor of IBM products, but is involved in numerous other leading brands. Its Mercury Mobility venture provides innovative content for mobile phones, and its Comms+ business is engaged in marketing and advertising, and has evolved into a specialised agency for some of the major mobile phone manufacturers and retail outlets.

Latest business results (June 2004, full year)

Booming nationwide demand for electronics and telecommunications devices helped the company to a big jump in sales and profits. Mobile phone revenues were up 41%, with profits soaring 90%, as demand for phones and accessories exceeded expectations. The result was also affected by inventory write-offs that bit into profits in the previous year. IT product revenues rose 39%, but profits fell 30%, which the company largely attributed to a re-allocation of group costs. There was a particularly strong performance from specialist IT components distributor Cassa Australia, acquired by Cellnet in July 2003, which increased its revenues by 54%.

Outlook

Cellnet operates in a highly competitive and rapidly evolving industry, and it must stay nimble to prosper. Much of its success has been due to its diversity, with a wide variety of manufacturers whose products it distributes. This has allowed it to continue to grow, despite the loss of a $20-million distribution contract with Nokia. It also faces the loss of a deal with Hutchison, which is moving to direct distribution of its products. The company is seeking to diversify further, with the launch in June 2004 of a consumer electronics business, Cellnet Consumer Products. This division has a distribution arrangement with Sony for audio accessories, and Cellnet hopes to use this as a springboard for greater penetration of this high-growth industry. The company is also working to strengthen its presence in NSW and Victoria, with new warehouses in both states.

CLT Year to 30 June	2003	2004
Revenues ($mn)	318.4	446.6
Mobile phones & accessories (%)	62	62
IT products (%)	38	38
EBIT ($mn)	8.9	14.6
EBIT margin (%)	2.8	3.3
Gross margin (%)	10.1	8.8
Operating profit before tax ($mn)	7.7	13.5
Profit after tax ($mn)	5.3	9.1
Earnings per share (¢)	10.6	18.3
Cash flow per share (¢)	14.7	22.8
Dividend (¢)	7	11.5
Percentage franked	100	100
Net tangible assets per share ($)	0.94	0.97
Interest cover (times)	7.4	13.2
Return on equity (%)	10.6	16.7
Debt-to-equity ratio (%)	~	38.0
Current ratio	2.1	1.7

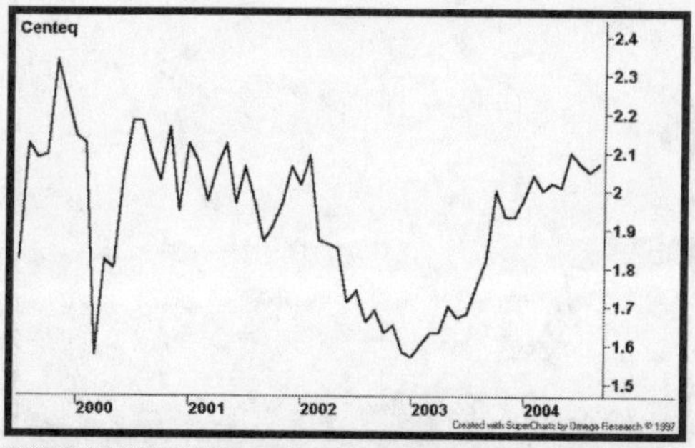

www.centralequity.com.au

Central Equity Limited

Share price ($)	2.07	
12-month high ($)	2.15	
12-month low ($)	1.72	
Market capitalisation ($mn)	180.2	
Price-to-NTA-per-share ratio	0.9	
5-year share price return (% p.a.)	7.2	
Sector: Financials	**Company**	**Sector**
Price-earnings ratio (times)	5.3	12.9
Dividend yield (%)	6.3	5.2

Melbourne-based property developer Central Equity was founded in 1987, and has been responsible for more than $2.3 billion worth of residential property developments in the city. It has achieved renown for its pioneering inner-city apartment projects, including the conversion of older buildings into residential properties. It has also moved into medium-density housing in Melbourne's inner suburbs. Altogether, it has sold more than 7,000 homes and apartments in the city. Its real estate subsidiary, Melbourne Inner City Management, has an extensive business managing many of the properties the company has sold.

Latest business results (June 2004, full year)

Rising construction costs bit into profits, which rose only modestly — albeit, to record levels — despite a 25% increase in sales revenues. The company completed construction of three projects in Melbourne's riverside Southbank precinct — Southpoint in August 2003 and The Sentinel and Victoria Tower in November 2003. At the end of June 2004 the company had an additional $185 million of contracted sales which had not been brought to account as sales revenue or reflected in the company's financial statements. This was sharply down from $433 million in June 2003 and $495 million in June 2002.

Outlook

Central Equity was a prime stock market beneficiary of the prolonged housing boom, and of the trend towards inner-city living. However, it is now suffering from the after-effects of this boom, with an easing in demand and rising costs, though there are indications that the housing slowdown means that costs are no longer escalating as much as previously. It has two Southbank projects in the final stages of completion, Melbourne Tower and City Tower. With fears of a slump in the inner-city apartment market, the company is working to expand its product range. Its land subdivision interests have grown with the acquisition of 186 hectares of land at Pakenham, Mernda and Point Cook, which will yield a total of around 2,000 blocks, with an estimated end sales value of approximately $250 million. These parcels of land to be developed as housing estates are at various stages of the planning process, with the Mernda project scheduled to be released to the market during 2004.

CEQ Year to 30 June	2003	2004
Revenues ($mn)	224.4	281.7
EBIT ($mn)	42.5	41.2
EBIT margin (%)	18.9	14.6
Gross margin (%)	24.8	22.0
Operating profit before tax ($mn)	46.9	48.0
Profit after tax ($mn)	32.8	33.6
Earnings per share (¢)	38.0	39.0
Cash flow per share (¢)	39.4	41.1
Dividend (¢)	13	13
Percentage franked	100	100
Net tangible assets per share ($)	2.13	2.39
Interest cover (times)	~	~
Return on equity (%)	19.1	17.2
Debt-to-equity ratio (%)	46.6	21.3
Current ratio	1.7	1.9

Coates Hire Limited

Share price ($)	3.81	
12-month high ($)	3.89	
12-month low ($)	2.40	
Market capitalisation ($mn)	798.9	
Price-to-NTA-per-share ratio	2.3	
5-year share price return (% p.a.)	21.9	
Sector: Industrials	**Company**	**Sector**
Price-earnings ratio (times)	14.9	14.8
Dividend yield (%)	3.4	4.2

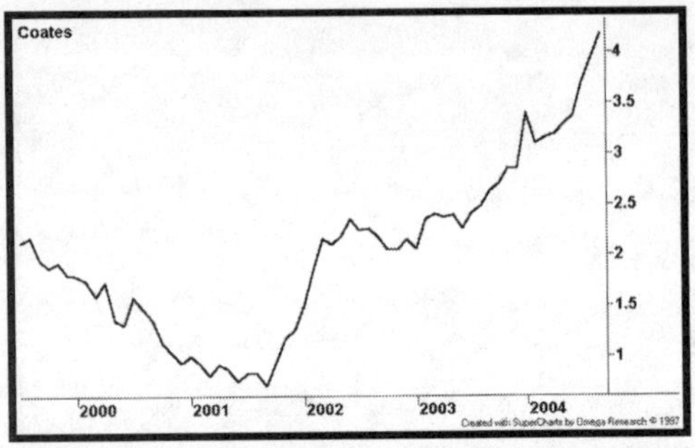

www.coates.com.au

Sydney-based Coates Hire Limited is Australia's largest hire equipment company with more than 130 branches. Following the acquisition of its largest rival Wreckair, it now has around a third of the market. Domestically, it divides its operations into four businesses: Coates Hire provides a large range of general equipment; Coates Shorco Sykes supplies specialist pumps and excavation support equipment; Coates Prestige provides portable buildings and toilets; and Coates Conrent is a leading supplier of construction hoists. It sold much of its British business in August 2004, but retains a small operation in Indonesia.

Latest business results (June 2004, full year)

The company achieved a superb result, with a strong rise in sales and a big jump in profits. Most of the growth was organic, although there was a contribution from about $40 million of new acquisitions made during the year. The core Coates Hire business saw strong growth, thanks in particular to a continuing series of major infrastructure projects around Australia. Of the company's specialist businesses, Coates Conrent had its best year ever. Acquisitions by Coates Shorco Sykes helped it capitalise on strong activity in the resources industry. Coates Prestige again used its strong industry position and sound reputation to continue a trend of growing revenue and improved margins. Uncertain conditions in Indonesia (which represents less than 1% of total company sales) led to a 40% decline in revenues, and business there fell into the red. British business was much improved, though not yet in profit, but the decision was nevertheless made to sell much of that division.

Outlook

Several years of acquisitions and productivity improvements continue to hand Coates superior growth, at exactly the time when the construction and resources industries are booming. The company's problem now is to manage its growth — through further acquisitions and internal organic expansion — so that it can take advantage of new opportunities but avoid being caught out with huge amounts of surplus equipment when the cycle turns. It has retained its profitable British business servicing the offshore oil and gas industry, and hopes to expand this to the Asia-Pacific region.

COA Year to 30 June	2003	2004
Revenues ($mn)	378.4	456.9
EBIT ($mn)	43.1	78.6
EBIT margin (%)	11.4	17.2
Operating profit before tax ($mn)	32.5	68.3
Profit after tax ($mn)	33.2	52.1
Earnings per share (¢)	16.7	25.6
Cash flow per share (¢)	51.5	59.8
Dividend (¢)	11	13
Percentage franked	89	100
Net tangible assets per share ($)	1.49	1.64
Interest cover (times)	4.1	7.6
Return on equity (%)	11.3	15.9
Debt-to-equity ratio (%)	35.8	40.0
Current ratio	1.0	1.1

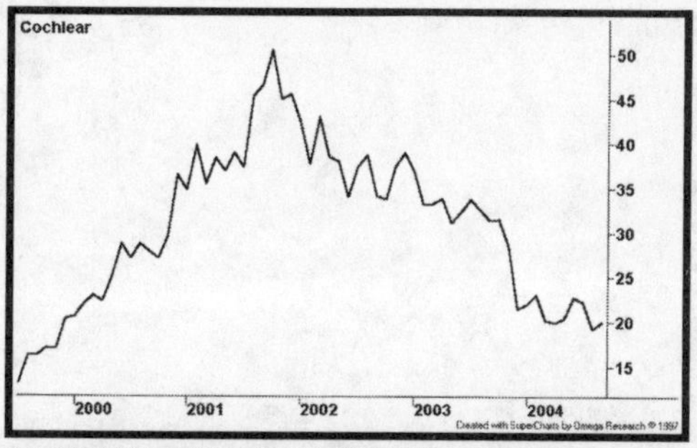

www.cochlear.com.au

Cochlear Limited

Share price ($)	18.78	
12-month high ($)	34.50	
12-month low ($)	18.20	
Market capitalisation ($mn)	1,029.1	
Price-to-NTA-per-share ratio	7.7	
5-year share price return (% p.a.)	6.9	
Sector: Health care	**Company**	**Sector**
Price-earnings ratio (times)	27.5	35.8
Dividend yield (%)	4.2	1.8

Sydney-based Cochlear, founded in 1981, has up to two-thirds of the world market for cochlear bionic-ear implants, which are intended to assist the communication ability of people suffering from severe hearing impediments. It has sold some 57,000 of its Nucleus 22 and Nucleus 24 implant systems in around 80 countries. Overseas business accounts for over 95% of sales and profits.

Latest business results (June 2004, full year)

Cochlear's high-growth trajectory came to a crashing halt, as profits plunged. Most of the damage was done in the US, where market share was down. Revenues for the Americas region fell 23% to $109 million, and EBIT slumped from $36.4 million to just $8.9 million. In part, this was because a leading US competitor had been forced out of the market in the previous year, handing Cochlear an unusually large gain in sales in that year. The strength of the dollar was also a significant factor. European sales slipped 5% to $93 million, with EBIT down 28% to $21.2 million, though, in local currencies, business actually improved. Asia Pacific — which includes Australian sales — saw revenues rise 4% to nearly $51 million, with EBIT jumping 53% to $5.8 million. The previous year had seen Asian business hurt by the SARS epidemic. Total unit sales for the year were flat at 9,306.

Outlook

Cochlear enjoyed a surging share price for some years, but this too has come crashing down, along with profits. Investors are also concerned about apparent turmoil in the key US market, where the company has been hurt by the resurgence of its main rival, Advanced Bionics, which has been gaining market share, as well as by the defection of a key executive to that company, and by news that the US Department of Justice has launched an investigation into Cochlear's relationship with health care professionals. However, Cochlear management believe they have turned the company around, and that it is heading back towards its high-growth path. New marketing executives have been appointed for all regions, and the company has acquired its distributors' businesses in key markets in Europe and Asia, in order to strengthen marketing. Late in September 2004, Cochlear's shares surged on reports of problems at Advanced Bionics.

COH Year to 30 June	2003	2004
Revenues ($mn)	288.6	252.5
EBIT ($mn)	80.1	45.5
EBIT margin (%)	27.8	18.0
Gross margin (%)	74.6	69.6
Operating profit before tax ($mn)	80.0	47.3
Profit after tax ($mn)	58.2	36.8
Earnings per share (¢)	110.0	68.2
Cash flow per share (¢)	124.6	85.7
Dividend (¢)	77	79
Percentage franked	100	100
Net tangible assets per share ($)	2.26	2.43
Interest cover (times)	576.6	~
Return on equity (%)	59.7	28.4
Debt-to-equity ratio (%)	~	~
Current ratio	1.8	1.9

Coffey International Limited

Share price ($)	6.18	
12-month high ($)	6.18	
12-month low ($)	4.35	
Market capitalisation ($mn)	79.4	
Price-to-NTA-per-share ratio	5.3	
5-year share price return (% p.a.)	48.0	
Sector: Industrials	**Company**	**Sector**
Price-earnings ratio (times)	10.3	14.8
Dividend yield (%)	7.1	4.2

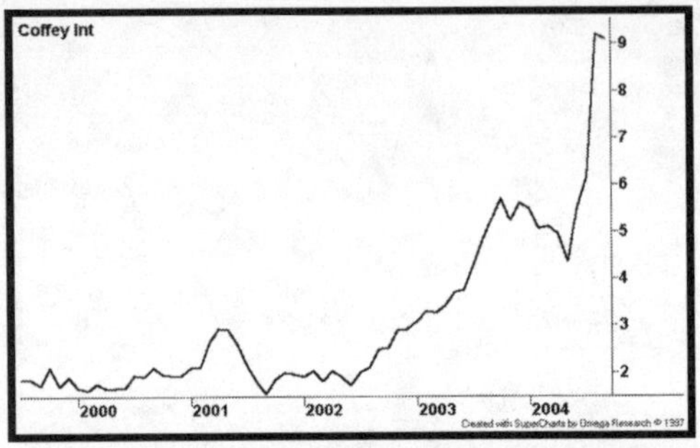

www.coffey.com.au

Sydney-based Coffey, established in 1959, has grown through acquisition from its roots as a specialist scientific and engineering consulting partnership into a diverse group of consulting and project management businesses. Its consulting group operates through a string of offices in Australia and South-East Asia, and offers particular expertise in geotechnical engineering, environmental engineering, hydrogeology, hydrology, natural resources, geophysics, mining and civil engineering. Its international development business group, based in Adelaide, offers project management and administration expertise in the areas of water supply and sanitation, governance, health, community development, land services, tourism, agriculture and the environment.

Latest business results (June 2004, full year)

The combination of recent acquisitions and continuing strong organic growth handed Coffey a record profit result. A buoyant domestic infrastructure market helped the consulting group to another year of strong business. It was also assisted by the acquisition during the year of two companies, Soil & Rock Engineering and IT Environmental (Australia). The international development business group saw good profits, especially in the second half, thanks to several major contract wins during the year. There was a particularly strong contribution from Coffey MPW, which specialises in international development projects, and which won important projects in Tonga, Sri Lanka and Mongolia.

Outlook

Coffey has launched itself upon a growth path, and it continues to expand through acquisition. The latest addition is the environmental planning consultancy Enesar Consulting, acquired in mid-2004. The company's own forecast is for profit growth of 15% to 20% in the June 2005 year, with strong organic growth for all businesses. Thanks to its prominent presence in the mining industry, Coffey is a major beneficiary of prevailing boom conditions. It is also benefiting greatly from a string of major new infrastructure projects from both the government and private sectors. It has experienced delays on some Iraq projects, but stresses that the financial impact will be minimal. It is working to boost shareholder value, including a more generous policy on dividend payouts and plans for a share split, to make the shares more marketable.

COF Year to 30 June	2003	2004
Revenues ($mn)	110.5	131.0
International development (%)	63	53
Consulting (%)	37	47
EBIT ($mn)	8.1	10.8
EBIT margin (%)	7.4	8.2
Operating profit before tax ($mn)	7.8	10.4
Profit after tax ($mn)	5.1	7.0
Earnings per share (¢)	45.0	59.7
Cash flow per share (¢)	55.4	72.0
Dividend (¢)	27	44
Percentage franked	100	100
Net tangible assets per share ($)	1.25	1.17
Interest cover (times)	28.4	32.6
Return on equity (%)	32.1	32.5
Debt-to-equity ratio (%)	~	18.7
Current ratio	1.5	1.3

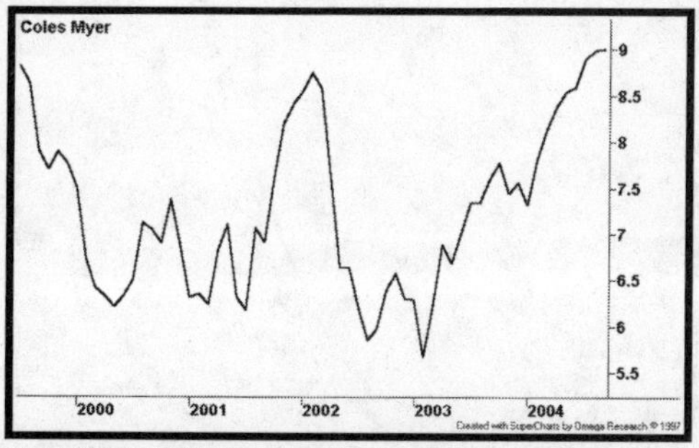

www.colesmyer.com.au

Coles Myer Limited

Share price ($)	8.87	
12-month high ($)	9.18	
12-month low ($)	7.21	
Market capitalisation ($mn)	10,857.8	
Price-to-NTA-per-share ratio	3.8	
5-year share price return (% p.a.)	7.4	
Sector: Consumer staples	**Company**	**Sector**
Price-earnings ratio (times)	17.5	16.8
Dividend yield (%)	3.3	3.7

Melbourne-based Coles Myer is Australia's largest retailer and one of the biggest in the world. It operates more than 2,500 stores, including Coles, Myer, Megamart, Kmart, Target, Bi-Lo, Coles Express, Liquorland, Vintage Cellars, Theo's Liquor, Harris Technology and Officeworks.

Latest business results (July 2004, full year)

Coles Myer enjoyed an excellent year, with all its main business groups reporting stronger sales and double- or triple-digit profit growth. The core food and liquor division recorded 8.5% sales growth, with EBIT up 12.5%, which was its strongest profit growth in six years. The Kmart and Officeworks division saw sales up 7.1% and EBIT up 30.9%. Target reported sales up 7.7% and EBIT jumping 64%. The Myer and Megamart division saw EBIT surge 140.9% on just a 2.5% sales increase, and despite continuing losses at Megamart. The new Coles Express fuel and convenience store business was profitable in its first year of operations.

Outlook

Coles Myer believes it is on track to deliver an $800 million after-tax profit in July 2006, although it remains to be seen whether recent superb conditions — including a strong domestic economy, a firm dollar and the government family assistance package — can easily be replicated. Part of its growth has come from the 598 new Coles Express sites — offering discounted petrol — with sales in July 2004 of $3.2 billion and a goal of $4.5 billion in July 2005. The supermarkets business is placing a growing emphasis on higher-margin house-brand products. Already, the company offers over 4,000 house-brand products, and expects these to represent 30% of total supermarket sales by 2007. It plans to enhance its Myer department stores with the introduction of Virgin-brand entertainment centres. The loss-making Megamart business is being restructured, with new store layouts, a new marketing campaign and a stronger focus on customer service. Coles Myer believes the ending of its popular shareholder's discount card in July 2004 has had only a marginal impact on sales, and has contributed to earnings growth, and it has introduced a loyalty card for regular Myer shoppers. There has been market speculation that Coles Myer will launch a takeover bid for liquor retailer Australian Leisure and Hospitality.

CML Year to 25 July*	2003	2004
Revenues ($mn)	27,016.6	32,266.8
Food & liquor (%)	61	56
Kmart & Officeworks (%)	16	14
Myer & Megamart (%)	12	10
Coles Express (%)	0	10
Target (%)	10	9
EBIT ($mn)	680.4	888.1
EBIT margin (%)	2.5	2.8
Gross margin (%)	27.4	25.4
Operating profit before tax ($mn)	617.2	874.6
Profit after tax ($mn)	429.5	616.5
Earnings per share (¢)	36.0	50.7
Cash flow per share (¢)	78.3	94.1
Dividend (¢)	26	29
Percentage franked	100	100
Net tangible assets per share ($	2.16	2.31
Interest cover (times)	10.8	65.8
Return on equity (%)	12.1	15.7
Debt-to-equity ratio (%)	6.6	3.1
Current ratio	1.4	1.2

* 27 July 2003

Colorado Group Limited

Share price ($)	5.35	
12-month high ($)	5.67	
12-month low ($)	3.20	
Market capitalisation ($mn)	494.5	
Price-to-NTA-per-share ratio	5.0	
3-year share price return (% p.a.)	54.3	
Sector: Consumer discretionary	**Company**	**Sector**
Price-earnings ratio (times)	16.4	23.8
Dividend yield (%)	3.0	1.5

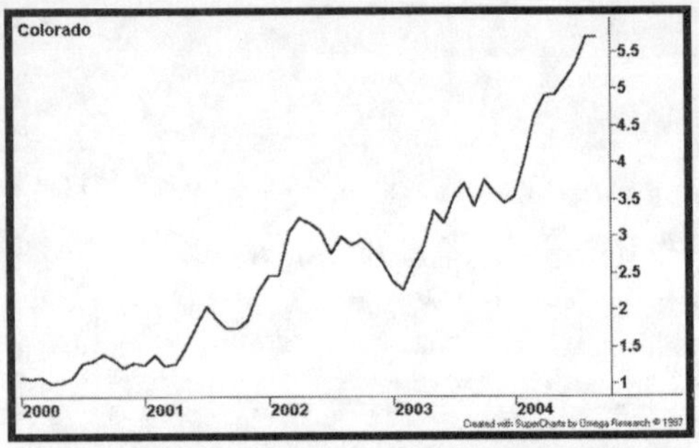

www.coloradogroup.com.au

Brisbane-based Colorado, with roots dating back to the establishment of the first Williams shoe store in Ballarat in 1864, is a prominent footwear and apparel retailer and wholesaler. It comprises 400 stores in Australia and New Zealand, across five divisions — Colorado Adventurewear, Mathers Shoes, Williams the Shoemen, Diana Ferrari and Jag.

Latest business results (July 2004, half-year)

Continuing strong consumer spending and the impact of the stronger dollar propelled Colorado to a stunning rise in profits. The company was also a beneficiary of government family assistance payments. Each of the company's five divisions contributed to the result, with double-digit sales growth from Jag, and excellent profit performances from the two biggest divisions, Williams the Shoemen and Colorado Adventurewear. The Mathers Shoes business turned in a much-improved result, after a poor performance in the previous year.

Outlook

Colorado continues to benefit from a buoyant economy and the strength of its popular, middle-market brands, and it has already announced that it expects 2005 profits to be at least 30% higher than in 2004. However, management has cautioned that part of the recent strong profit gain has been the result of a short-term profit spike from currency hedging. It believes it can achieve continuing firm growth through organic expansion, and plans to open at least 16 new stores in the January 2005 second half. However, it might also close some stores whose costs are becoming too high, due mainly to rapidly escalating rents. It is achieving particular success with a series of larger 'lifestyle' stores for the Colorado division, and it plans more of these. With no net debt, it is also eager to grow by acquisition, and management has already indicated that Colorado might expand into the accessories business. The company is installing a $10-million electronic inventory management system to improve efficiency. If suitable acquisition opportunities fail to present themselves, the company may arrange some kind of capital return to shareholders.

CDO Year to 31 January*	2003	2004
Revenues ($mn)	439.1	440.8
EBIT ($mn)	34.5	42.5
EBIT margin (%)	7.9	9.6
Gross margin (%)	48.2	50.9
Operating profit before tax ($mn)	32.7	41.5
Profit after tax ($mn)	22.5	28.8
Earnings per share (¢)	26.1	32.6
Cash flow per share (¢)	39.3	46.3
Dividend (¢)	12	16
Percentage franked	100	100
Interest cover (times)	18.9	40.3
Return on equity (%)	29.1	29.3

* 1 February 2003

Half-year to 31 July**	2003	2004
Revenues ($mn)	192.5	208.1
Operating profit before tax ($mn)	7.8	19.3
Profit after tax ($mn)	5.3	13.7
Earnings per share (¢)	6.0	15.2
Dividend (¢)	3	6
Percentage franked	100	100
Net tangible assets per share ($)	0.78	1.07
Debt-to-equity ratio (%)	4.4	~
Current ratio	1.9	2.4

** 2 August 2003

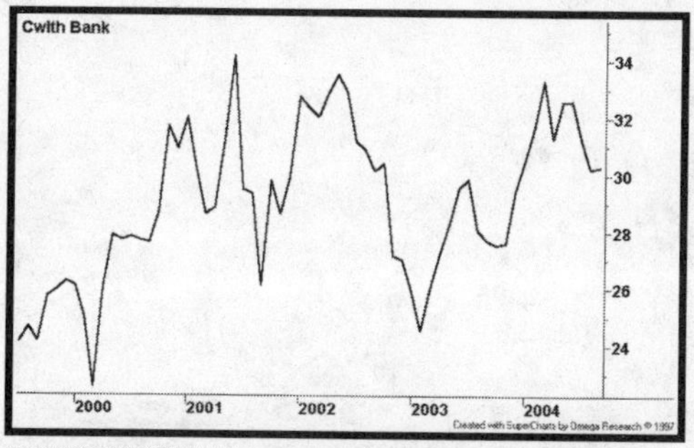

www.commbank.com.au

Commonwealth Bank of Australia

Share price ($)	28.87	
12-month high ($)	33.54	
12-month low ($)	27.00	
Market capitalisation ($mn)	36,853.1	
Price-to-NTA-per-share ratio	2.1	
5-year share price return (% p.a.)	9.8	
Sector: Financials	**Company**	**Sector**
Price-earnings ratio (times)	14.1	12.9
Dividend yield (%)	6.3	5.2

Australia's second-largest bank, with over seven million retail customers, the CBA is the country's top provider of home loans, personal loans and credit cards, and the largest holder of deposits. It is also Australia's largest fund manager, through Commonwealth Financial Services and Colonial First State, and the third-largest life insurer. Commonwealth Securities has become Australia's largest online stockbroker. It has significant interests in New Zealand through ASB Bank.

Latest business results (June 2004, full year)

The bank realised a strong rise in profits, with growth across all areas of its operations. However, there was a slight decline in second-half profit, due to heavy spending on the 'Which New Bank' growth initiative. The bank's lending strengths were the key to the strong full-year figure. Total lending assets increased by 18% to $206 billion, reflecting 20% and 35% increases in Australian and New Zealand home lending balances respectively and a 13% improvement in institutional and business lending balances. The bank actually boosted its share of the domestic home lending business to more than 23%. Despite fears of a housing downturn, the bank claimed that asset quality strengthened during the year, and the bad and doubtful debts expense was reduced by 10%. Strong investment markets fuelled an improved performance for the funds management business. Funds under management grew 11% to $110 billion, including a more than doubling to $7 billion of funds in the FirstChoice master trust. A booming insurance environment and improved efficiencies led to 8% growth in premiums and a 98% jump in profits.

Outlook

The Commonwealth Bank powers ahead. However, its strong position in domestic banking means the bank could suffer disproportionately in the event of a downturn in housing. In order to deliver continued growth the bank has launched its 'Which New Bank' strategy, which it estimates could cost $1.5 billion over three years, and incorporates a major refurbishment of many branches, staff retrenchments, new technology and an extensive program of staff retraining. The bank believes this will deliver annual EPS growth of at least 10% over several years, along with productivity improvements of 4% to 6% and enhanced market shares for its businesses.

CBA Year to 30 June	2003	2004
Operating income ($mn)	9,399.0	10,491.0
Net interest income ($mn)	5,026.0	5,410.0
Operating expenses ($mn)	5,551.0	6,249.0
Operating profit before tax ($mn)	2,976.0	3,843.0
Profit after tax ($mn)	2,012.0	2,572.0
Earnings per share (¢)	160.6	204.8
Dividend (¢)	154	183
Percentage franked	100	100
Non-interest income to total income (%)	46.5	48.4
Net tangible assets per share ($)	11.96	14.00
Cost-to-income ratio (%)	59.1	59.6
Return on equity (%)	10.3	12.1
Return on assets (%)	0.8	0.9

Computershare Limited

Share price ($)	3.23	
12-month high ($)	3.76	
12-month low ($)	2.04	
Market capitalisation ($mn)	1,822.5	
Price-to-NTA-per-share ratio	N/A	
5-year share price return (% p.a.)	–2.7	
Sector: Information technology	**Company**	**Sector**
Price-earnings ratio (times)	22.7	28.7
Dividend yield (%)	2.5	2.5

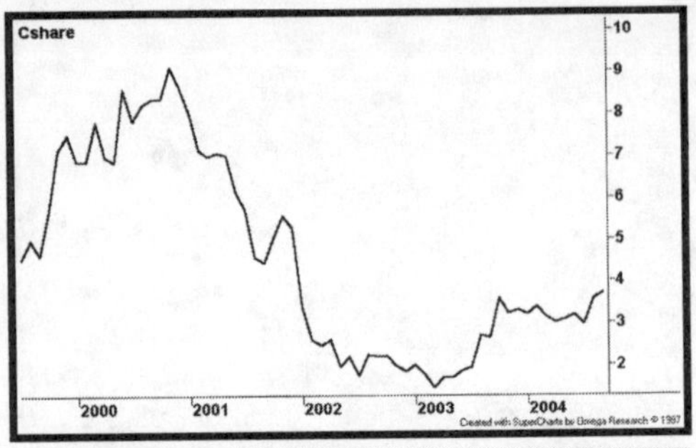

www.computershare.com.au

Melbourne-based Computershare, established in 1978, is one of the world's leading financial services and technology providers for the global securities industry, offering services to listed companies, investors, employees, exchanges and other financial institutions. It is the world's only global share registry/transfer agent, managing more than 80 million shareholder accounts for over 13,000 corporations in 12 countries. In Australia it arranges registry services for more than half of all companies, as well as 80% of those in New Zealand, 60% in Canada, 50% in Germany and significant proportions in Britain, Ireland, South Africa, the United States and Hong Kong.

Latest business results (June 2004, full year)

Profits came racing back, after a period of slump, as the company reaped the benefits of a series of stringent restructuring and consolidation initiatives. The results also benefited from buoyant stock markets domestically and in some other countries, and would have been higher still but for the strength of the dollar. A new revenue stream — mutual funds — contributed to the result, following the $180 million acquisition of Georgeson Shareholder Communications, an American shareholder communications company. All regions showed strength, with North America and South Africa moving out of the red and into profit, and Australia, New Zealand, Europe and Asia boosting their profits by substantial amounts.

Outlook

Computershare was, for a time, one of the fastest-growing large companies on the ASX, with a rapidly appreciating share price and a very high price-earnings ratio. However, declining revenues, following the stock market slump that started in 2000, along with high restructuring costs, sent profits — and the share price — plunging. The company now believes it is back on a growth track, with significant benefits still set to flow from the recent restructuring. Its target for the June 2005 year is for revenue growth of 10% and EPS growth of 20%. It is working to boost its new businesses in Germany and India, and is also looking for more acquisitions, particularly in continental Europe. Among recent new business, Computershare has won the contract to manage the listing and share transfer work for News Corporation's proposed relocation to the US.

CPU Year to 30 June	2003	2004
Revenues ($mn)	694.5	871.2
EBIT ($mn)	69.3	116.1
EBIT margin (%)	10.0	13.3
Operating profit before tax ($mn)	64.6	110.7
Profit after tax ($mn)	45.8	77.8
Earnings per share (¢)	8.4	14.2
Cash flow per share (¢)	19.6	25.2
Dividend (¢)	5	8
Percentage franked	100	100
Net tangible assets per share ($)	0.27	~
Interest cover (times)	14.7	21.4
Return on equity (%)	7.4	13.2
Debt-to-equity ratio (%)	13.2	36.6
Current ratio	1.6	1.0

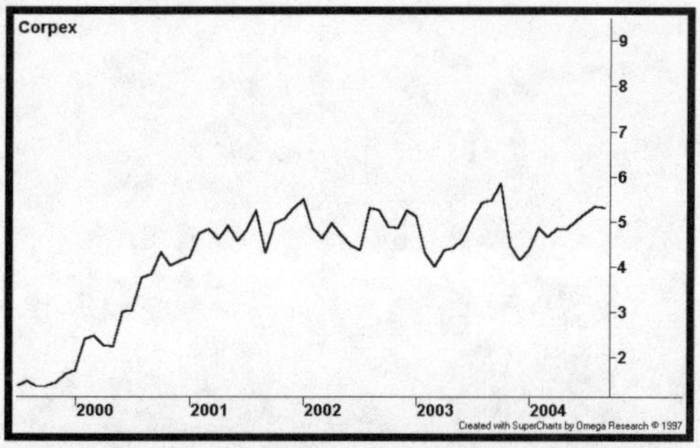

www.ce.com.au

Corporate Express Australia Limited

Share price ($)	5.19	
12-month high ($)	5.91	
12-month low ($)	3.79	
Market capitalisation ($mn)	991.0	
Price-to-NTA-per-share ratio	9.8	
5-year share price return (% p.a.)	34.3	
Sector: Industrials	**Company**	**Sector**
Price-earnings ratio (times)	21.6	14.8
Dividend yield (%)	2.5	4.2

Sydney-based Corporate Express, a 52%-owned subsidiary of the Dutch-based office provisions giant Buhrmann, has become Australia's largest distributor of office supplies to business. As well as basic office provisions, its products and services include information technology (IT) solutions, business furniture, janitorial supplies, print services, promotional marketing, and liquor, coffee and kitchen supplies. It services some 38,000 corporate customers from a string of regional offices throughout Australia and New Zealand.

Latest business results (June 2004, half-year)

The buoyant economy and the company's growth strategies delivered a strong mid-term boost to sales and profits. Management announced that the company had improved market share across all its business categories. Part of the growth came from four acquisitions — three office products businesses and one promotional marketing business — during the period. Sales of private-brand products were up by more than 19%.

Outlook

Corporate Express has achieved exceptional growth over an extended period through an aggressive policy of corporate acquisition. Many of the more than 40 businesses it has acquired have been small, niche office-supply distributors, lacking the capital to expand, but with solid customer bases. The company has said that it will continue this acquisition policy, though some concerns have been expressed that quality takeover targets are now becoming scarce. The company also continues to expand the range of products and services it is able to offer its corporate customers. Recently, these include the supply and servicing of copiers, facsimiles and printers and consumables for specialty printers. Corporate Express also continues to boost its offering of private-brand products, which are generally cheaper than branded products. The successful roll-out of a third-generation client online ordering system, NetXpress III, is expected to lay the groundwork for a steady boost to productivity. The company has also established the new CE Direct business, which targets small and medium-sized businesses, where Corporate Express has been comparatively weak.

CXP Year to 31 December	2002	2003
Revenues ($mn)	758.0	896.3
EBIT ($mn)	63.2	68.7
EBIT margin (%)	8.3	7.7
Gross margin (%)	23.5	23.2
Operating profit before tax ($mn)	62.9	67.5
Profit after tax ($mn)	43.4	45.7
Earnings per share (¢)	22.8	24.0
Cash flow per share (¢)	28.2	30.6
Dividend (¢)	8	13
Percentage franked	100	100
Interest cover (times)	168.7	57.3
Return on equity (%)	33.5	28.4
Half-year to 30 June	**2003**	**2004**
Revenues ($mn)	407.6	470.0
Operating profit before tax ($mn)	32.0	41.7
Profit after tax ($mn)	21.5	28.3
Earnings per share (¢)	11.3	14.8
Dividend (¢)	5	7
Percentage franked	100	100
Net tangible assets per share ($)	0.47	0.53
Debt-to-equity ratio (%)	~	~
Current ratio	1.4	1.4

COVENTRY GROUP LIMITED

Share price ($)	5.90	
12-month high ($)	6.50	
12-month low ($)	5.35	
Market capitalisation ($mn)	207.0	
Price-to-NTA-per-share ratio	1.4	
5-year share price return (% p.a.)	17.3	
Sector: Consumer discretionary	**Company**	**Sector**
Price-earnings ratio (times)	13.9	23.8
Dividend yield (%)	5.8	1.5

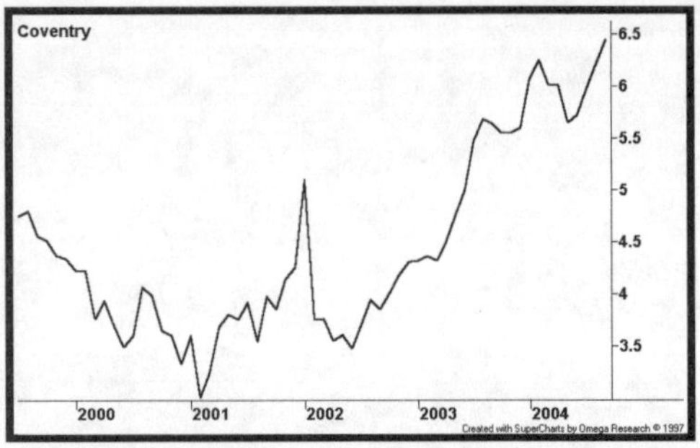

www.cgl.com.au

With roots that back to its establishment as a small motor accessory business in the 1920s, Perth-based Coventry Group is today a diversified industrial company with activities across Australia and New Zealand. Its major business is automotive parts distribution. The other main business, industrial products distribution, involves a wide range of specialist parts and equipment. Two minor businesses are bitumen products — asphalt manufacture and application, road profiling, and the manufacture and spraying of bituminous products — and the manufacture and distribution of automotive industrial gaskets.

LATEST BUSINESS RESULTS (JUNE 2004, FULL YEAR)

Coventry achieved a healthy increase in profits on just a moderate sales rise. The key factor was the core automotive parts business, with EBIT surging more than 90%, thanks to strength from the Western Australian-based Coventrys operation, with a particular assist from the state's booming resources industry. The division was also helped by a 29% decline in the trading loss for Coventry Auto Parts. The industrial products business realised 16% profit growth, helped by a number of strategic supply initiatives, a buoyant resources sector and strong New Zealand sales. Growing competition forced down bitumen profits, but gasket profits were strongly up.

OUTLOOK

Despite the big jump in automotive parts profits, margins for this business remain low, and the company is struggling to boost them. The strength of the Western Australian economy is helping, as is the state's powerful resources industry. However, the South Australian business, Motor Traders, has been hurt by competition, and the loss-making Coventry Auto Parts continues to struggle, particularly in NSW. In mid-2004, Coventry acquired three auto-parts distributors in Queensland and the Northern Territory, and it expects these to add $2 million to annual EBIT. The industrial products business continues to benefit from strong demand in New Zealand, but domestically is facing growing levels of competition from smaller entrants into the market. Competition also continues in the bitumen business, and the company is seeking new market opportunities in a bid to boost sales. The gasket business, though small, is very profitable and the company believes that further improvements in production capacity and efficiencies are set to boost margins even higher.

CYG Year to 30 June	2003	2004
Revenues ($mn)	415.5	433.9
Automotive parts distribution (%)	55	55
Industrial products distribution (%)	39	39
EBIT ($mn)	18.7	23.1
EBIT margin (%)	4.5	5.3
Gross margin (%)	36.1	37.1
Operating profit before tax ($mn)	16.9	21.9
Profit after tax ($mn)	10.8	14.8
Earnings per share (¢)	31.5	42.5
Cash flow per share (¢)	55.1	65.0
Dividend (¢)	30	34
Percentage franked	100	100
Net tangible assets per share ($)	3.98	4.15
Interest cover (times)	10.1	19.6
Return on equity (%)	6.9	9.1
Debt-to-equity ratio (%)	14.4	7.4
Current ratio	3.4	3.3

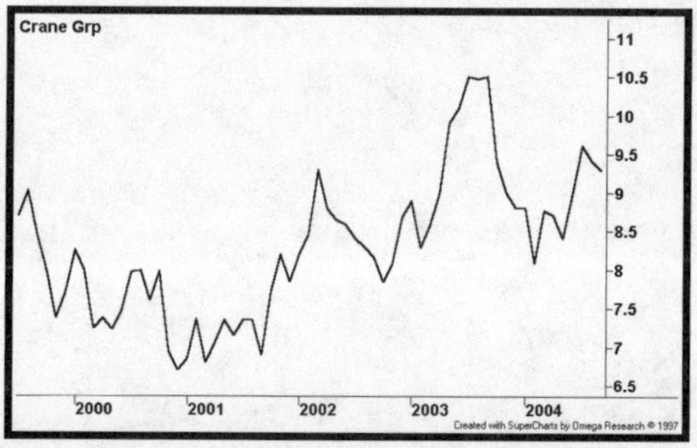

www.crane.com.au

Crane Group Limited

Share price ($)	9.75	
12-month high ($)	11.05	
12-month low ($)	8.02	
Market capitalisation ($mn)	546.3	
Price-to-NTA-per-share ratio	2.1	
5-year share price return (% p.a.)	8.3	
Sector: Industrials	**Company**	**Sector**
Price-earnings ratio (times)	14.7	14.8
Dividend yield (%)	6.2	4.2

Sydney-based Crane, founded in 1867, is a prominent manufacturer and distributor of non-ferrous metal products and of plastic pipeline systems. Its Tradelink division is Australia's largest distributor of plumbing supplies, with 189 outlets, and its CDNZ division is a leading New Zealand plumbing and electrical supplies distribution business, with 118 branches. In August 2003, Crane acquired Milnes Holdings, a rival plastic pipelines manufacturer.

Latest business results (June 2004, full year)

The buoyant housing market pushed revenues higher, but profits fell as the company encountered problems with its Tradelink business. Sales in this division rose 9%, but profits fell in half, due particularly to disruptions caused by the implementation of a major new IT system. The Iplex plastic pipelines business achieved a strong gain in sales and profits, though much of this was attributable to an 11-month contribution from the new Milnes Holdings acquisition. The metals divisions saw a slight dip in sales and profit, with a strong performance from the company's aluminium operations offset by weakness in copper and brass manufacturing and in metals distribution. However, New Zealand was very strong, reflecting that country's upbeat building sector, with sales in Australian dollar terms up 10% and profits surging by 27%. The company reported a $51 million after-tax significant loss, mainly attributable to a major restructuring of its operations.

Outlook

In June 2004 Crane announced its big corporate restructure plan, aimed at boosting profits. It is shaking up its management structure and has announced some big write-downs of assets. The company has expressed concern that its Tradelink operation is considerably less profitable than rival businesses such as Reece Holdings, and it is closing under-performing stores and streamlining others. It is also cutting 200 Tradelink jobs. It is cutting 100 jobs in New Zealand and is closing or merging seven stores there. The metals business will also see staff numbers cut and the closure of some business units. Despite expectations of a big jump in its IT costs, the company believes that it can deliver higher profits in the June 2005 year.

CRG Year to 30 June	2003	2004
Revenues ($mn)	1,911.7	2,087.7
Tradelink (%)	33	33
Iplex (%)	21	24
Metals (%)	27	24
CDNZ (%)	19	19
EBIT ($mn)	96.2	90.6
EBIT margin (%)	5.0	4.3
Gross margin (%)	20.2	20.6
Operating profit before tax ($mn)	75.9	64.3
Profit after tax ($mn)	46.4	35.9
Earnings per share (¢)	89.2	66.3
Cash flow per share (¢)	161.1	161.3
Dividend (¢)	60	60
Percentage franked	100	100
Net tangible assets per share ($)	6.03	4.54
Interest cover (times)	4.7	3.4
Return on equity (%)	11.8	9.0
Debt-to-equity ratio (%)	57.5	70.3
Current ratio	1.5	1.7

CSR Limited

Share price ($)	2.30	
12-month high ($)	2.44	
12-month low ($)	1.73	
Market capitalisation ($mn)	2,086.1	
Price-to-NTA-per-share ratio	2.0	
5-year share price return (% p.a.)	24.7	
Sector: Materials	**Company**	**Sector**
Price-earnings ratio (times)	13.5	14.3
Dividend yield (%)	4.8	2.6

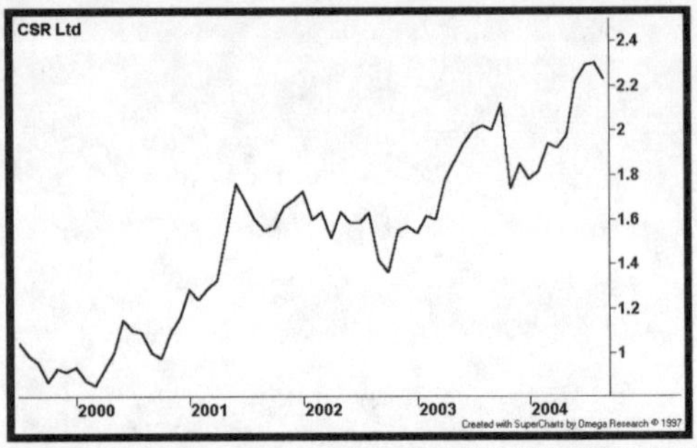

www.csr.com.au

CSR, founded in 1855 as a sugar refiner, returned to its roots with the 2003 demerger of its Rinker construction materials business into a separate company, also listed on the stock exchange. CSR now operates in three separate industries: it is one of the world's leading sugar producers; it makes building products, such as bricks, pavers, plasterboard and roofing tiles; and it owns 70% of Gove Aluminium Finance, which holds more than a third of the equity of NSW's Tomago Aluminium Smelter.

Latest business results (March 2004, full year)

The Rinker demerger took place in March 2003. However, for comparison purposes, the company has adjusted its March 2003 results to exclude Rinker operations. A 17% fall in raw sugar prices pushed company revenues and profits down, despite a slightly larger sugarcane crop. A softening of the building market also saw a dip in building product profits. However, a strong rise in aluminium prices, along with the company's successful currency hedging strategies, boosted aluminium division profits by 14%. The company also reported a $16 million profit (before interest and tax) from property developments.

Outlook

Following the Rinker demerger, CSR is working to restructure and rationalise its remaining businesses. This includes the redevelopment of selected land holdings, and the company expects a growing earnings stream from this business in coming years. However, in the short term its fortunes are quite dependent on trends in the global sugar market, and it should benefit from the government's $444 million sugar industry reform program, announced in April 2004. It is building a $100-million electricity plant at its Pioneer sugar mill in North Queensland, to generate renewable electricity from sugarcane waste fibre. The company will be affected by a slowdown in residential construction, though it expects this to be at least partly offset by continued growth in the home renovations market, and it believes efficiency gains and cost reductions will sustain profits. It is also boosting its glasswool production capacity in China, from 8,000 to 14,000 tonnes per year. A three-year, $76-million project has been launched to expand output of the Tomago aluminium smelter by 15%.

CSR Year to 31 March	2003	2004
Revenues ($mn)	2,051.2	1,970.8
Building products (%)	43	46
Sugar — milling (%)	30	27
Aluminium (%)	21	23
Sugar — ethanol & refining (%)	4	3
EBIT ($mn)	275.1	262.7
EBIT margin (%)	13.4	13.3
Gross margin (%)	28.7	28.9
Operating profit before tax ($mn)	256.5	249.7
Profit after tax ($mn)	171.7	160.2
Earnings per share (¢)	18.3	17.1
Cash flow per share (¢)	29.7	28.5
Dividend (¢)	11	11
Percentage franked	70	70
Net tangible assets per share ($)	1.10	1.13
Interest cover (times)	14.8	20.2
Return on equity (%)	15.9	14.9
Debt-to-equity ratio (%)	19.7	14.3
Current ratio	1.2	1.2

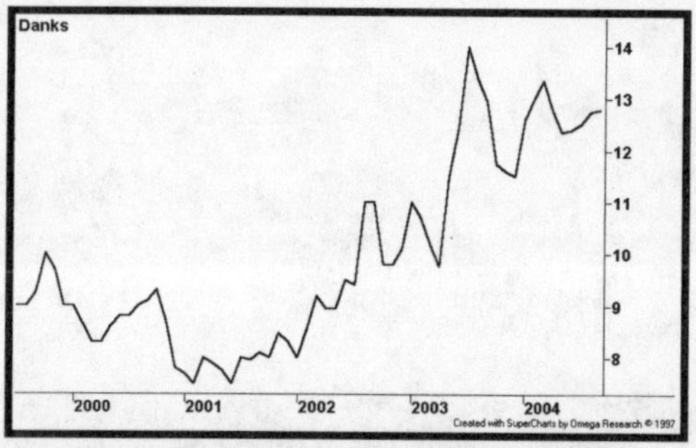

www.danks.com.au

Danks Holdings Limited

Share price ($)	12.40	
12-month high ($)	13.99	
12-month low ($)	11.00	
Market capitalisation ($mn)	80.6	
Price-to-NTA-per-share ratio	1.5	
5-year share price return (% p.a.)	13.0	
Sector: Consumer discretionary	**Company**	**Sector**
Price-earnings ratio (times)	15.1	23.8
Dividend yield (%)	4.4	1.5

Melbourne-based Danks Holdings has roots that date back to 1859, and is Australia's largest independent hardware wholesale distributor, with six warehouses in Victoria, NSW and Western Australia. It carries a range of some 25,000 products, which it distributes to more than 730 group stores, all independently owned. These include HOME Timber and Hardware stores, Thrifty-Link Hardware stores and Plants Plus Garden Centre nurseries. It also distributes its products to more than 1,000 other independent retailers.

Latest business results (June 2004, full year)

The housing and home renovations boom handed Danks its eighth straight revenues gain, with product sales rising nearly 13%. However, the competitive conditions prevailing in the market hit profits, which rose only modestly. Thanks to the company's marketing initiatives it was able to boost its group store numbers, though management expressed concern that this growth has led to concerns over distribution. The results also included a one-off $1.8 million profit from the sale of a property that had been the base for the company's now-discontinued steel products distribution business.

Outlook

The company is still managed conservatively by the original Danks family, who have progressively restructured its operations in order to remain competitive against the growing power of the giant warehouse stores of rivals like Bunnings and, increasingly, Mitre 10. The particular focus of the company has been on the attractions of the smaller, more personalised stores within its group. However, it remains to be seen whether the company is able to maintain its growth record in the face of a housing downturn, although it seems that the home renovations business remains sound. There has been a heavy investment in information technology systems, with the aim of streamlining the ordering and distribution processes, though the company has stated that it is experiencing difficulties in running its warehouses as efficiently as it would like. It has begun the planning to create much larger consolidated distribution centres, which it believes will be a major contributor to a better profit in the future. The company has achieved significant customer acceptance of its house-branded product ranges under the JDS and the Plumbworx labels. Danks shares are very thinly traded.

DKS Year to 30 June	2003	2004
Revenues ($mn)	449.3	527.9
EBIT ($mn)	8.6	8.8
EBIT margin (%)	1.9	1.7
Gross margin (%)	9.8	9.2
Operating profit before tax ($mn)	7.6	7.8
Profit after tax ($mn)	5.2	5.3
Earnings per share (¢)	80.1	82.0
Cash flow per share (¢)	112.4	114.6
Dividend (¢)	55	55
Percentage franked	100	100
Net tangible assets per share ($)	7.90	8.45
Interest cover (times)	8.2	8.9
Return on equity (%)	10.5	10.0
Debt-to-equity ratio (%)	18.8	8.6
Current ratio	1.9	1.8

Downer EDI Limited

Share price ($)	3.21	
12-month high ($)	3.96	
12-month low ($)	2.76	
Market capitalisation ($mn)	904.2	
Price-to-NTA-per-share ratio	1.8	
5-year share price return (% p.a.)	18.7	
Sector: Industrials	**Company**	**Sector**
Price-earnings ratio (times)	10.8	14.8
Dividend yield (%)	4.2	4.2

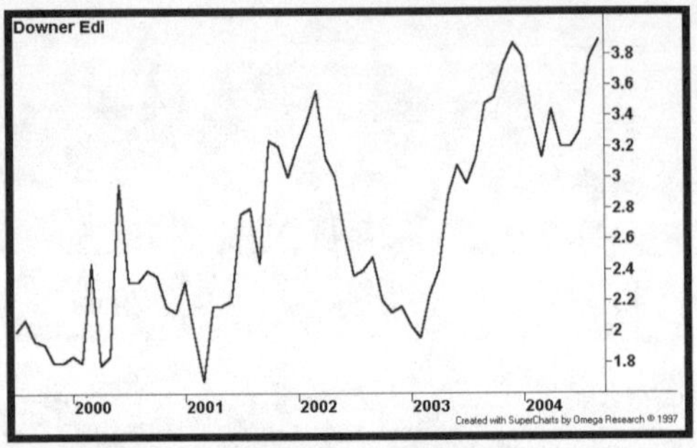

www.downeredi.com.au

Sydney-based Downer EDI — Australia's second-largest listed engineering, infrastructure and resource services company (after Leighton Holdings) — has grown through a long series of mergers in Australia and New Zealand. It provides engineering and infrastructure management services to the public and private power, rail, road, telecommunications, mining and mineral processing sectors in Australia, New Zealand, Asia and the Pacific. It operates through five broad divisions: Works Infrastructure, Downer Engineering, Roche Mining, Century Resources and EDI Rail.

Latest business results (June 2004, full year)

Revenues and profits were up for the seventh straight year. Most of the good gain came from the company's powerhouse engineering operations, with revenues up 30% and profit soaring 90%. In part, this was due to a full year's contribution from CPG Corporation, a leader in facilities management and engineering consultancy that was formerly part of Singapore's public works department, and was acquired in early 2003. However, it also reflected strong performances from power and telecommunications business. The strong infrastructure market prevailing in Australia and New Zealand led to a 19% lift in revenues in infrastructure, with profit up 51%. However, the company's mining business was hit by one-off problems at one contract, and profits fell sharply.

Outlook

Downer EDI is ideally placed to take full advantage of a growing number of major rail and transport infrastructure projects that are being promoted in Australia and New Zealand. The company is also well-positioned to benefit from the continued buoyancy of the resources sector. It is now working on ways to develop regular annuity-type income from its projects, perhaps in the form of an infrastructure fund. At the end of June 2004 the company's order book had swelled 16% from a year earlier to $6.4 billion, and it also reported that by late-August 2004 it had risen still further to $6.8 billion. Downer EDI has a small but growing business in Asia, and is using its CPG acquisition as a base for moves into the growth markets of China and India. The company is also looking to make further acquisitions, particularly in the power and rail industries.

DOW Year to 30 June	2003	2004
Revenues ($mn)	2,573.5	3,112.3
Mining & resources (%)	35	34
Engineering (%)	31	29
Infrastructure services (%)	21	21
Rail (%)	11	13
EBIT ($mn)	124.8	138.6
EBIT margin (%)	4.8	4.5
Operating profit before tax ($mn)	94.7	109.2
Profit after tax ($mn)	66.6	81.5
Earnings per share (¢)	27.5*	29.6
Cash flow per share (¢)	76.8*	72.3
Dividend (¢)	11.6*	13.6
Percentage franked	41	50
Net tangible assets per share ($)	1.77*	1.75
Interest cover (times)	4.2	4.7
Return on equity (%)	9.1	10.3
Debt-to-equity ratio (%)	39.0	40.9
Current ratio	1.4	1.4

* adjusted for a 1:4 share consolidation

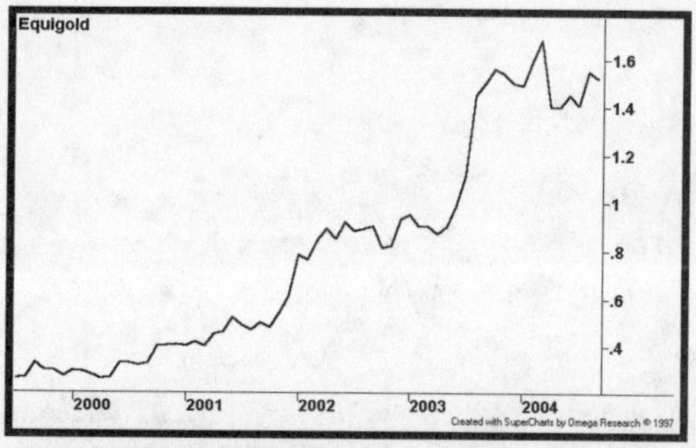

www.equigold.com.au

EQUIGOLD NL

Share price ($)	1.45	
12-month high ($)	1.72	
12-month low ($)	1.28	
Market capitalisation ($mn)	215.4	
Price-to-NTA-per-share ratio	2.9	
5-year share price return (% p.a.)	40.7	
Sector: Materials	**Company**	**Sector**
Price-earnings ratio (times)	12.9	14.3
Dividend yield (%)	4.8	2.6

Perth company Equigold, founded in 1993, initially mined for gold in Vietnam and Ghana. It later acquired interests in gold projects in Western Australia and Queensland, and its current production is at Mount Rawdon in south-east Queensland and at Kirkalocka near Mount Magnet in Western Australia. Since 1996 the company has been actively exploring for gold in the Ivory Coast, leading to the discovery of a significant gold deposit at Bonikro.

LATEST BUSINESS RESULTS (JUNE 2004, FULL YEAR)

Equigold achieved a record profit, thanks to increased gold production at Mount Rawdon and the first full year of production at Kirkalocka. Total gold production of 156,556 ounces was 24% more than in the previous year, though the price received of $583 per ounce was little changed from $581 in the previous year. At Mount Rawdon the company produced 89,102 ounces of gold, up 9% from the previous year, due to the increase in mill throughput as a result of the crushing circuit upgrade completed part way through the prior year. The production cost of $370 per ounce, was up from $338 in the previous year. At Kirkalocka the company produced 67,454 ounces, up 49% from the previous year, at a cost of $341 per ounce, which was down from $359 in the June 2003 year.

OUTLOOK

Equigold has great hopes for its Ivory Coast resource, estimated at more than one million ounces. A full feasibility study is due to report by the end of 2004, and the company envisages launching production by the end of 2005, at an annual rate of 130,000 to 150,000 ounces a year for seven to eight years. However, among the risks of this project is the uncertain political climate prevailing in the Ivory Coast. In the year to June 2005, Equigold expects production at its two domestic mines to reach a total of around 161,000 ounces, at a cost of about $360 to $370 per ounce. Only 18,000 ounces of this gold has been hedged, and company profits will be highly geared to the gold price. Domestically, Equigold has gold reserves of approximately 1.5 million ounces.

EQI Year to 30 June	2003	2004
Revenues ($mn)	75.3	93.0
EBIT ($mn)	19.8	23.2
EBIT margin (%)	26.3	25.0
Operating profit before tax ($mn)	18.6	23.7
Profit after tax ($mn)	12.3	16.7
Earnings per share (¢)	8.7	11.2
Cash flow per share (¢)	14.9	18.9
Dividend (¢)	5	7
Percentage franked	100	100
Net tangible assets per share ($)	0.45	0.51
Interest cover (times)	16.8	~
Return on equity (%)	21.2	23.3
Debt-to-equity ratio (%)	12.5	~
Current ratio	1.3	1.3

Fairfax (John) Holdings Limited

	Company	Sector
Share price ($)	3.79	
12-month high ($)	3.90	
12-month low ($)	3.05	
Market capitalisation ($mn)	3,400.7	
Price-to-NTA-per-share ratio	N/A	
5-year share price return (% p.a.)	2.3	
Sector: Consumer discretionary	**Company**	**Sector**
Price-earnings ratio (times)	16.2	23.8
Dividend yield (%)	4.4	1.5

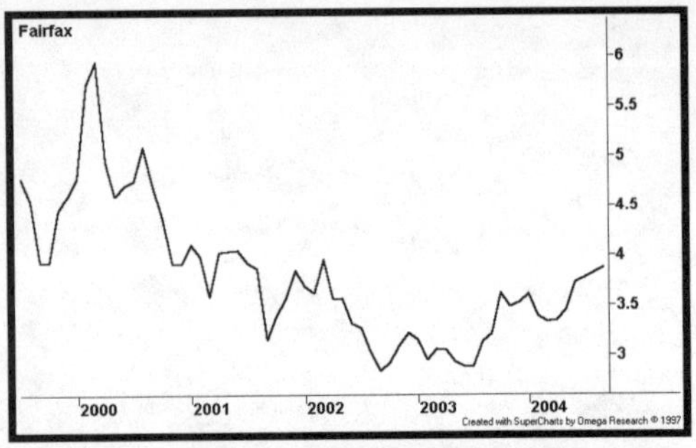

www.fxj.com.au

John Fairfax Holdings is one of Australia's leading media companies. It publishes *The Sydney Morning Herald*, Melbourne's *The Age*, *The Australian Financial Review* and *BRW*, *Shares* and *Personal Investor* magazines, as well as local and specialist newspapers and magazines. It also provides a range of online services through its Fairfax Digital subsidiary. In mid-2003, it acquired New Zealand's largest publishing business from Independent Newspapers, including a string of metropolitan and regional newspapers, and 13 magazine titles. Fairfax also owns the publishing house Text Media and 43% of AAP Information Services.

Latest business results (June 2004, full year)

The company reported a giant jump to its profits, driven in part by its NZ acquisition, but also reflecting the strength of the domestic media business. Metropolitan newspapers benefited from a 3.7% gain in advertising revenues and a marginal increase in circulation revenues. The group's regional publications showed strong double-digit profit growth, thanks to productivity gains and new acquisitions. Fairfax Digital posted a 50% expansion of revenues, and was cash flow positive for the first time. NZ operations achieved healthy gains, with profits considerably higher than forecast at the time of acquisition.

Outlook

The publishing business has high fixed costs, and profits are greatly affected by economic conditions. Small increases in advertising and circulation can translate into a big rise in profits, and the reverse is also true. However, thanks in particular to the NZ acquisition, the company's operations have become more balanced than previously. Australian metropolitan newspapers are now only 50% of revenues, compared to 70% a year before, and Fairfax is therefore less dependent on the advertising cycles of Sydney and Melbourne. In addition, after considerable start-up difficulties, the major new Melbourne printing facility at Tullamarine is operating well, which will bring significant cost savings. A series of new labour agreements, in both the printing and editorial areas, has boosted productivity. Fairfax Digital continues to blossom, attracting millions of readers monthly to its online news services and its fast-growing classified advertising sites. The NZ operation continues to grow faster than expected.

FXJ Year to 30 June	2003	2004
Revenues ($mn)	1,208.4	1,765.9
EBIT ($mn)	201.3	368.2
EBIT margin (%)	16.7	20.9
Gross margin (%)	62.1	67.1
Operating profit before tax ($mn)	177.8	296.3
Profit after tax ($mn)	125.5	207.6
Earnings per share (c)	16.6	23.4
Cash flow per share (c)	25.8	33.1
Dividend (c)	13	16.5
Percentage franked	100	100
Net tangible assets per share ($)	~	~
Interest cover (times)	8.6	5.1
Return on equity (%)	8.0	10.8
Debt-to-equity ratio (%)	67.4	52.7
Current ratio	0.3	1.0

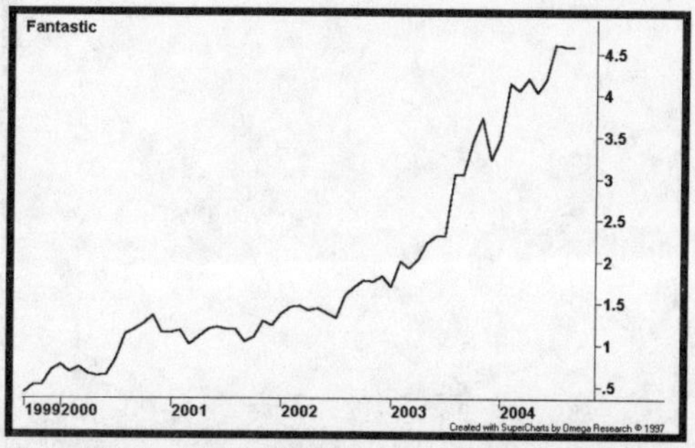

www.fantasticfurniture.com.au

Fantastic Holdings Limited

Share price ($)	4.60	
12-month high ($)	4.75	
12-month low ($)	2.98	
Market capitalisation ($mn)	369.4	
Price-to-NTA-per-share ratio	11.8	
5-year share price return (% p.a.)	65.4	
Sector: Consumer discretionary	**Company**	**Sector**
Price-earnings ratio (times)	21.9	23.8
Dividend yield (%)	2.2	1.5

Sydney-based furniture manufacturer and retailer Fantastic Holdings evolved from a struggling furniture chain that was acquired in 1996 by a group of partners, including managing director Julian Tertini, who earlier had helped launch Freedom Furniture. Today, Fantastic is one of Australia's leading budget furniture chains, with a total of 54 company-owned and franchised stores in NSW, ACT, Victoria and Tasmania, operating under the Fantastic Furniture and Plush banners.

Latest business results (June 2004, full year)

Fantastic achieved another surge in profits, its fifth consecutive earnings increase since listing on the ASX in 1999. Seven new stores — three Fantastic Furniture outlets and four Plush stores — were opened during the year, and contributed to the result. Nevertheless, on a like-for-like basis, sales were up an impressive 16%.

Outlook

Fantastic has achieved great success in the budget furniture sector through a policy of careful planning and strict cost containment. Its lounge factory produced 113,000 sofas in the June 2004 year, and the company believes its production strategies have allowed it to raise productivity to levels where it can compete on cost with cheap imports from Asia. It has moved its import centre to larger premises and is developing an integrated computer system to streamline the entire manufacturing, sales and delivery process. In mid-2004 it acquired a large property in Victoria for development as a bulky goods value centre and testing ground. The company believes that rental fees being demanded for quality bulky goods store sites have become excessive, which limits the number of new outlets it can open, although it plans 12 new stores in the June 2005 year. It expects a market correction for bulky goods store rentals, and it feels well-placed to take advantage of this. Looking further ahead, it plans sharp increases in store numbers in NSW and Victoria, as well as strong moves into Queensland and Western Australia. It is also looking to a big expansion into New Zealand. Thanks to its emphasis on the budget sector, the company believes it will weather the effects of any slowdown in consumer spending on furniture if interest rates rise.

FAN Year to 30 June	2003	2004
Revenues ($mn)	134.2	183.0
EBIT ($mn)	14.9	21.9
EBIT margin (%)	11.1	12.0
Gross margin (%)	38.4	40.5
Operating profit before tax ($mn)	15.2	22.3
Profit after tax ($mn)	10.6	15.7
Earnings per share (¢)	14.2*	21.0
Cash flow per share (¢)	15.0*	22.2
Dividend (¢)	7*	10.3
Percentage franked	100	100
Net tangible assets per share ($)	0.31*	0.39
Interest cover (times)	~	~
Return on equity (%)	52.5	56.8
Debt-to-equity ratio (%)	~	~
Current ratio	2.0	2.1

* figures adjusted for an 11:10 share split

FKP Limited

Share price ($)	2.87	
12-month high ($)	3.00	
12-month low ($)	2.01	
Market capitalisation ($mn)	382.9	
Price-to-NTA-per-share ratio	1.6	
5-year share price return (% p.a.)	30.8	
Sector: Financials	**Company**	**Sector**
Price-earnings ratio (times)	9.3	12.9
Dividend yield (%)	5.2	5.2

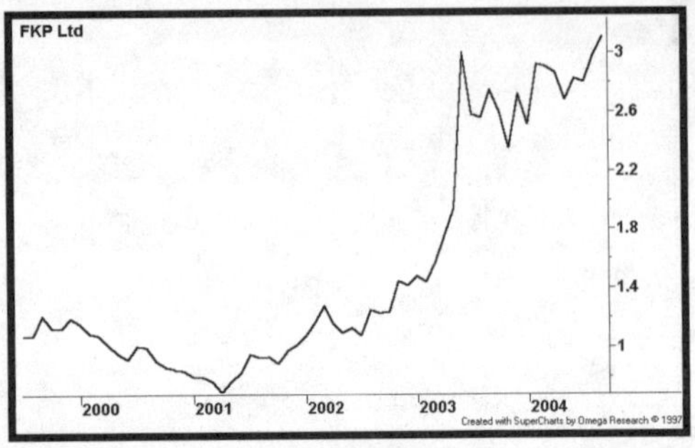

www.fkp.com.au

FKP, formerly called Forrester Kurts Properties, is a leading Queensland-based property developer, with activities that encompass construction, low-, medium- and high-density residential developments, commercial and retail projects, master planned residential communities and the ownership and management of retirement villages. It is active in all eastern states. Its subsidiary, Australian Retirement Homes, has become a leader in the aged-care industry, with 28 retirement community properties, making FKP Australia's largest owner/operator of retirement villages. The company also manages two property trusts.

Latest business results (June 2004, full year)

The property boom handed FKP a strong lift in profits. Residential sales soared 80%, with strong contributions from company developments at the Gold Coast, Sunshine Coast and Brisbane. Land subdivision sales were also strong, up 34%, thanks to record sales on the Sunshine Coast and good results from the Ocean Acres development in coastal Victoria. The company also achieved record retirement village sales — 128 units worth $35 million, up from 87 units worth $19 million in the previous year. Commercial, retail and industrial property sales revenues fell 73%, due mainly to some significant one-off sales in the previous year. External construction revenues were also sharply down, as the company concentrated on its in-house activities.

FKP Year to 30 June	2003	2004
Revenues ($mn)	294.1	263.7
Residential development (%)	25	36
Land subdivision (%)	16	25
Aged care services (%)	12	22
Commercial development (%)	28	9
Construction (%)	14	6
EBIT ($mn)	39.9	59.2
EBIT margin (%)	13.6	22.4
Gross margin (%)	17.6	27.2
Operating profit before tax ($mn)	38.7	53.0
Profit after tax ($mn)	26.7	36.7
Earnings per share (¢)	23.5	30.8
Cash flow per share (¢)	24.7	32.3
Dividend (¢)	12	15
Percentage franked	100	100
Net tangible assets per share ($)	1.53	1.80
Interest cover (times)	32.6	9.6
Return on equity (%)	16.2	17.5
Debt-to-equity ratio (%)	12.1	51.4
Current ratio	2.2	2.0

Outlook

FKP believes it can achieve profit growth of at least 10% in the June 2005 year. It has taken a controlling 85% stake in listed retirement village operator Forest Place Group, giving FKP 4,000 retirement village units under management and a further 1,000 under development. The company now derives 18% of its earnings from recurring income streams such as retirement villages and funds management, and aims to raise this tò 50% by 2008. It is planning to create a stapled structure joining its FKP shares with units in the company's second property trust. It believes this will give it greater access to development capital, and will also enable it to pay higher dividends. It continues to win major contracts, and has been selected as the successful tenderer for stage two of Brisbane's $300 million Newstead Rziverpark Gateway development.

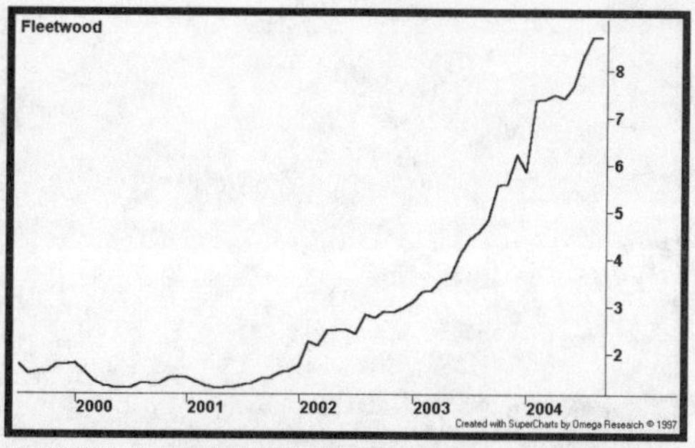

www.fleetwood.com.au

Fleetwood Corporation Limited

Share price ($)	8.39	
12-month high ($)	8.44	
12-month low ($)	4.35	
Market capitalisation ($mn)	379.0	
Price-to-NTA-per-share ratio	5.7	
5-year share price return (% p.a.)	48.2	
Sector: Consumer discretionary	**Company**	**Sector**
Price-earnings ratio (times)	18.7	23.8
Dividend yield (%)	2.1	1.5

Western Australian company Fleetwood, established in 1964, is a leader in the caravan, recreational vehicle and portable accommodation businesses. Its Coromal Caravans division is the second-largest caravan manufacturer in Australia and its Windsor Caravans business is the fourth-largest. Its Camec Group is Australia's largest caravan spare parts and accessories manufacturer and retailer. Fleetwood Durabuilt is one of the largest park home and transportable home manufacturers in Western Australia, Fleetwood Portables is one of Australia's largest providers of portable accommodation to the resources industry, and Flexiglass Challenge is Australia's largest manufacturer of canopies for utility vehicles. Fleetwood has sold its caravan parks division and its Hertz Campervan rental business.

Latest business results (June 2004, full year)

Fleetwood generated its eleventh successive record profit, as it struggled to keep up with the booming demand for its caravans. Profits for its recreational vehicles division — mainly caravans — rocketed ahead 75%, following a 46% jump in the previous year. Manufactured accommodation profits were up 27%, thanks to increased activity in the resources industry and strong demand by retirees for park homes.

Outlook

With its business geared to three areas with high growth potential — recreation, resource development and retirement — Fleetwood has been expanding rapidly, and the shares have performed very strongly. Its acquisition of Windsor Caravans has helped it strengthen its East Coast presence, though demand is such that there is a seven-month order backlog. Fleetwood is working to boost capacity and it is also continually streamlining the production process, with steadily improving margins. With most caravan purchasers aged over 55, Fleetwood is a big beneficiary of this growing demographic. It is also benefiting from moves towards recreation park living. In Western Australia it has an overwhelming share of the market for the supply of park homes, and it is boosting its presence in other states. The company's other major source of revenue — on-site manufactured accommodation for resource project workers — is also flourishing, thanks to the ongoing resources boom, with a string of profitable new contracts in prospect.

FWD Year to 30 June	2003	2004
Revenues ($mn)	188.5	231.1
Recreational vehicles (%)	62	65
Manufactured accommodation (%)	33	31
EBIT ($mn)	18.7	31.2
EBIT margin (%)	9.9	13.5
Gross margin (%)	23.0	26.8
Operating profit before tax ($mn)	16.6	29.4
Profit after tax ($mn)	11.2	20.2
Earnings per share (¢)	29.1	44.8
Cash flow per share (¢)	44.8	61.8
Dividend (¢)	14	18
Percentage franked	100	100
Net tangible assets per share ($)	1.20	1.47
Interest cover (times)	9.0	17.1
Return on equity (%)	17.4	22.9
Debt-to-equity ratio (%)	24.3	26.3
Current ratio	1.9	1.8

Flight Centre Limited

Share price ($)	19.85	
12-month high ($)	23.00	
12-month low ($)	17.27	
Market capitalisation ($mn)	1,891.7	
Price-to-NTA-per-share ratio	7.3	
5-year share price return (% p.a.)	12.2	
Sector: Consumer discretionary	**Company**	**Sector**
Price-earnings ratio (times)	22.7	23.8
Dividend yield (%)	3.1	1.5

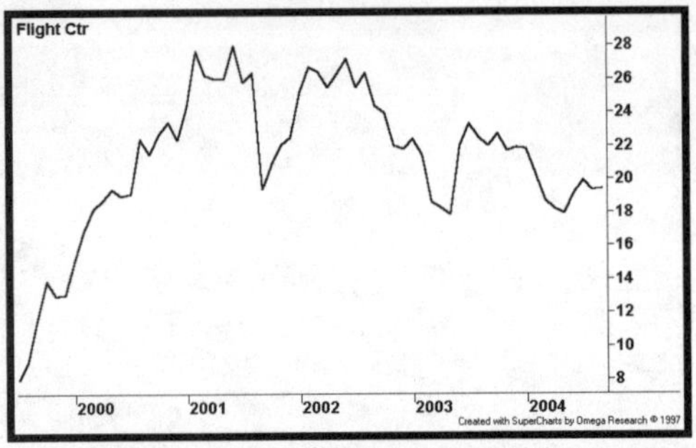

www.flightcentre.com.au

Brisbane-based Flight Centre is the largest independent retail travel agency in Australia and New Zealand, and has an estimated 20% market share. It operates under various brands, including Escape Travel, Student Flights, Travel Associates, Overseas Working Holidays, Cruiseabout, FCm Travel Solutions and Campus Travel, as well as several online brands. It has expanded to South Africa, Britain, Canada and the US.

Latest business results (June 2004, full year)

Flight Centre continues to expand and to boost its profits, despite ongoing uncertainties in the global travel business. Strong domestic consumer spending was the key to the good results, with Australian leisure travel boosting its profits by 50%. Domestic corporate travel was also strong, though profits were dented by an increase in some low-margin business and by restructuring expenses. British business was strong, but profits were down in both New Zealand and South Africa. The former was hurt by the cancellation of a NZ–Fiji charter holiday program, while South African business was affected by the loss of bonus payments from the country's major carrier. America and Canada remained in the red, despite a marked improvement in US operations. Shop numbers grew 12% during the year to 1,139, broken down as follows: Australia 646, New Zealand 140, UK 124, Canada 115, South Africa 88, US 17, others 9.

Outlook

Flight Centre has net cash holdings of more than $200 million, which will enable it to continue its expansion program. It plans to open 172 new shops by June 2005, including 94 in Australia, 23 in New Zealand, 20 in Britain and 17 in Canada, and it is working on expansion in Asia. It sees particular scope in the corporate travel sector, and has consolidated its corporate service brands under the FCm Travel Solutions banner, with plans to expand globally. Concerned that some airlines, such as the new Qantas subsidiary Jetstar, pay only low — or no — agent commissions, it is trying to move more strongly into higher-margin businesses such as package tours, hotel bookings, cruises and car hire. Its target is that these businesses should contribute 50% of company revenues within three years, up from 35% at present.

FLT Year to 30 June	2003	2004
Revenues ($mn)	605.9	774.3
EBIT ($mn)	96.6	117.8
EBIT margin (%)	15.9	15.2
Operating profit before tax ($mn)	102.3	121.3
Profit after tax ($mn)	70.0	81.9
Earnings per share (¢)	77.0	87.4
Cash flow per share (¢)	110.3	129.3
Dividend (¢)	43.5	61
Percentage franked	100	100
Net tangible assets per share ($)	2.13	2.73
Interest cover (times)	~	~
Return on equity (%)	23.2	20.7
Debt-to-equity ratio (%)	~	~
Current ratio	1.4	1.3

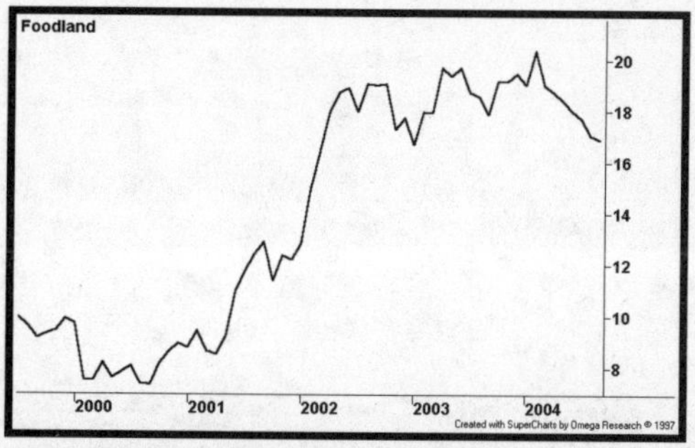

www.fal.com.au

Foodland Associated Limited

Share price ($)	16.73	
12-month high ($)	21.05	
12-month low ($)	16.69	
Market capitalisation ($mn)	1,953.6	
Price-to-NTA-per-share ratio	6.7	
5-year share price return (% p.a.)	19.5	
Sector: Consumer staples	**Company**	**Sector**
Price-earnings ratio (times)	13.7	16.8
Dividend yield (%)	5.7	3.7

Perth-based Foodland is one of Australia's leading grocery retailers and wholesalers. Its Australian supermarket division, Action, operates 81 supermarkets in Western Australia, Queensland and northern NSW. In Western Australia the group is a leading grocery wholesaler. In New Zealand it operates 150 supermarkets in the Countdown, Foodtown, Woolworths and Price Chopper banner groups and 26 Woolworths outlets at Gull convenience stores. In November 2003, it sold Farmers Holdings, its New Zealand department store chain and consumer finance provider.

Latest business results (August 2004, full year)

Revenues were down, due to the sale during the year of Farmers Holdings, but Foodland overcame strong competitive pressures to post a good rise in profits. However, the result included an after-tax profit of $39 million from the Farmers sale and from property disposals. Supermarket profits rose nearly 9%. New Zealand was especially firm, thanks to the benefits of store re-branding and refurbishments, leading to significant market share increases. However, Australian business was hit by strong competition from the discounted petrol schemes of rivals, and the February–August 2004 second half saw a marked decline in the profitability of domestic retail operations.

Outlook

After a period of strong growth — spurred on by some large acquisitions in Australia and New Zealand — Foodland's expansion has slowed. Domestically, its businesses are being hurt by stepped-up competition from its major rivals, Woolworths and Coles Myer, whose petrol discount schemes have hurt Foodland sales. Queensland has been a particular battleground, with petrol discounts of up to 10 cents per litre in some places, although the company believes this activity has peaked. Nevertheless, Foodland has seen its market share decline in the state. In its home state it has been able to boost market share through the acquisition of five former Newmart stores, though costs have been hit by the expense of introducing a new customer loyalty program. New Zealand operations remain strong, and the company believes that it is on track to continue to boost market share there. It is moving into pharmaceutical retailing in New Zealand. Foodland's share price has been supported by speculation of a takeover bid by Woolworths or Coles Myer.

FOA Year to 1 August*	2003	2004
Revenues ($mn)	6,385.8	6,026.5
Supermarkets — New Zealand (%)	48	52
Supermarkets — Australia (%)	18	21
Franchise & supply (%)	19	19
Farmers Holdings (%)	10	2
EBIT ($mn)	256.2	260.1
EBIT margin (%)	4.0	4.3
Gross margin (%)	17.0	15.7
Operating profit before tax ($mn)	191.4	225.9
Profit after tax ($mn)	120.1	142.7
Earnings per share (¢)	103.3	122.0
Cash flow per share (¢)	225.1	234.1
Dividend (¢)	85	96
Percentage franked	100	100
Net tangible assets per share ($)	2.01	2.49
Interest cover (times)	4.0	7.6
Return on equity (%)	13.2	14.4
Debt-to-equity ratio (%)	98.8	36.1
Current ratio	1.3	1.5

* 3 August 2003

Foster's Group Limited

Share price ($)	4.61	
12-month high ($)	4.90	
12-month low ($)	4.22	
Market capitalisation ($mn)	9,268.2	
Price-to-NTA-per-share ratio	4.1	
5-year share price return (% p.a.)	5.1	
Sector: Consumer staples	**Company**	**Sector**
Price-earnings ratio (times)	20.3	16.8
Dividend yield (%)	4.2	3.7

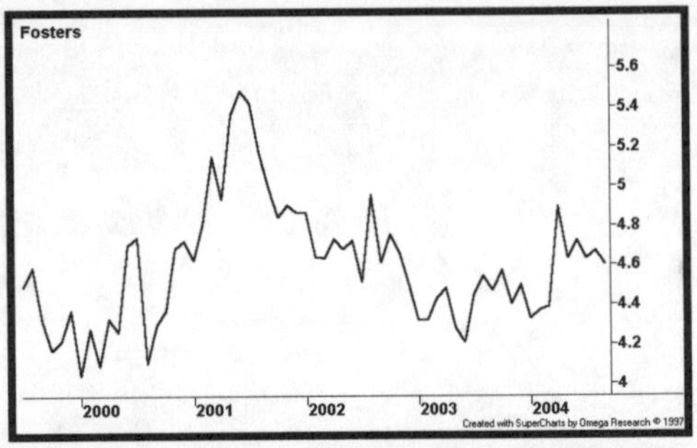

www.fosters.com.au

Melbourne-based Foster's, one of the world's leading brewers and winemakers, operates within four broad groupings: Beringer Blass Wine Estates is the company's international wine business; Carlton and United Breweries dominates the Australian beer market and has extensive hotel interests; Foster's Brewing International manages the Foster's Lager premium beer brand in more than 150 countries; and the Lensworth Group manages the company's extensive property assets. The group has brewing operations and wine operations in numerous countries. It has sold its pub business, Australian Leisure and Hospitality.

Latest business results (June 2004, full year)

Profits fell, as the company was hit by turmoil in its once high-flying wine business. There was a good result from the domestic beer business, with profits up nearly 10%, thanks to higher prices and tighter cost controls. Beer volumes actually edged down, but this was offset by stronger demand for spirits and for high-margin, ready-to-drink mixed liquors. International beer profits rose more than 10%, with Foster's Lager, currently the number seven international premium beer brand, increasing volume by 8.5%, compared to global beer industry growth of around 2%. However, wine profits plunged 32%, due particularly to oversupply and extreme price competition in the North American market, compounded by the strength of the dollar. Foster's realised a large $553 million pre-tax profit — treated as a significant item — from the sale of Australian Leisure and Hospitality.

FGL Year to 30 June	2003	2004
Revenues ($mn)	4,637.8	3,908.1
Beer (%)	40	51
Wine (%)	41	40
Leisure & hospitality (%)	18	8
EBIT ($mn)	972.0	780.8
EBIT margin (%)	21.0	20.0
Gross margin (%)	48.1	48.3
Operating profit before tax ($mn)	818.8	685.9
Profit after tax ($mn)	568.1	469.4
Earnings per share (¢)	27.5	22.7
Cash flow per share (¢)	37.9	32.6
Dividend (¢)	18.75	19.25
Percentage franked	100	100
Net tangible assets per share ($)	0.97	1.13
Interest cover (times)	6.3	8.2
Return on equity (%)	13.2	10.4
Debt-to-equity ratio (%)	58.9	36.1
Current ratio	1.3	1.2

Outlook

Its beer business provides stable cash flow and profit, but with limited growth prospects, and Foster's had been depending on its wine activities to build the company. It is now working to restructure this business, including new products and promotions, and it believes excess US inventories have been largely cleared. However, it does not expect much improvement before 2005. The company is also working to revitalise its under-performing global wine club operations, and has indicated that it might sell this business. It is also planning to sell its Lensworth property division. It expects just single-digit EPS growth in the June 2005 year — with about half of this from share buybacks — before returning to double-digit levels in the June 2006 year.

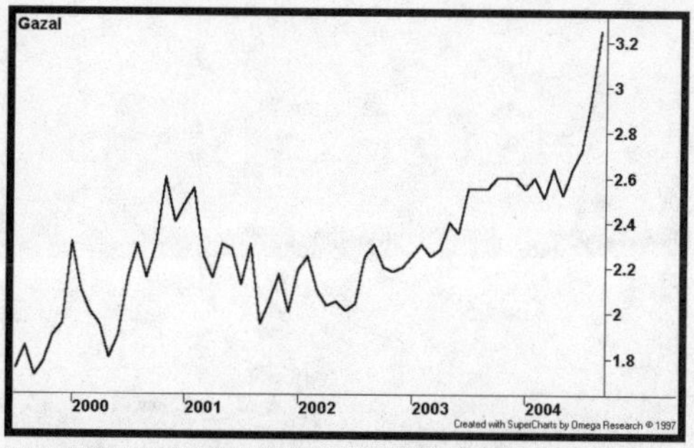

www.gazal.com.au

Gazal Corporation Limited

Share price ($)	2.75	
12-month high ($)	2.80	
12-month low ($)	2.40	
Market capitalisation ($mn)	162.6	
Price-to-NTA-per-share ratio	3.4	
5-year share price return (% p.a.)	19.6	
Sector: Consumer discretionary	**Company**	**Sector**
Price-earnings ratio (times)	14.6	23.8
Dividend yield (%)	5.1	1.5

Sydney-based Gazal, founded in 1958, is one of Australia's largest publicly listed clothing companies, specialising mainly in business shirts, men's casual wear and surf wear, ladies' intimate apparel and school wear. It owns the Mambo label, and in Australia it is a licence holder for such well-known brands as Nautica, Van Heusen, Lovable, Crystelle, Maui and Sons, Bisley, Paramount, Midford, Oroton, Stamina, Tigerlily, Mariner and Kookai. It also makes house-brand merchandise for major retailers, and it has some sales in Europe. The controlling Gazal family hold more than 60% of the shares. It has sold its Asian manufacturing operation.

Latest business results (June 2004, full year)

Revenues fell — reflecting Gazal's sale of its Asian business — but strong domestic consumer demand and the dollar's strength helped the company to a firm rise in profits. Excluding Asian operations, sales increased by nearly 6%. The company's key brands generally produced strong results. The Trade Secret factory outlets business also had a solid year. The company's drive to boost its share of the workwear market continued, with the Bisley brand delivering significant growth. The Davenport underwear business, acquired in November 2003, which includes the Calvin Klein, Nancy Ganz, Playboy and Virgin Ware brands, contributed positively to earnings, as did the Trent Nathan fashion lifestyle brand acquired in October 2003. However, the Mambo label performed poorly, with results well down on the previous year.

Outlook

Gazal is benefiting from the strength of the domestic economy and high levels of consumer spending. It is also a beneficiary of the appreciation of the dollar. It hopes to embark on a new strategy of acquiring its own high-profile brands and developing these as intellectual assets with long-term value. However, its Mambo acquisition has fallen short of expectations, though the company believes that new marketing initiatives and operational changes will deliver improved results in the June 2005 year. It expects substantial growth for the Bisley workwear business, as well as for the Kenneth Cole sportswear operation, which was launched in July 2004. The company in mid-2004 appointed Rothschild Australia as financial advisers, and is assessing a number of potential acquisitions.

GZL Year to 30 June	2003	2004
Revenues ($mn)	194.7	193.0
EBIT ($mn)	16.0	18.4
EBIT margin (%)	8.2	9.5
Gross margin (%)	43.8	50.4
Operating profit before tax ($mn)	14.2	16.2
Profit after tax ($mn)	9.7	10.8
Earnings per share (¢)	17.0	18.8
Cash flow per share (¢)	23.3	26.2
Dividend (¢)	14	14
Percentage franked	100	100
Net tangible assets per share ($)	0.94	0.81
Interest cover (times)	8.5	8.4
Return on equity (%)	11.8	11.9
Debt-to-equity ratio (%)	27.8	36.5
Current ratio	2.2	2.0

Great Southern Plantations Limited

Share price ($)	3.10	
12-month high ($)	3.37	
12-month low ($)	1.35	
Market capitalisation ($mn)	757.4	
Price-to-NTA-per-share ratio	1.7	
5-year share price return (% p.a.)	17.5	
Sector: Materials	**Company**	**Sector**
Price-earnings ratio (times)	7.0	14.3
Dividend yield (%)	3.2	2.6

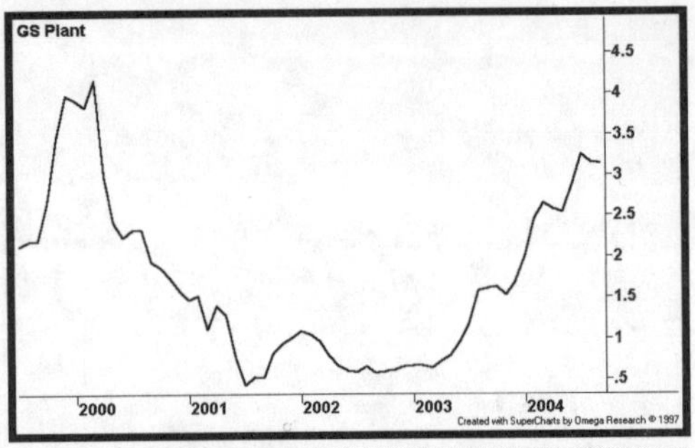

www.great-southern.com.au

Perth-based Great Southern Plantations, founded in 1987, is an agribusiness investment manager, providing investors with tax-effective investment products. It manages a total of 52,000 hectares of eucalypt plantations at three locations — the Great Southern region in the south west of Western Australia, the Green Triangle region in the south west of Victoria, and in an area located between Gladstone and Bundaberg on Queensland's Capricorn Coast. In 2004, it launched its first viticulture project, on 170 hectares of land in the Frankland River wine region of Western Australia.

Latest business results (June 2004, full year)

The company delivered a huge increase in revenues and profits, thanks to expanded operations, a greatly stepped-up marketing effort and a steady growth in investor appreciation of the attractions of its products. Sales of eucalypt plantation products totalled approximately $227 million, and the company's first viticulture project closed oversubscribed, having raised more than $16 million. Under Great Southern's accounting rules, around $60 million of the revenues will be deferred until future years, while more than $16 million in revenues from previous years was added to the June 2004 figure. The company claimed that its market share in the managed investment scheme industry has grown to an estimated 37%.

Outlook

Great Southern Plantations is a big beneficiary of renewed investor interest in managed schemes targeting agriculture. This follows a period when it seemed that Australian Taxation Office rulings might derail the schemes. The company is also a beneficiary of government moves to substantially boost timber plantation acreage in Australia, under the 'Vision 2020' program, which envisages a further 1.5 million hectares of plantations nationwide. In March 2004, the company announced that it had bought the rights to acquire a further 55,000 hectares of plantable land, in Western Australia and Victoria, and this will form the base of future long-term growth. In January 2004, Great Southern announced its first hardwood woodchip contract — a three-year deal with Japan's Nichimen Corporation to export more than 500,000 tonnes of woodchip over three years — and it expects further similar contracts as its plantations mature.

GTP Year to 30 June	2003	2004
Revenues ($mn)	95.7	204.2
EBIT ($mn)	58.3	131.1
EBIT margin (%)	60.9	64.2
Operating profit before tax ($mn)	59.5	132.7
Profit after tax ($mn)	41.4	93.2
Earnings per share (¢)	20.7	44.1
Cash flow per share (¢)	20.8	44.3
Dividend (¢)	7	10
Percentage franked	100	100
Net tangible assets per share ($)	1.13	1.84
Interest cover (times)	~	~
Return on equity (%)	19.9	27.6
Debt-to-equity ratio (%)	~	~
Current ratio	1.4	1.0

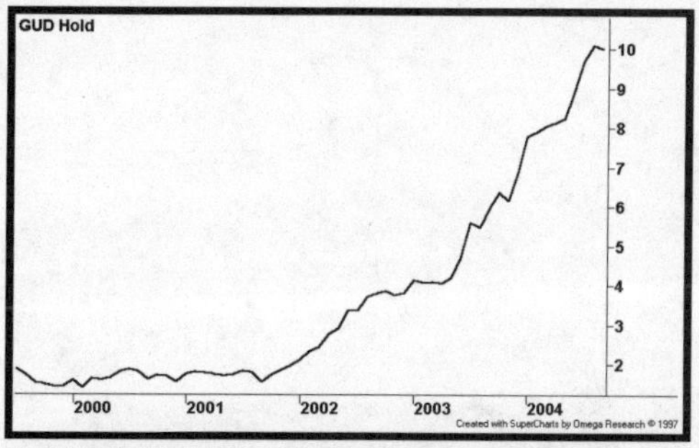

www.gud.com.au

GUD Holdings Limited

Share price ($)	9.84	
12-month high ($)	10.20	
12-month low ($)	5.40	
Market capitalisation ($mn)	615.2	
Price-to-NTA-per-share ratio	7.1	
5-year share price return (% p.a.)	54.6	
Sector: Consumer discretionary	**Company**	**Sector**
Price-earnings ratio (times)	14.3	23.8
Dividend yield (%)	4.1	1.5

GUD, based in Melbourne and founded in 1940, is a diversified manufacturer and distributor with five broad product lines: Sunbeam small electrical appliances; Victa lawnmowers; Ryco, Wesfil and Goss automotive filtration and associated products; Davey water pumps, pump sets and water pressure systems; and Lock Focus security products and associated hardware. It exports to more than 50 countries.

Latest business results (June 2004, full year)

New product initiatives, its continuing restructuring program and the strength of the domestic economy all combined to hand GUD another powerful rise in profits, despite just a modest gain in sales revenues. The core Sunbeam Victa division was the star, with EBIT surging 66%, on a lift in sales of just 11%. Sunbeam boosted its market share, with particularly strong growth from coffee machines, electric blankets, irons and portable heaters. Victa reported significantly improved results, on the back of new product launches and a market recovery as the drought eased. Despite flat sales, the Ryco Wesfil division saw EBIT up 21%, thanks to restructuring gains and the benefits from Wesfil's acquisition in the first half of its Queensland distributor. Davey boosted EBIT 12% on just a 1% increase in sales, due to productivity gains and new products. The small Lock Focus business saw sales and profits edge down, in the face of lower demand from most major customers. GUD reported as a significant item an $8.9 million pre-tax restructuring charge.

Outlook

GUD shares have been superb performers on the strength of the company's continuing expansion, and the question now is to what degree this growth can continue. As long as consumer spending remains firm it seems likely that the company will continue to prosper, with a stream of new products and continuing restructuring initiatives providing strong earnings support. The Sunbeam business is benefiting from a new wave of higher-margin premium products, such as the Sunbeam Café series of coffee makers. The new Razor range of alloy-based mowers is helping provide higher profits for Victa. The $15 million acquisition of the spa pool products manufacturer Spa-Quip is seen as boosting the Davey division.

GUD Year to 30 June	2003	2004
Revenues ($mn)	372.4	393.8
Sunbeam Victa (%)	54	56
Ryco/Wesfil (%)	23	22
Davey (%)	19	18
Lock Focus (%)	4	3
EBIT ($mn)	44.3	62.6
EBIT margin (%)	11.9	15.9
Gross margin (%)	35.9	39.3
Operating profit before tax ($mn)	40.6	60.2
Profit after tax ($mn)	27.4	41.7
Earnings per share (¢)	45.0	68.6
Cash flow per share (¢)	61.3	88.1
Dividend (¢)	26	40
Percentage franked	100	100
Net tangible assets per share ($)	1.26	1.39
Interest cover (times)	11.9	25.8
Return on equity (%)	22.1	31.0
Debt-to-equity ratio (%)	16.5	12.3
Current ratio	1.7	1.7

Gunns Limited

Share price ($)	13.38	
12-month high ($)	14.05	
12-month low ($)	11.01	
Market capitalisation ($mn)	1,151.0	
Price-to-NTA-per-share ratio	2.6	
5-year share price return (% p.a.)	71.4	
Sector: Materials	**Company**	**Sector**
Price-earnings ratio (times)	10.7	14.3
Dividend yield (%)	3.7	2.6

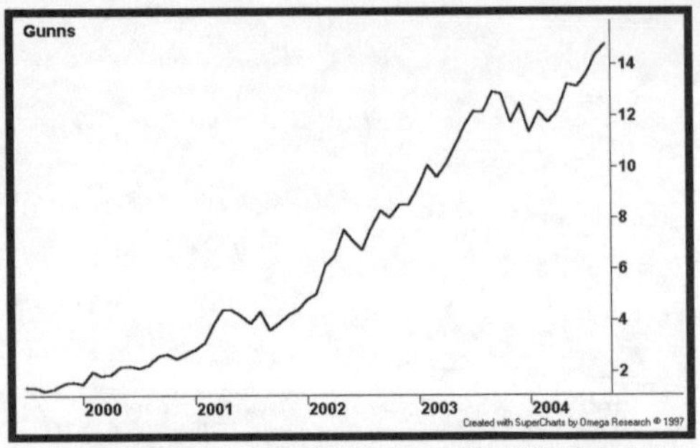

www.gunns.com.au

Launceston timber company Gunns was founded in 1875, and claims to be one of Australia's oldest companies. It manages over 90,000 hectares of plantations, and is Australia's largest hardwood producer, with five sawmills around Tasmania. It also maintains two veneer factories in Tasmania and one in New Zealand. It operates four woodchip export ports in Tasmania, and woodchip sales to Asian pulp mills are a major activity. Other businesses include six Gunns Mitre 10 hardware stores in Northern Tasmania, the building contracting company Hinman Wright and Manser, and Tamar Ridge Wines. The Gunns Plantations subsidiary offers managed investment products in timber plantations to the public.

Latest business results (June 2004, full year)

In a solid environment for the forestry industry, sales and profits showed good increases, although much of the earnings gain came about through accounting rules requiring the revaluation of the company's forest resource. It was the Gunns managed investment business — less than 10% of total turnover — that showed the most powerful growth, with revenues up 35% and EBIT surging by 74%, thanks to an increased level of woodlot development and the release of the company's new viticulture project, based on its acquisition of Tamar Ridge in 2003.

Outlook

The forestry industry has enjoyed buoyant conditions over several years, reflected in the soaring Gunns share price. The outlook remains firm, with Asian demand for Australian wood fibre continuing to rise. The company has various initiatives intended to meet growing demand. It has bought three sawmills in Western Australia from Wesfarmers, and sees these as helping promote growth in the June 2005 year. It is also actively seeking further acquisitions outside Tasmania. In mid-2004 it announced the start of a feasibility study into the development of a $1-billion eucalyptus pulp mill in Tasmania, with results due in early 2005. Gunns also hopes to boost the Tamar Ridge Wines business, with new capital investment and the development of new markets in Asia, where Gunns already enjoys a significant presence. The company's managed investment business has enormous potential, as can be seen from the success of companies such as Timbercorp and Great Southern Plantations.

GNS Year to 30 June	2003	2004
Revenues ($mn)	605.7	649.7
EBIT ($mn)	130.3	174.4
EBIT margin (%)	21.5	26.8
Gross margin (%)	26.6	21.8
Operating profit before tax ($mn)	106.2	151.5
Profit after tax ($mn)	74.0	105.3
Earnings per share (¢)	91.8	125.3
Cash flow per share (¢)	111.5	144.8
Dividend (¢)	40	50
Percentage franked	100	100
Net tangible assets per share ($)	4.26	5.19
Interest cover (times)	5.4	7.6
Return on equity (%)	25.8	26.4
Debt-to-equity ratio (%)	84.2	64.5
Current ratio	1.0	1.0

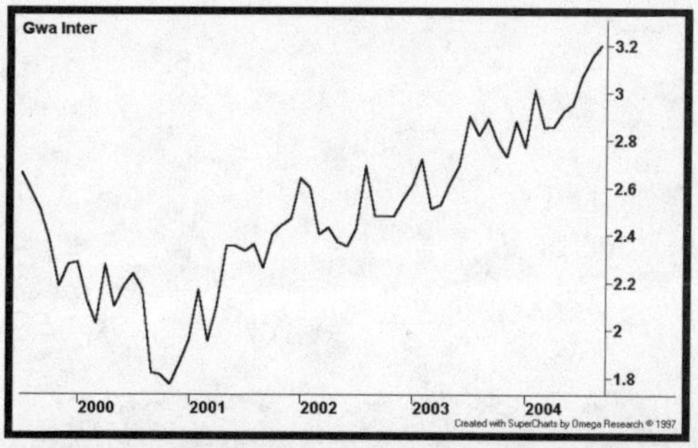

www.gwail.com.au

GWA International Limited

Share price ($)	3.11	
12-month high ($)	3.25	
12-month low ($)	2.67	
Market capitalisation ($mn)	860.0	
Price-to-NTA-per-share ratio	12.3	
5-year share price return (% p.a.)	10.3	
Sector: Industrials	**Company**	**Sector**
Price-earnings ratio (times)	13.9	14.8
Dividend yield (%)	5.8	4.2

Brisbane-based GWA is a manufacturer of a wide range of household products, including 90% of Australia's toilets. Its Caroma division is a leading supplier of bathroom fittings, and has operations in Asia, Europe and America. The Sebel contract furniture business provides seating for stadiums and auditoriums, and also operates in several countries. In addition, the company makes Rover lawn mowers, Dorf Clark tapware, Dux hot water systems and Gainsborough door fittings, and it owns the Wisa Beheer cistern producer in the Netherlands.

Latest business results (June 2004, full year)

The firm economy and strong domestic housing sector helped GWA to its third consecutive record profit. The primary driver of growth was the high-margin building fixtures and fittings business, comprising the Caroma, Dorf Clark, Gainsborough and Dux brands, with sales revenues edging up 1% and profits up nearly 7%. There was a particularly strong performance for Caroma products, underpinned by strong domestic demand from the dwelling, non-dwelling, renovation and replacement sectors. However, Caroma's export sales to Asia and North America were hurt by the exchange rate. Most other brands in this division were also strong, though Dorf Clark performed below expectations. The Sebel commercial furniture business is the company's largest exporter, and was hit by the higher dollar, although domestic sales were firm. Favourable seasonal conditions meant that Rover mowers enjoyed strong demand, with an excellent lift in sales revenues and profits.

Outlook

GWA itself concedes that the construction sector has reached the peak of the current cycle. Its own forecast is for domestic demand for its building fixtures and fittings products to decline by 4% to 5% in the June 2005 year. In response, it is placing emphasis on innovative new product ranges — from both Caroma and Dorf Clark — that help reduce household water consumption, and it is already seeing strong market take-up of these. It has strong hopes for its Caroma's Smartflush range of toilets, to be released in 2005, which have the capacity to save 38,000 litres of water per year in an average household. With exports expanding, the currency will play a growing role in the company's results.

GWT Year to 30 June	2003	2004
Revenues ($mn)	659.6	667.9
Building fixtures & fittings (%)	83	83
Commercial furniture (%)	11	10
EBIT ($mn)	90.9	99.5
EBIT margin (%)	13.8	14.9
Gross margin (%)	44.2	46.3
Operating profit before tax ($mn)	78.6	88.4
Profit after tax ($mn)	55.0	62.1
Earnings per share (¢)	19.8	22.3
Cash flow per share (¢)	29.9	33.3
Dividend (¢)	15.5	18
Percentage franked	100	100
Net tangible assets per share ($)	0.20	0.25
Interest cover (times)	7.4	9.0
Return on equity (%)	13.7	14.7
Debt-to-equity ratio (%)	50.2	37.2
Current ratio	2.5	3.1

Harvey Norman Holdings Limited

Share price ($)	2.92	
12-month high ($)	3.47	
12-month low ($)	2.53	
Market capitalisation ($mn)	3,128.2	
Price-to-NTA-per-share ratio	2.7	
5-year share price return (% p.a.)	1.1	
Sector: Consumer discretionary	**Company**	**Sector**
Price-earnings ratio (times)	17.5	23.8
Dividend yield (%)	2.6	1.5

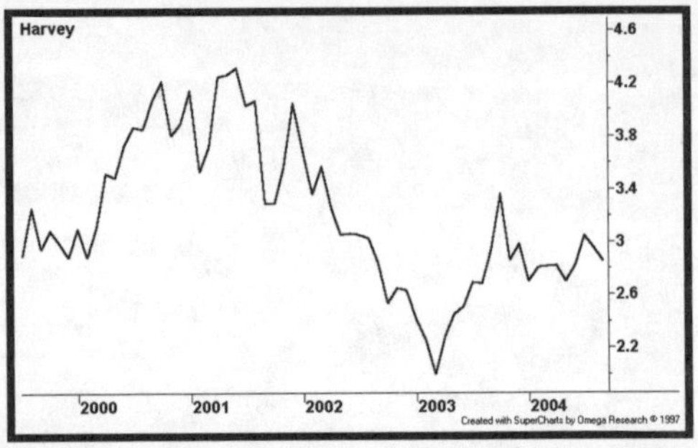

www.harveynorman.com.au

Harvey Norman operates a chain of more than 180 retail stores specialising in electrical and electronic goods, home appliances, furniture, flooring, carpets and manchester, throughout Australia and New Zealand, under the Harvey Norman and Domayne banners. Many of the stores are independently held as part of a franchise operation, from which Harvey Norman receives income for advisory and advertising services. It also receives rental income from property investments, from its own stores and from the provision of finance to franchisees and customers. It has bought controlling stakes in Rebel Sport and in the Singapore retailer Pertama, and operates in Slovenia and Ireland.

Latest business results (June 2004, full year)

Booming retail conditions — especially for home electronics products — handed Harvey Norman another boost to sales and profits, aided by its continuing expansion. The main contributory factors were a 39% increase in sales from New Zealand company-owned stores to $97 million, a 79% increase in sales revenues from the Slovenian company-owned store to $32 million, a 10% rise in sales revenues from Rebel Sport and $45 million in revenues from its two new Irish stores. Singapore sales rose in local currency, but were down in Australian dollars. Retail sales by Harvey Norman franchisees — which are not part of the company's results — rose 12% to $3.25 billion. Nine new stores or complexes were opened in Australia and five in New Zealand.

HVN Year to 30 June	2003	2004
Revenues ($mn)	1,382.0	1,751.7
Franchising & corporate (%)	22	29
Retail — New Zealand (%)	18	19
Retail — Asia (%)	26	18
Retail — Rebel Sport (%)	20	17
Non-franchised retail (%)	7	9
Property (%)	5	5
Retail — Slovenia (%)	1	2
EBIT ($mn)	256.7	296.3
EBIT margin (%)	18.6	16.9
Gross margin (%)	25.9	25.1
Operating profit before tax ($mn)	233.3	269.3
Profit after tax ($mn)	151.0	176.1
Earnings per share (¢)	14.3	16.6
Cash flow per share (¢)	20.6	23.7
Dividend (¢)	5	7.5
Percentage franked	100	100
Net tangible assets per share ($)	0.90	1.09
Interest cover (times)	11.0	11.0
Return on equity (%)	17.0	16.6
Debt-to-equity ratio (%)	37.7	36.3
Current ratio	1.8	1.7

Outlook

Harvey Norman is a major beneficiary of the continuing Australian appetite for the latest high-tech gadgets. As a big importer, the company also gains from the strong dollar. It sees a new stream of growth coming from urban living complexes modelled on the newly-opened 17,800-square-metre Domayne Alexandria and Space Furniture retail outlet in Sydney. However, it is also now increasingly looking overseas for growth, and this has led to volatility in the share price. New Zealand operations are strong, and Singapore has turned the corner into profit. The trial store in Slovenia has been a big success, moving into profit in only its second year of trading. The company is considering further expansion in Europe, and has also initiated talks on opening in China and India.

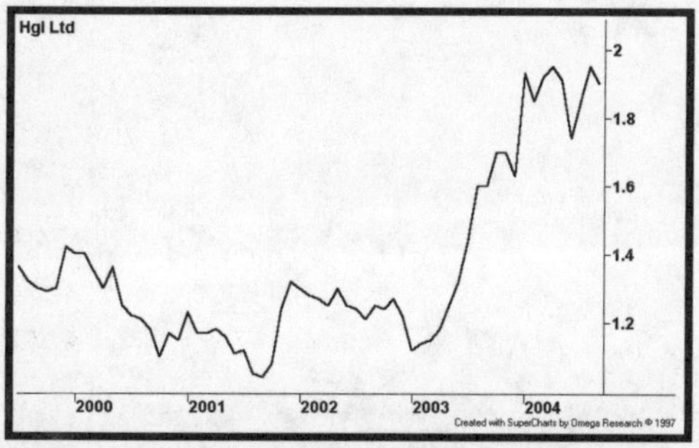

www.hgl.com.au

HGL Limited

Share price ($)	1.91	
12-month high ($)	2.05	
12-month low ($)	1.43	
Market capitalisation ($mn)	94.3	
Price-to-NTA-per-share ratio	1.7	
5-year share price return (% p.a.)	16.3	
Sector: Industrials	**Company**	**Sector**
Price-earnings ratio (times)	9.0	14.8
Dividend yield (%)	4.5	4.2

Sydney-based HGL is a small diversified investment group that specialises in acquiring and rejuvenating under-performing niche companies. In recent years it has been targeting those in the import and distribution business, and it is now part-owner of 11 of these, including firms that specialise in eyewear, fabrics, cosmetics, headwear and imaging equipment. Generally, the companies are partially owned by their management or other industry experts, who work in partnership with HGL executives. HGL also participates in public company investing and the funds management sector, through its 38% interest in the boutique fund manager MMC Asset Management, its 40% interest in the manager of listed investment company MMC Contrarian and its 6% stake in the listed investment company Hunter Hall International.

Latest business results (March 2004, half-year)

Profits roared ahead, though mainly thanks to revaluations and capital gains from listed investments of $3.7 million after tax. Excluding revaluations and capital gains, the after-tax profit rose from $1.5 million in the March 2003 half to $2.6 million. The earnings before interest and tax (EBIT) from the company's import and distribution businesses increased to $6.2 million, from $4.4 million in the March 2003 half. This improvement was mainly as a result of two large acquisitions made in the second half of the September 2003 year. EBIT from continuing import and distribution businesses rose from $4.4 million to $4.6 million. The company did not buy any new businesses during the March 2004 half, despite reaching an advanced stage of due diligence on two transactions that did not proceed.

Outlook

HGL's growth prospects depend to a large degree on management's success in identifying high-potential, under-performing niche businesses that require fresh capital and business know-how. HGL management must also then negotiate a satisfactory partnership deal with the new entity's owners. The company's target is businesses where the return on capital employed is likely to exceed 20% in a reasonably short period of time, and it hopes to invest $30 million in such businesses over the next few years.

HNG Year to 30 September	2002	2003
Revenues ($mn)	114.6	116.2
EBIT ($mn)	14.6	15.2
EBIT margin (%)	12.7	13.1
Gross margin (%)	47.6	45.3
Operating profit before tax ($mn)	14.4	14.9
Profit after tax ($mn)	8.0	9.9
Earnings per share (¢)	17.2	21.2
Cash flow per share (¢)	25.8	25.2
Dividend (¢)	12	8.6
Percentage franked	0	100
Interest cover (times)	75.9	42.3
Return on equity (%)	17.7	19.5
Half-year to 30 March	**2003**	**2004**
Revenues ($mn)	39.5	50.7
Operating profit before tax ($mn)	2.9	11.1
Profit after tax ($mn)	2.0	6.3
Earnings per share (¢)	4.3	13.0
Dividend (¢)	4.2	4.2
Percentage franked	100	100
Net tangible assets per share ($)	1.00	1.09
Debt-to-equity ratio (%)	~	~
Current ratio	4.0	3.6

Hills Industries Limited

Share price ($)	4.06	
12-month high ($)	4.10	
12-month low ($)	3.55	
Market capitalisation ($mn)	574.2	
Price-to-NTA-per-share ratio	3.1	
5-year share price return (% p.a.)	19.5	
Sector: Industrials	**Company**	**Sector**
Price-earnings ratio (times)	18.0	14.8
Dividend yield (%)	5.5	4.2

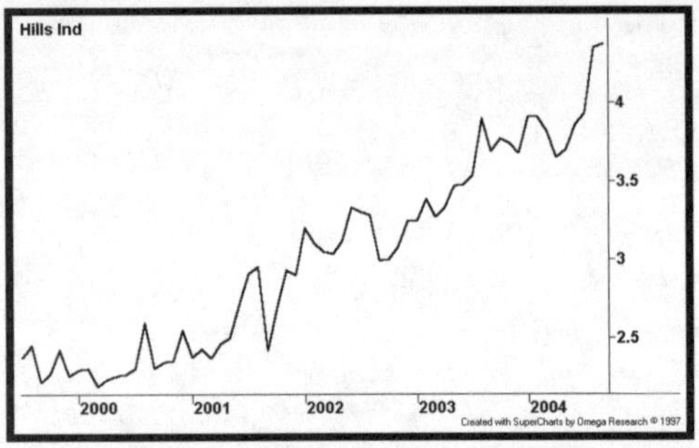

www.hills.com.au

Adelaide-based Hills, founded in 1946, is famous for its clothes hoists. However, it also manufactures a diverse range of other products, including garden equipment, structural tubing, a wide range of commercial and industrial steel products, closed circuit TV systems, satellite dishes, electronic security systems and television antennas. It owns 47% of the listed metal products manufacturer Korvest.

Latest business results (June 2004, full year)

A buoyant domestic economy, with continuing strength in housing and construction, handed Hills another solid result. The best performance came from the electronic security and entertainment division, with a 27% jump in EBIT on a 4% rise in sales. There was a particular boost from the new Foxtel pay TV digitalisation program, for which Hills is a key supplier. The division was also assisted by the closure of some loss-making businesses in the previous year, and by the strength of the dollar in the first half. The building and industrial products division also realised an excellent result, with revenues up 14% and EBIT surging 17%, and increased market shares for many products. There was an especially fine contribution from the Orrcon structural tubing business. However, the home and hardware products division saw revenues edge down 3% and EBIT slip 1%. Despite the strength of the domestic market, profitability was dented by competition from Chinese-made products, and exports were hurt by problems in the British market.

HIL Year to 30 June	2003	2004
Revenues ($mn)	660.6	713.6
Building & industrial (%)	50	54
Electronic security & entertainment (%)	25	24
Home & hardware (%)	25	22
EBIT ($mn)	54.2	58.5
EBIT margin (%)	8.2	8.2
Gross margin (%)	34.0	34.8
Operating profit before tax ($mn)	49.8	54.0
Profit after tax ($mn)	27.2	31.1
Earnings per share (¢)	20.7	22.5
Cash flow per share (¢)	34.5	36.8
Dividend (¢)	21	22.5
Percentage franked	100	100
Net tangible assets per share ($)	1.17	1.31
Interest cover (times)	12.5	12.9
Return on equity (%)	17.5	16.6
Debt-to-equity ratio (%)	27.9	26.9
Current ratio	1.8	2.0

Outlook

Hills has become a major beneficiary of the strength in the domestic construction industry, with a threefold surge in profits for its building and industrial products division over three years, and sales revenues up 81%. While the domestic non-residential and engineering construction sectors remain strong, this division should prosper, though rising steel prices are a concern. The electronics business has also returned to high-growth mode, with the Foxtel digitalisation program a particular incentive. A restructuring of British operations is intended to restore profits there, and Hills will also benefit from the continuing strength of the domestic home renovations market. It sees great long-term potential in its K-Care business, which makes disability and rehabilitation equipment.

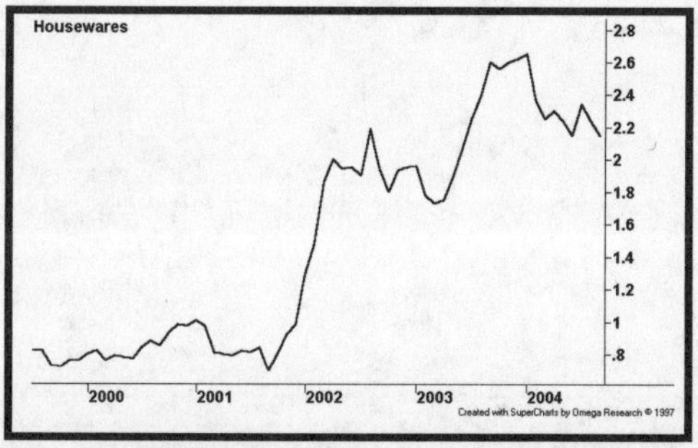

www.housewares.com.au

Housewares International Limited

Share price ($)	2.30	
12-month high ($)	2.79	
12-month low ($)	2.07	
Market capitalisation ($mn)	269.8	
Price-to-NTA-per-share ratio	3.3	
5-year share price return (% p.a.)	31.2	
Sector: Consumer discretionary	**Company**	**Sector**
Price-earnings ratio (times)	11.7	23.8
Dividend yield (%)	4.6	1.5

Melbourne-based Housewares International has evolved from its 1957 beginnings as a small local importer into a large distributor of household products in several countries. Its wholly owned brands include Breville, Kambrook, Ronson and Goldair for home appliances, and Arcosteel, alex liddy, Baccarat, Forum, Mayfair & Jackson and Pronto for kitchenware. Its distribution companies include Metro Marketing in the US and a 50% stake in Anglo Canadian in Canada. In 2003, it acquired the Sabco household cleaning goods company.

Latest business results (June 2004, full year)

Strong domestic consumer spending helped Housewares to a firm increase in its profits. The figure would have been higher but for the considerable costs involved in a major restructuring of the company's homeware businesses and of integrating the Sabco acquisition. There was weakness from the homeware businesses, but a strong contribution from electrical products. The Metro Marketing operation in the US realised a 25% increase in profits, following the successful introduction of the Breville brand, though in Australian dollars the gain was only minor.

Outlook

Housewares International is rapidly transforming itself into a global marketer of a wide variety of household goods. Its Sydney design centre is responsible for a stream of new product initiatives, which are manufactured in China, with an office in Hong Kong as a global marketing base. The company's particular objective is to gain success the huge North American market, and it is aiming to establish Breville there as one of the top three brands at specialty gourmet stores by 2008. After a marketing effort of just 18 months, more than 2,500 North American stores now stock a limited range of Breville products. South Africa is another particular target of the company, and it also hopes to develop sales in Europe. With an increasing amount of its business being transacted offshore — both production and sales — exchange rate trends will become an ever-growing factor in the company's success. After some years of little movement, the shares came to life after Housewares International's 2002 acquisition of Breville, which doubled its size. More recently, there has been stock market speculation that the company could become a takeover target.

HWI Year to 30 June	2003	2004
Revenues ($mn)	456.0	457.6
EBIT ($mn)	35.7	39.0
EBIT margin (%)	7.8	8.5
Gross margin (%)	38.2	40.8
Operating profit before tax ($mn)	30.9	34.0
Profit after tax ($mn)	20.9	22.9
Earnings per share (¢)	18.6	19.7
Cash flow per share (¢)	22.6	24.2
Dividend (¢)	10	10.5
Percentage franked	100	100
Net tangible assets per share ($)	0.65	0.69
Interest cover (times)	7.3	7.9
Return on equity (%)	15.6	15.2
Debt-to-equity ratio (%)	30.9	39.8
Current ratio	2.9	3.1

Iluka Resources Limited

Share price ($)	4.48	
12-month high ($)	4.73	
12-month low ($)	3.84	
Market capitalisation ($mn)	1,043.0	
Price-to-NTA-per-share ratio	1.2	
5-year share price return (% p.a.)	9.9	
Sector: Materials	**Company**	**Sector**
Price-earnings ratio (times)	12.2	14.3
Dividend yield (%)	4.9	2.6

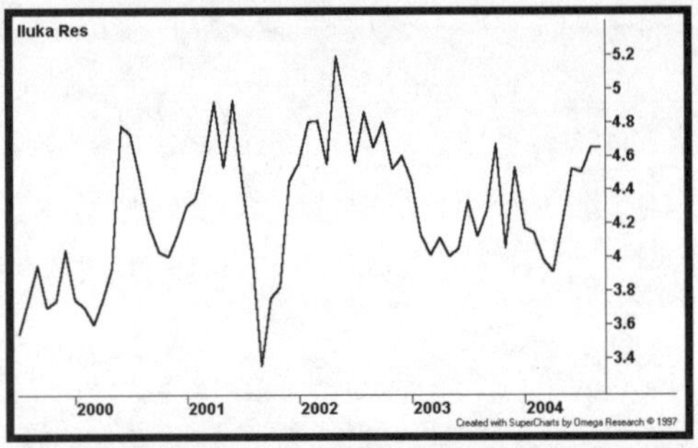

www.iluka.com

Perth-based Iluka is the world's second-largest producer and processor of titanium minerals — used in paint pigments and other protective coatings — and the world's largest miner and processor of zircon, which is used in ceramics and refractories. It also has a coal mining joint venture. It has production and processing operations in Australia and the US, and extensive mineral exploration activities in several countries. It owns half the equity of the listed Queensland mineral sands producer Consolidated Rutile.

Latest business results (June 2004, half-year)

Sales and the pre-tax profit rose solidly, with the company gaining from higher sales volumes and prices, further cost reductions and efficiency improvements from its business improvement program, the achievement of a significant performance turnaround in American operations and higher profits from foreign currency hedging. All this was partially offset by the appreciation of the Australian dollar, which hurt US dollar denominated sales, a book loss on US dollar borrowings and a period of low-grade and high-cost remnant mining at the Capel operations in Western Australia. However, the June 2003 after-tax profit result had been helped by some remaining tax credits. These were no longer available in June 2004, and the tax bill rose substantially, with just a modest post-tax profit gain.

ILU Year to 31 December	2002	2003
Revenues ($mn)	894.5	786.0
EBIT ($mn)	128.4	105.4
EBIT margin (%)	14.4	13.4
Gross margin (%)	23.9	18.9
Operating profit before tax ($mn)	102.1	90.8
Profit after tax ($mn)	109.0	85.2
Earnings per share (¢)	48.6	36.6
Cash flow per share (¢)	92.0	86.2
Dividend (¢)	22	22
Percentage franked	9	42
Interest cover (times)	4.9	7.2
Return on equity (%)	14.4	10.0
Half-year to 30 June	**2003**	**2004**
Revenues ($mn)	358.5	392.6
Operating profit before tax ($mn)	40.0	62.2
Profit after tax ($mn)	36.7	38.0
Earnings per share (¢)	15.8	16.3
Dividend (¢)	10	10
Percentage franked	92	87
Net tangible assets per share ($)	3.63	3.80
Debt-to-equity ratio (%)	43.5	39.7
Current ratio	2.2	1.6

Outlook

Iluka sees December 2004 full-year profits as being roughly in line with those of December 2003. However, the longer term outlook is more positive. The company continues its cost-cutting initiatives, aimed at boosting annual pre-tax profit by at least $40 million. It expects to begin production at its new Murray Basin mineral sands acquisition in 2005. It also expects a substantial increase in production from its Capel operation, following the establishment of a new mine there. The Capel mine has significantly higher mineral grades than the company has been achieving recently. However, reduced hedging levels mean exchange rates will be a significant influence on the results.

Five-year chart not available

www.incitecpivot.com.au

Incitec Pivot Limited

Share price ($)	19.00	
12-month high ($)	19.30	
12-month low ($)	15.10	
Market capitalisation ($mn)	1,107.3	
Price-to-NTA-per-share ratio	2.7	
5-year share price return (% p.a.)	N/A	
Sector: Materials	**Company**	**Sector**
Price-earnings ratio (times)	16.9	14.3
Dividend yield (%)	0.0	2.6

Melbourne-based Incitec Pivot was formed in June 2003 from the merger of two of Australia's largest fertiliser manufacturers and distributors — the listed company Incitec and its unlisted rival Pivot — both with histories dating back more than 80 years. With manufacturing facilities in Queensland, Victoria and New South Wales, major distribution facilities throughout the eastern seaboard of Australia, and annual production of around three million tonnes, the new company is a major force in the rural economy. Incitec's former parent, Orica, owns 70% of the new company, and much of the balance is held by the farming community. The shares are very thinly traded.

Latest business results (March 2004, half-year)

The results, as released by the company, are for Pivot only until May 2003 — which explains the lack of dividends — then for the new company from June 2003. It reported that, on a like-for-like basis, the after-tax profit soared from $5.1 million in the March 2003 half — the sum of Incitec's and Pivot's profits — to $20.2 million in March 2004. Better weather conditions helped the good result, along with merger synergies of $18 million. Sales volumes rose 5% and sales revenues were up 8%. Significant items of $3.6 million after tax related to merger restructuring and implementation costs.

Outlook

The new company has become the dominant force in the Australian fertiliser industry, with roughly a 50% national market share, and more than 70% of the eastern seaboard market. It believes it will take at least one more year to make a full recovery from the drought, suggesting continuing growth in demand, though much depends on weather conditions. Currency also has an impact on profits, with a weaker dollar generally more favourable. With the merger completed, the new company is now looking for expansion opportunities, though with many small farmer shareholders, it has also expressed its desire to maintain high dividend payouts.

IPL Year to 30 September*	2002	2003
Revenues ($mn)	604.2	686.3
EBIT ($mn)	45.6	59.3
EBIT margin (%)	7.5	8.6
Gross margin (%)	22.1	31.4
Operating profit before tax ($mn)	31.9	52.4
Profit after tax ($mn)	21.2	35.1
Earnings per share (¢)	121.1	112.7
Cash flow per share (¢)	208.4	191.0
Dividend (¢)	0	0
Percentage franked	~	~
Interest cover (times)	3.3	8.7
Return on equity (%)	15.1	9.7
Half-year to 31 March*	**2003**	**2004**
Revenues ($mn)	181.7	420.3
Operating profit before tax ($mn)	6.4	28.9
Profit after tax ($mn)	3.7	20.2
Earnings per share (¢)	21.4	34.7
Dividend (¢)	0	20
Percentage franked	~	100
Net tangible assets per share ($)	10.77	7.02
Debt-to-equity ratio (%)	99.2	22.7
Current ratio	1.1	1.3

* Results are for Pivot only to May 2003 and for Incitec Pivot from June 2003.

Institute of Drug Technology Australia Limited

Share price ($)	2.32	
12-month high ($)	2.72	
12-month low ($)	1.75	
Market capitalisation ($mn)	100.6	
Price-to-NTA-per-share ratio	3.8	
5-year share price return (% p.a.)	18.8	
Sector: Health care	**Company**	**Sector**
Price-earnings ratio (times)	23.2	35.8
Dividend yield (%)	3.0	1.8

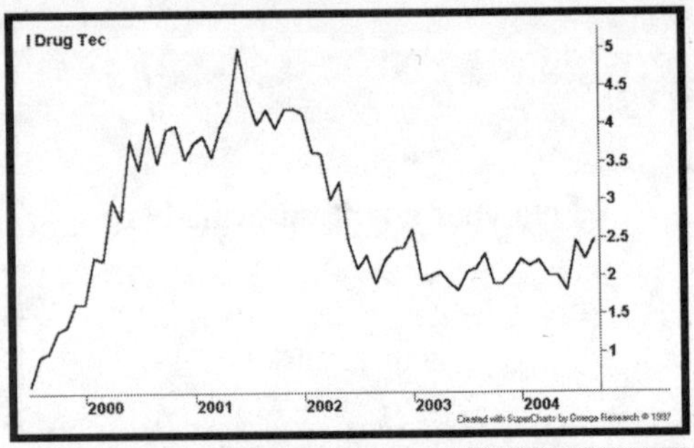

www.idtaus.com.au

Melbourne-based Institute of Drug Technology Australia (IDT), established in 1975, is a small, well-regarded developer and manufacturer of active pharmaceutical ingredients (APIs) for local and international companies. It also provides technical consulting and clinical trial services to the pharmaceuticals, chemical and biotechnology industries. In addition, it operates a research and development business for clients. Its Melbourne manufacturing facilities and laboratories have been licensed by the Australian Therapeutic Goods Administration and the United States Food and Drug Administration for production of APIs, and the company has developed a strong reputation for its dedicated facilities for the development and production of anti-cancer drugs. Through its CMAX division, IDT offers early-stage clinical trial services from a base at the Royal Adelaide Hospital.

Latest business results (June 2004, full year)

Sales revenues dipped, but the company managed a small rise in profits, its 10th straight earnings gain. A competitive market forced down sales and profits for generic APIs. However, a combination of increased funding to the Australian biotechnology sector and the company's growing international reputation led to strong demand for CMAX's contract clinical trial services. There was also growth in the areas of contract API and finished product manufacture.

Outlook

IDT is spending heavily to expand its operations, giving it the potential to win growing amounts of business. It has invested nearly $7 million over two years on facilities and equipment, and plans to augment these with even more API and finished-product manufacturing facilities, to meet future opportunities under discussion with new and existing clients. In addition, three new contracts are expected to provide strong growth in revenues and profit. The first is a major contract with a US pharmaceutical company for the supply of finished dosage pharmaceutical product for the US and international markets. The second, announced in mid-2004, is with Pfizer, the world's largest pharmaceuticals manufacturer, for the development and production of a new drug candidate. Also in mid-2004, the company won a contract for a development project with an American specialty pharmaceuticals company involving the development of a new range of pharmaceutical finished products.

IDT Year to 30 June	2003	2004
Revenues ($mn)	25.5	25.2
EBIT ($mn)	6.0	6.0
EBIT margin (%)	23.5	23.9
Gross margin (%)	70.8	72.9
Operating profit before tax ($mn)	6.0	6.1
Profit after tax ($mn)	4.2	4.3
Earnings per share (¢)	9.9	10.0
Cash flow per share (¢)	15.0	15.7
Dividend (¢)	6	7
Percentage franked	100	100
Net tangible assets per share ($)	0.57	0.61
Interest cover (times)	~	~
Return on equity (%)	17.0	15.7
Debt-to-equity ratio (%)	~	~
Current ratio	3.4	3.2

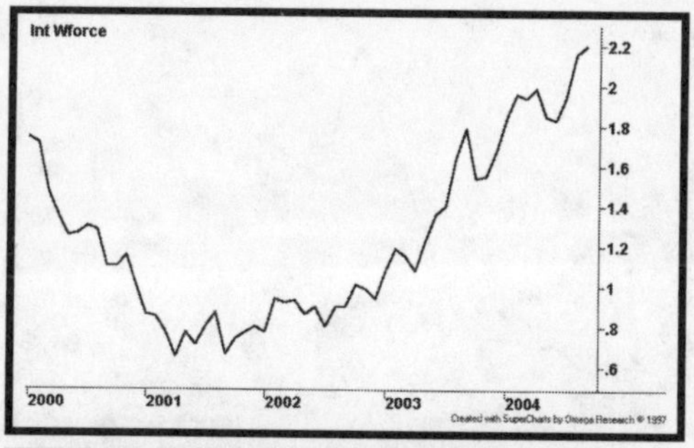

www.intgroup.com.au

Integrated Group Limited

Share price ($)	2.09	
12-month high ($)	2.09	
12-month low ($)	1.40	
Market capitalisation ($mn)	153.1	
Price-to-NTA-per-share ratio	4.8	
5-year share price return (% p.a.)	32.8	
Sector: Industrials	**Company**	**Sector**
Price-earnings ratio (times)	12.4	14.8
Dividend yield (%)	4.8	4.2

Perth-based Integrated Group, founded in 1992 as Integrated Workforce, is a labour hire company, with a particular specialty in the supply of blue-collar workers for industry. It has expanded rapidly, through acquisition and organic growth, and now does business nationwide. It has also branched into the provision of support and maintenance services for the oil and gas sector, through its Total Marine Services division and its 50% stake in Integrated Maintenance Services (IMS).

Latest business results (June 2004, full year)

Integrated Group recorded further strong profit growth, due especially to a surge in business for the company's core labour hire operations. Revenues for the workforce division rose 20%, and despite pressure on labour hire margins throughout the year the company saw division profits rise 36%, thanks to efficiency and productivity gains, particularly in the area of workers compensation management. By contrast, marine division revenues fell 16%. This largely reflected the fact that June 2003 results had been boosted by several large-scale projects that were not replicated in the June 2004 year. However, productivity gains and a higher margin business mix led to just a slight dip in profits for the division. In its accounts, the company did not recognise the profit from its 50% interest in IMS, pending the resolution of a legal dispute between IMS and a client.

Outlook

Integrated Group's moves since 2001 to diversify away from labour hire and into maintenance services have proven successful, despite the decline in the June 2004 accounts of revenues and profits for this business. Though representing less than a third of company revenues, the marine services division brings in around half of company profits, and the outlook is very rosy, thanks to the buoyant Australian oil and gas sector. The company is also continuing to boost its workforce division, in order to expand the range of services it can offer clients. In mid-2004, Integrated Group announced the $3.5-million acquisition of the Corpfit Training Solutions group, a nationwide organisation providing workplace training across a range of industries, and the company has declared its intention to pursue further similar acquisitions.

IWF Year to 30 June	2003	2004
Revenues ($mn)	311.8	331.2
Workforce division (%)	61	69
Marine division (%)	39	31
EBIT ($mn)	16.2	17.6
EBIT margin (%)	5.2	5.3
Operating profit before tax ($mn)	14.8	16.4
Profit after tax ($mn)	10.0	11.8
Earnings per share (¢)	16.5	16.9
Cash flow per share (¢)	24.1	23.5
Dividend (¢)	9	10
Percentage franked	100	100
Net tangible assets per share ($)	0.34	0.44
Interest cover (times)	11.7	14.8
Return on equity (%)	31.9	24.0
Debt-to-equity ratio (%)	18.1	17.9
Current ratio	1.2	1.4

ION Limited

Share price ($)	1.63	
12-month high ($)	2.55	
12-month low ($)	1.31	
Market capitalisation ($mn)	423.7	
Price-to-NTA-per-share ratio	1.5	
5-year share price return (% p.a.)	48.0	
Sector: Consumer discretionary	**Company**	**Sector**
Price-earnings ratio (times)	6.8	23.8
Dividend yield (%)	7.4	1.5

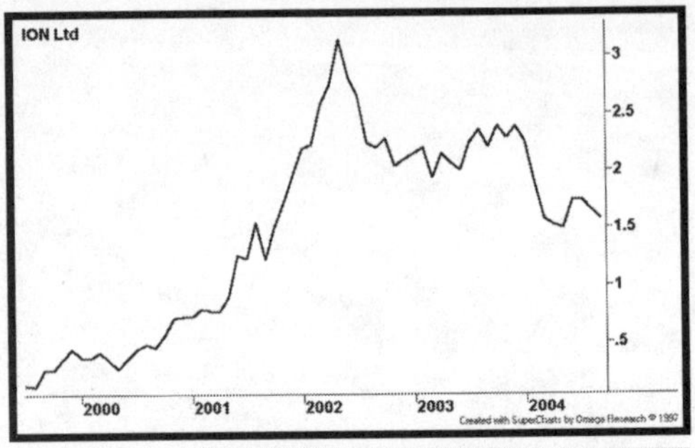

www.ionlimited.com.au

Melbourne-based ION, built up through a series of recent acquisitions, operates in two broad areas. Its automotive group manages plants in South Australia, NSW, Victoria and New Zealand producing auto wheels, suspension, automatic and manual transmissions, speciality wheels, hollow castings, cylinder heads, manifolds and oilpans, with leading global car makers among its customers. Its energy services group operates more than 300 road tankers distributing petroleum products, chemicals, LPG, bitumen, propylene and anhydrous ammonia for oil, chemical and gas companies. It also performs aviation refuelling and manages terminal operations.

Latest business results (June 2004, full year)

Revenues and profits edged up. The star performer was the company's energy services business, with sales up 74% and EBIT soaring more than threefold, thanks to its transformation with the acquisition of fuel-handling equipment manufacturer Liquip and the full-year impact of Stevenson Transport, acquired in 2003, together with the winning of new business and the improvement in drought conditions in eastern Australia. But sales and profit were down for the company's auto business, following reduced demand from Ford in the US and from Ssangyong in South Korea. The company also recorded a net after-tax loss from significant items of $26.5 million, due particularly to commissioning difficulties at its new Wingfield plant in Adelaide.

Outlook

ION has long-term contracts with key vehicle makers, including the supply of alloy wheels for Harley-Davidson motorcycles, differentials and alloy blocks for Holden and premium wheels for Ford in the US. It is also receiving business from South Korean, Malaysian and Chinese auto companies. Large levels of capital spending have been needed to build new plants to meet these orders, and concerns about ION's rapid expansion and growing capital requirements have led to share price volatility. In September 2004 the shares plunged on a company forecast of sharply lower first-half profits. The company is making solid progress with its energy services business. Thanks to several acquisitions, ION has become the Australian leader in the transportation of petrol and LPG, and is prominent in transporting other dangerous goods.

ION Year to 30 June	2003	2004
Revenues ($mn)	654.2	671.2
Automotive systems (%)	52	45
Light metal castings (%)	34	31
Energy services (%)	14	24
EBIT ($mn)	80.9	85.2
EBIT margin (%)	12.4	12.7
Gross margin (%)	23.2	21.7
Operating profit before tax ($mn)	73.1	74.3
Profit after tax ($mn)	53.1	55.2
Earnings per share (¢)	24.9	24.1
Cash flow per share (¢)	37.3	37.2
Dividend (¢)	11.25	12
Percentage franked	100	100
Net tangible assets per share ($)	1.05	1.11
Interest cover (times)	10.3	7.8
Return on equity (%)	26.1	20.9
Debt-to-equity ratio (%)	63.2	66.1
Current ratio	1.0	1.0

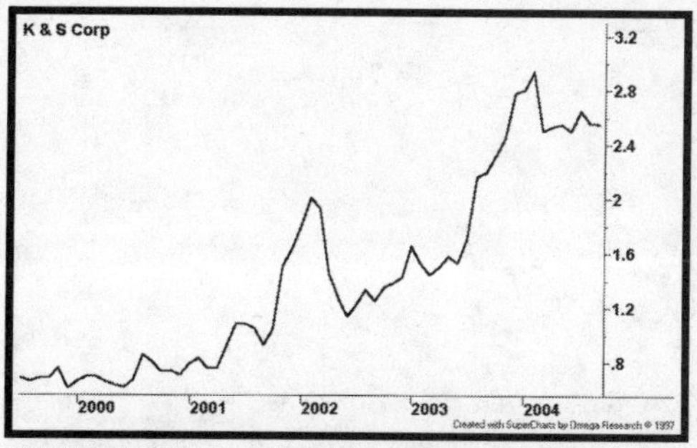

www.ksgroup.com.au

K&S Corporation Limited

Share price ($)	2.58	
12-month high ($)	3.20	
12-month low ($)	1.79	
Market capitalisation ($mn)	154.7	
Price-to-NTA-per-share ratio	2.7	
5-year share price return (% p.a.)	40.6	
Sector: Industrials	**Company**	**Sector**
Price-earnings ratio (times)	12.7	14.8
Dividend yield (%)	4.3	4.2

Based in Mt Gambier, and with a history stretching back more than 55 years, K&S is one of Australia's leading transport, warehousing and logistics companies, with a strategy directed towards large national contracts. It controls one of the largest company-owned fleets in Australia, as well as owning over 160,000 square metres of warehousing and a large range of rail and sea containers. It operates through four divisions: K&S Freighters is involved in road, rail and coastal sea forwarding; K&S Integrated Distribution handles warehousing, storage and local distribution; K&S Agencies manages Ampol fuel distribution throughout regions of South Australia and Victoria; and K&S (NZ) provides distribution throughout New Zealand. The company chairman, Allan Scott, owns more than 60% of the equity. In December 2003, K&S bought Cochrane's Transport in New Zealand.

Latest business results (June 2004, full year)

The company overcame rising fuel costs to post a solid rise in its profits, although sales revenues were flat, restrained by the costs of restructuring the loss-making activities of its Sydney warehousing business. Domestically, there was particular strength from the timber, metals and paper sectors. Thanks to the restructuring of its Sydney operations, the warehousing business turned a small profit.

Outlook

The ongoing strength of the domestic economy has provided a strong boost to K&S, which at the same time has been expanding its operations. However, it has been forced to introduce fuel surcharges, to recover its extra fuel costs. It has made a series of strong moves into New Zealand, winning a major contract with timber giant Fletcher Challenge, and its acquisition of Cochrane's Transport has turned it into a key provider of logistics services to the dairy, kiwi fruit and paper industries. Domestically, its warehousing business has been successful in gaining an important new contract with Coca Cola in Melbourne for distribution services, from July 2004. This business also continues to benefit from its restructuring, which is part of the company's tactic of focusing on larger strategic customers. As part of its expansion program, the company has bought a 23-hectare site in Melbourne's fast-growing Laverton area, for future development as a transport terminal and warehouse facility.

KSC Year to 30 June	2003	2004
Revenues ($mn)	293.3	295.7
EBIT ($mn)	17.9	20.1
EBIT margin (%)	6.1	6.8
Gross margin (%)	14.6	8.8
Operating profit before tax ($mn)	15.3	17.6
Profit after tax ($mn)	11.1	12.2
Earnings per share (¢)	18.4*	20.3
Cash flow per share (¢)	37.9*	43.0
Dividend (¢)	8*	11
Percentage franked	100	100
Net tangible assets per share ($)	0.92*	0.95
Interest cover (times)	6.9	8.1
Return on equity (%)	20.2	19.5
Debt-to-equity ratio (%)	39.9	52.7
Current ratio	1.0	0.9

* adjusted for a 2-for-1 share split

Leighton Holdings Limited

Share price ($)	8.88	
12-month high ($)	11.94	
12-month low ($)	7.62	
Market capitalisation ($mn)	2,451.5	
Price-to-NTA-per-share ratio	2.9	
5-year share price return (% p.a.)	16.6	
Sector: Industrials	**Company**	**Sector**
Price-earnings ratio (times)	21.9	14.8
Dividend yield (%)	5.1	4.2

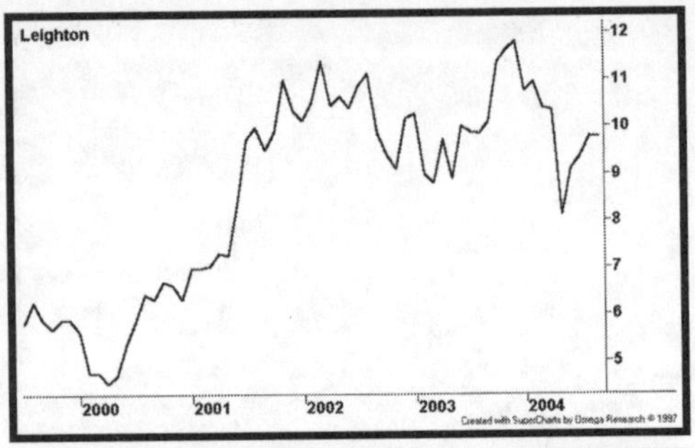

www.leighton.com.au

Founded in 1949, Leighton is Australia's largest project development and contracting group. It incorporates Leighton Contractors, Thiess Contractors, Leighton Asia, Leighton Properties and John Holland, and employs more than 10,000 people at sites around the Asia-Pacific region and in South America. The German construction company Hochtief owns 53% of Leighton's shares.

Latest business results (June 2004, full year)

Revenues were flat, but profits fell sharply, as the company experienced severe cost blow-outs on the Spencer Street Station project in Melbourne and the Sydney Hilton refurbishment, and was forced to write off an investment in the Southland Colliery, following the closure of the mine. Engineering and infrastructure revenues rose 23%, reflecting strong contributions from some major domestic infrastructure projects, and building and property development revenues surged 36%. But mining and resources revenues slumped 22%, following the suspension of the Stanwell Magnesium Plant project in Queensland. Asian business grew, thanks to mining projects in Indonesia and infrastructure projects in Hong Kong and the Philippines. The company's order book surged 35% to $13 billion — with a near-doubling of Asian orders to $3.1 billion — including the Lane Cove Tunnel project in Sydney, $1.7 billion worth of extensions to mining contracts in Indonesia, some large construction projects in Hong Kong and Macau, and the Perth-Mandurah railway in Western Australia.

Outlook

Leighton continues to benefit from the infrastructure boom and from its strengths in Asia, and it also stands to gain from the ongoing resources boom. Its own forecast is for an after-tax profit of around $180 million in the June 2005 year. Transport infrastructure is likely to be a key driver of growth, with a number of large road and rail projects continuing to boost profits, and Leighton is part of consortia short-listed for Melbourne's $2 billion Mitcham-Frankston Freeway. It sees contract coal mining as underpinning the mining and resources sector. Its huge net cash holdings of more than $500 million have given rise to speculation that it is seeking a major acquisition. The shares have been volatile, plunging on the announcement of declining profits, but supported by speculation that majority shareholder Hochtief might make a full takeover bid.

LEI Year to 30 June	2003	2004
Revenues ($mn)	4,848.5	4,834.4
Civil & building (%)	48	58
Mining & resources (%)	39	31
Environmental (%)	3	4
Telecommunications	6	3
EBIT ($mn)	222.2	164.6
EBIT margin (%)	4.6	3.4
Operating profit before tax ($mn)	222.5	161.4
Profit after tax ($mn)	140.0	110.0
Earnings per share (¢)	51.7	40.6
Cash flow per share (¢)	169.2	148.4
Dividend (¢)	44	45
Percentage franked	100	100
Net tangible assets per share ($)	3.06	3.02
Interest cover (times)	~	50.2
Return on equity (%)	17.0	12.9
Debt-to-equity ratio (%)	~	~

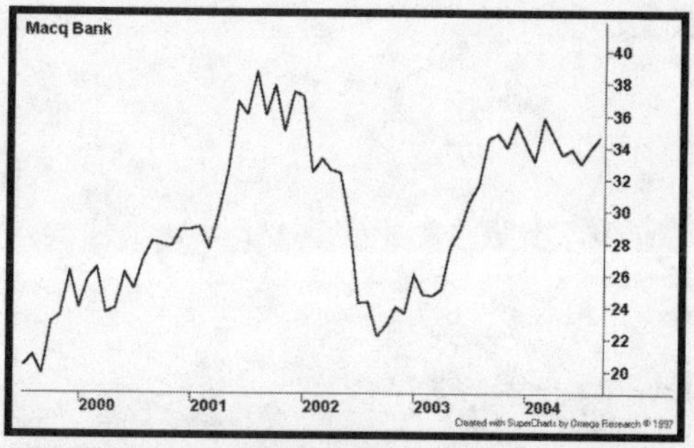

www.macquarie.com.au

Macquarie Bank Limited

Share price ($)	32.30	
12-month high ($)	37.40	
12-month low ($)	30.70	
Market capitalisation ($mn)	7,058.6	
Price-to-NTA-per-share ratio	2.5	
5-year share price return (% p.a.)	15.6	
Sector: Financials	**Company**	**Sector**
Price-earnings ratio (times)	13.9	12.9
Dividend yield (%)	3.8	5.2

Macquarie, established in 1969 as Hill Samuel Australia, a subsidiary of a British merchant bank, is now Australia's leading locally owned investment bank. Its activities are divided into six operating groups that span four broad business segments: Asset and Wealth Management involves the distribution and manufacture of funds management products; Financial Markets incorporates the bank's trading in fixed income, equities, currency, commodities and derivative products; Investment Banking encompasses corporate finance, advisory, underwriting, facilitation, broking and real estate/property development activities; and Lending includes banking activities, mortgages, margin lending and leasing. Its extensive international business accounts for more than 30% of company income.

Latest business results (March 2004, full year)

Buoyant global financial markets delivered Macquarie a superb result. All business groups showed gains, with the core investment banking group seeing profits up 46%, on the back of strong markets and the bank's fund management strengths. Total assets under management increased by $11 billion to $63 billion, with significant increases from the bank's specialist infrastructure and property funds. Macquarie is now the third largest fund manager in Australia. The treasury and commodities group achieved an 18% profit gain, with strong results from the metals and mining, the foreign exchange and the debt markets divisions. Macquarie's strength in the Hong Kong warrants market helped the equity markets group to a record profit. Altogether, international income rose 61%.

Outlook

Macquarie continues to grow, though the bank has already said it does not see profits expanding greatly in the March 2005 year, with much dependent on market conditions. The roll-out of a succession of infrastructure funds around the world is expected to provide a steady and stable source of management fee income. The bank also sees great potential from the acquisition of ING's Asian equities businesses, which included the addition of approximately 450 new staff. This business will be known as Macquarie Securities Asia and is expected to strengthen Macquarie's existing equities distribution capabilities and provide opportunities to broaden Macquarie's investment banking activities in the Asia-Pacific region. Within a few years it is possible that half the bank's income will be derived offshore.

MBL Year to 31 March	2003	2004
Operating income ($mn)	1,890.0	2,465.0
Net interest income ($mn)	247.0	270.0
Operating expenses ($mn)	1,430.0	1,780.0
Operating profit before tax ($mn)	460.0	685.0
Profit after tax ($mn)	333.0	494.0
Earnings per share (¢)	164.8	233.0
Dividend (¢)	93	122
Percentage franked	87	90
Non-interest income to total income (%)	86.9	89.0
Net tangible assets per share ($)	10.69	13.03
Cost-to-income ratio (%)	75.7	72.2
Return on equity (%)	15.8	19.8
Return on assets (%)	1.1	1.3

Macquarie Goodman Management Limited

Share price ($)	3.34	
12-month high ($)	3.90	
12-month low ($)	1.91	
Market capitalisation ($mn)	920.9	
Price-to-NTA-per-share ratio	26.0	
5-year share price return (% p.a.)	72.3	
Sector: Financials	**Company**	**Sector**
Price-earnings ratio (times)	24.0	12.9
Dividend yield (%)	2.1	5.2

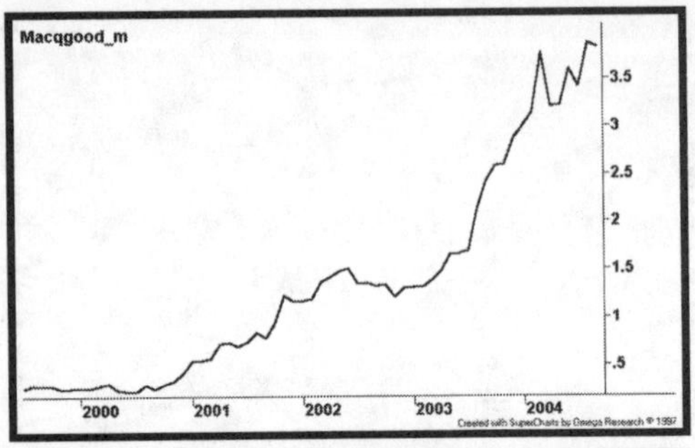

www.macquariegoodman.com.au

Sydney-based Macquarie Goodman Management evolved from a merger in 2000 of listed property developer Triden Corporation and the industrial property management business of Macquarie Bank. The company acquired management rights to the Macquarie Industrial Trust, which merged with the Goodman Hardie Industrial Property Trust. Today Macquarie Goodman operates in three broad business areas: its funds management business runs the Macquarie Goodman Industrial Trust (MGI) in Australia and the Macquarie Goodman Property Trust in New Zealand, and it has a 40–60 partnership with Ascendas Land in Singapore to run that country's first listed industrial property trust, Ascendas Real Estate Investment Trust; its development management business manages all aspects of the property development process; and its property services division acts as a property manager. Macquarie Bank owns 40% of the company's equity, and the Goodman family 19%.

Latest business results (June 2004, full year)

Revenues and profits soared. The funds management business was the star performer, with revenues tripling and pre-tax profit up fourfold. In large part this was due to the payment from the funds to the company of a $17.2 million performance fee, for exceeding certain benchmarks. There was a 56% increase in funds under management to $5.3 billion, including MGI's acquisition of the $615-million AMP Industrial Trust and a doubling of the Singapore property portfolio. The development management division saw sales up 77%, with profit rising 81%, and the property services group achieved sales growth of 14%, with profits up 17%.

MGM Year to 30 June	2003	2004
Revenues ($mn)	38.5	78.8
Funds management (%)	33	51
Development management (%)	31	26
Property services (%)	33	18
Investments (%)	3	5
EBIT ($mn)	21.5	55.0
EBIT margin (%)	55.9	69.7
Operating profit before tax ($mn)	22.3	53.4
Profit after tax ($mn)	17.0	37.0
Earnings per share (¢)	6.8	13.9
Cash flow per share (¢)	7.1	14.5
Dividend (¢)	5	7
Percentage franked	74	71
Net tangible assets per share ($)	0.07	0.13
Interest cover (times)	~	35.3
Return on equity (%)	24.3	35.2
Debt-to-equity ratio (%)	44.5	51.3
Current ratio	0.7	5.7

Outlook

Macquarie Goodman Management continues to grow. It is working to develop and enhance the attractions of properties in the Australian property trust. It views the fragmented industrial property of New Zealand as offering great potential for further acquisitions, and it also hopes to build on its success in Singapore with new industrial trusts in other Asian countries. The development management division has a total of 203,000 square metres of development works under way, with an estimated end value of $233 million. It has joined with Brickworks to develop a major new industrial and business estate at Eastern Creek in Sydney's west, subject to planning approvals.

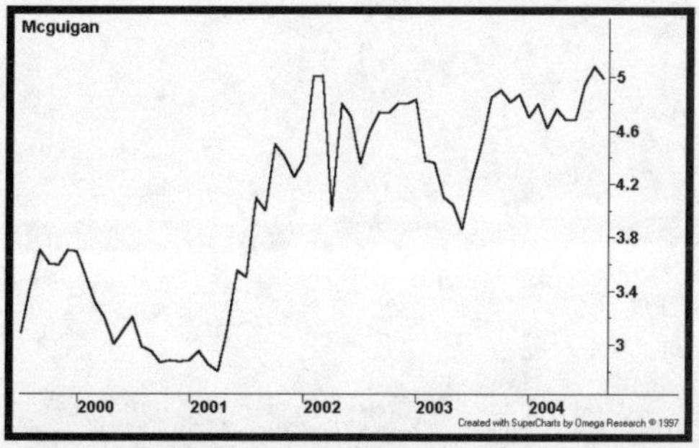

www.mcguiganwines.com.au

McGuigan Simeon Wines Limited

Share price ($)	4.90	
12-month high ($)	5.12	
12-month low ($)	4.40	
Market capitalisation ($mn)	535.1	
Price-to-NTA-per-share ratio	1.9	
5-year share price return (% p.a.)	9.7	
Sector: Consumer staples	**Company**	**Sector**
Price-earnings ratio (times)	12.8	16.8
Dividend yield (%)	4.8	3.7

McGuigan Simeon Wines was formed from the merger in 2002 of Brian McGuigan Wines — founded 10 years earlier — with Simeon Wines. It is now Australia's third-largest listed winery, with vineyards in many premium viticulture regions. Its labels include the Harvest range and the Black Label range. It is also Australia's largest seller of bulk wine and it manages vineyards. Exports are more than 40% of sales. Late in 2003 it acquired Miranda Wines.

Latest business results (June 2004, full year)

In a challenging environment for the wine industry, McGuigan Simeon posted an excellent result, based in particular on the growing strength of its brands. Domestically, bottled sales of $85 million were up 86%, reflecting the company's focus on higher-margin branded products, economies of scale and the acquisition of Miranda. However, bulk sales fell 19% to $67 million, primarily due to a change in contractual arrangements with a major customer from bulk wine purchasing to contract processing. Exports of branded bottled sales increased 24% to $44 million, thanks to strengthening distribution alliances with customers, particularly in the UK and Europe. However, with a decline in overseas bulk sales — due to a competitive market and the company's redirection of wine into the branded market — total export sales were flat.

Outlook

The company has grown through merger and acquisition to the point where it is now one of Australia's most successful wine companies. It offers wine at all price points, and claims to be one of the industry's lowest-cost producers, though it has vowed to continue driving down its cost base. The Miranda acquisition has allowed it to enter the domestic cask wine market, which represents 45% of domestic wine sales, by volume. It has also broadened the company's grape-buying and production base, and provided access to new domestic and export customers. The company continues to boost its presence in the branded market, where margins are highest, and with its low cost base is confident it can prosper even as the global wine industry endures a glut of red wines and heightened competition from a growing number of countries. It continues to seek our further acquisitions.

MGW Year to 30 June	2003	2004
Revenues ($mn)	283.5	305.7
Bottled wine (%)	29	41
Bulk wine & grapes (%)	42	31
Bulk in bottle (%)	18	14
Vineyard development (%)	10	14
EBIT ($mn)	55.8	61.6
EBIT margin (%)	19.7	20.1
Gross margin (%)	15.7	17.3
Operating profit before tax ($mn)	46.1	51.3
Profit after tax ($mn)	32.2	40.2
Earnings per share (¢)	33.3	38.2
Cash flow per share (¢)	44.3	50.2
Dividend (¢)	20	23.5
Percentage franked	100	100
Net tangible assets per share ($)	2.19	2.57
Interest cover (times)	5.7	6.0
Return on equity (%)	13.0	13.3
Debt-to-equity ratio (%)	65.4	44.7
Current ratio	2.4	2.2

McPherson's Limited

Share price ($)	4.43	
12-month high ($)	5.75	
12-month low ($)	3.60	
Market capitalisation ($mn)	254.3	
Price-to-NTA-per-share ratio	N/A	
5-year share price return (% p.a.)	47.1	
Sector: Industrials	**Company**	**Sector**
Price-earnings ratio (times)	14.7	14.8
Dividend yield (%)	4.3	4.2

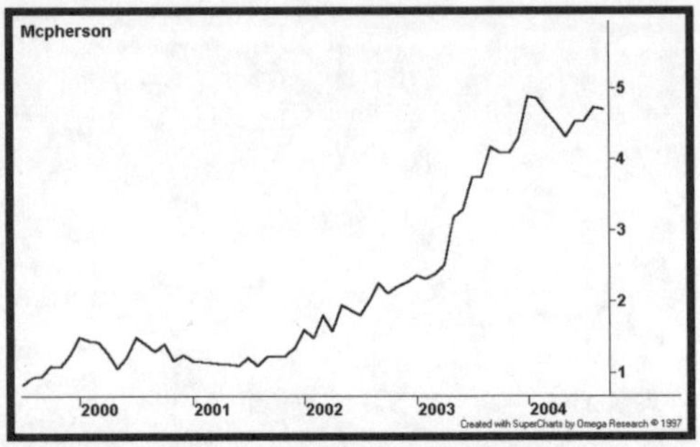

www.mcphersons.com.au

Melbourne-based McPherson's, established in 1860, operates in three broad areas. Its housewares division markets a wide range of kitchenware products, both within Australasia and internationally. Brand names include Wiltshire, Strachan, Grosvenor, Rodd and Crown Glassware. The Australasian business has a third of the kitchen knife and flatware cutlery markets. Overseas, trading as Richardson Sheffield and Regent-Sheffield, the company holds around 30% of the British and Canadian kitchen knife markets and 5% in the US. The company's second business is commercial printing. It is one of Australia's leading printers of books (including *Top Stocks*) and its William Brooks division has a contract to produce 50% of Telstra's *White* and *Yellow Pages* telephone directory requirements until June 2009. A third business, the distribution of hair care and beauty products, was launched in mid-2003 with the $101-million acquisition of Cork Asia Pacific.

Latest business results (June 2004, full year)

Sales and profits grew strongly, thanks mainly to the inclusion in the accounts of the new Cork Asia Pacific acquisition. The consumer products division — incorporating kitchenware and hair care products — increased sales by 67% to $217 million, with profit more than doubling. This came about despite $3.7 million in restructuring expenses for the division, including the relocation of the kitchenware business to Cork's Sydney premises. However, continuing competitive pressures in the printing industry led to a 6% decline in sales revenues to $112 million, with profits also edging down.

Outlook

McPherson's is now working to achieve the full integration of the Cork business into its other operations, with the aim of realising $6 million in synergies annually by June 2005. It has closed down its kitchenware warehouses at Bundoora in Melbourne and Matraville in Sydney, and transferred all activities to the Cork site at Kingsgrove in Sydney. The McPherson's subsidiary Richardson Sheffield has taken over marketing of Cork's products for the UK and European markets, which is expected to boost sales. McPherson's is now looking at further possible compatible acquisitions. It has undertaken a major re-equipment and restructuring program for its printing business, with the aim of reducing costs to address the problem of over-capacity within the industry.

MCP Year to 30 June	2003	2004
Revenues ($mn)	248.7	329.0
Consumer products (%)	52	66
Printing (%)	48	34
EBIT ($mn)	20.7	31.0
EBIT margin (%)	8.3	9.4
Operating profit before tax ($mn)	16.6	23.4
Profit after tax ($mn)	11.8	16.8
Earnings per share (¢)	29.1	30.2
Cash flow per share (¢)	43.4	48.7
Dividend (¢)	15	19
Percentage franked	100	100
Net tangible assets per share ($)	0.69	~
Interest cover (times)	5.1	4.1
Return on equity (%)	21.0	19.8
Debt-to-equity ratio (%)	68.6	74.1
Current ratio	2.4	2.0

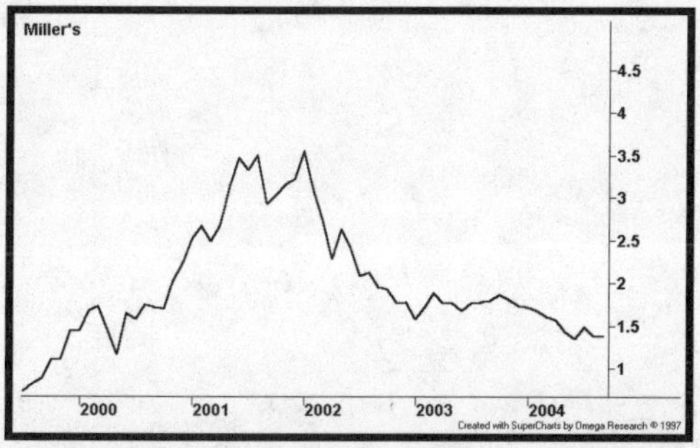

www.millersretail.com.au

Miller's Retail Limited

Share price ($)	1.41	
12-month high ($)	1.97	
12-month low ($)	1.27	
Market capitalisation ($mn)	340.3	
Price-to-NTA-per-share ratio	3.4	
5-year share price return (% p.a.)	13.3	
Sector: Consumer discretionary	**Company**	**Sector**
Price-earnings ratio (times)	16.0	23.8
Dividend yield (%)	6.7	1.5

Sydney-based Miller's is a retailer operating in two broad market segments: its discount variety group manages a national chain of 353 discount variety stores under the names Crazy Clark's, Go-Lo and Chickenfeed; and its apparel group operates 695 specialty apparel stores with the names Miller's Fashion Club, Katies, 1626, Crossroads and Silhouette. The company's Miller's Retail Club customer loyalty program has more than two million members.

Latest business results (June 2004, full year)

Profits fell sharply, as the company's variety business was hit by a fierce discounting war. Sales rose nearly 6%, though on a like-for-like store basis the increase was less than 1%. The apparel business enjoyed a solid year, with sales up 7%, or 4% on a like-for-like store basis, and profits (before interest, tax and goodwill amortisation) surging nearly 40%. However, at the discount variety division, a 5% sales rise actually translated to a 2% decline on a like-for-like store basis, and profits crashed 64%. The company reported as a significant item an asset write-down of $12.6 million, reflecting the reduced carrying value of its discount variety division's intangible assets (goodwill and brand name). A total of 78 stores were added during the period, and 46 were closed.

Outlook

Once a high-growth stock market favourite, Miller's is now limping, with sagging profits and share price, at a time when most Australian retailers are flourishing. A key problem is that there appear to be too many retailers operating at the cheaper end of the market, including Miller's, the New Zealand retailer Warehouse Group, Reject Shop, Target, Kmart, Big W and others. When their stores are in close proximity the discounting can be intense. However, Miller's itself has conceded that it has opened some stores in inappropriate locations and of the wrong size. It is working to streamline its internal logistics and supply chain. Its apparel business remains strong, with its Miller's Retail Club highly successful, and it is working to strengthen its brands through direct marketing and loyalty programs. It is also expanding into children's clothing and a menswear range, as well as footwear and manchester.

MRL Year to 30 June	2003	2004
Revenues ($mn)	1,049.7	1,109.9
Discount variety (%)	60	59
Apparel (%)	40	41
EBIT ($mn)	55.6	43.1
EBIT margin (%)	5.3	3.9
Gross margin (%)	43.7	43.4
Operating profit before tax ($mn)	45.8	32.8
Profit after tax ($mn)	30.5	21.3
Earnings per share (¢)	13.0	8.8
Cash flow per share (¢)	23.7	20.4
Dividend (¢)	9.5	9.5
Percentage franked	100	100
Net tangible assets per share ($)	0.37	0.41
Interest cover (times)	5.7	4.2
Return on equity (%)	15.1	10.0
Debt-to-equity ratio (%)	55.1	49.2
Current ratio	1.3	1.6

Monadelphous Group Limited

Share price ($)	6.27	
12-month high ($)	6.37	
12-month low ($)	4.17	
Market capitalisation ($mn)	118.7	
Price-to-NTA-per-share ratio	3.1	
5-year share price return (% p.a.)	24.5	
Sector: Industrials	**Company**	**Sector**
Price-earnings ratio (times)	14.1	14.8
Dividend yield (%)	4.8	4.2

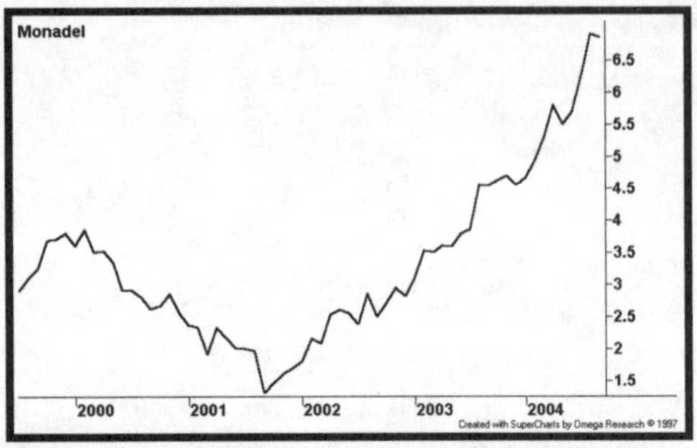

www.monadel.com.au

Perth-based Monadelphous is an engineering company that provides project management, construction, maintenance and support services to the mining, mineral processing and associated industries. It operates from branches at key mining and mineral processing centres throughout Australia. Although the mining sector has been the major focus of its work, it is becoming increasingly diversified, with growing involvement in the energy and government sectors.

Latest business results (June 2004, full year)

The strength of the resources sector led to excellent business for Monadelphous and a further jump in its profits. The highlight was new work won in the iron ore sector, notably a series of major contracts in Western Australia's Pilbara region valued at a total of $130 million, and either completed or substantially completed during the reporting period. However, revenues from the company's new Brisbane-based maintenance and industrial services division were down.

Outlook

As a small company, Monadelphous is gaining enormous benefits from the ongoing resources boom in Australia, and this has been reflected in its surging share price. The good news continues, with $200 million worth of new contracts won between January and July 2004, leading management to warn of the possibility of a looming shortage of skilled labour. The new business includes a $20 million contract for Comalco's bauxite operations at Weipa in Queensland, a $40 million contract for structural, mechanical and commissioning works at the Burrup Fertilisers Ammonia Plant Project in Karratha, Western Australia, a $30 million construction contract for Hamersley Iron's Parker Point expansion in Karratha, a $25 million contract for the design and construction of coal handling facilities at the Rolleston Coal Project in the Bowen Basin in Queensland, and a $50 million contract — the company's largest ever — for work on Hamersley Iron's Yandi iron ore plant in Western Australia. Monadelphous is also continuing to pursue its longer-term aim of boosting its maintenance and industrial services business, particularly in the eastern states markets, and in partnership with Fluor Australia has been awarded two large contracts, for Comalco's new alumina refinery in Gladstone, Queensland, and for WMC Resources' copper and uranium mine and processing facilities at Olympic Dam in South Australia.

MND Year to 30 June	2003	2004
Revenues ($mn)	243.7	220.8
EBIT ($mn)	10.1	11.9
EBIT margin (%)	4.1	5.4
Gross margin (%)	7.8	9.7
Operating profit before tax ($mn)	10.1	12.2
Profit after tax ($mn)	7.1	8.5
Earnings per share (¢)	38.2	44.5
Cash flow per share (¢)	66.5	66.5
Dividend (¢)	25	30
Percentage franked	100	100
Net tangible assets per share ($)	1.83	2.01
Interest cover (times)	~	~
Return on equity (%)	22.8	23.2
Debt-to-equity ratio (%)	~	~
Current ratio	1.5	1.5

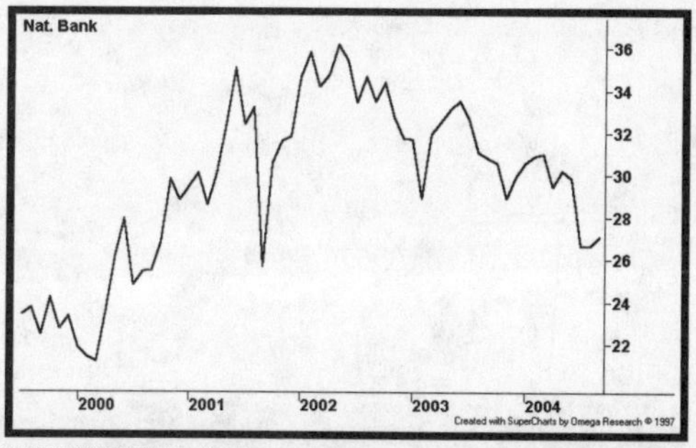

www.nabgroup.com

National Australia Bank Limited

Share price ($)	26.42	
12-month high ($)	32.70	
12-month low ($)	26.04	
Market capitalisation ($mn)	40,932.3	
Price-to-NTA-per-share ratio	1.7	
5-year share price return (% p.a.)	8.4	
Sector: Financials	**Company**	**Sector**
Price-earnings ratio (times)	10.1	12.9
Dividend yield (%)	6.2	5.2

The NAB, Australia's largest bank, is a world-class operation with a wide spread of financial activities. It owns the Clydesdale Bank, Yorkshire Bank and Northern Bank in Britain, along with the National Irish Bank and the Bank of New Zealand. Its MLC business is one of Australia's leading funds management operations.

Latest business results (March 2004, half-year)

Profits rose, though the result was a disappointment, given the strong economic environment. The key driver of profits was the bank's wealth management division, with after-tax profit up 37% from the March 2003 half, thanks to buoyant insurance operations and a booming funds management business. Strong equity markets meant that average funds under management rose by nearly 12%. Domestically, mainstream banking businesses were firm, with strong growth in housing lending partly offset by a fall in the overall net interest margin. Retail deposits rose by nearly 10%. But corporate and institutional banking was hit by a foreign currency options trading scandal, along with adverse currency movements, a higher charge for doubtful debts and reduced demand for debt market products. Overseas, New Zealand was firm, but European operations were hurt by the strength of the Australian dollar and by higher pension fund expenses. Significant items included a $315 million profit on the sale of equity holdings in AMP and St George Bank, and a $360 million loss from foreign currency options trading.

Outlook

NAB has been hit by a series of upheavals, including the options trading scandal, difficulties with its British operations and boardroom fighting. This has hit the share price, and is also hurting earnings. There is now speculation that the company's new management hopes to sell its European subsidiaries, in order to concentrate on Australia and New Zealand, though in the short term a weakening Australian dollar could boost earnings derived from Europe. NAB will continue to benefit from its powerhouse funds management and insurance operations, and it retains its strengths in small business and agribusiness lending.

NAB Year to 30 September	2002	2003
Operating income ($mn)	11,870.0	12,873.0
Net interest income ($mn)	7,222.0	7,419.0
Operating expenses ($mn)	5,949.0	6,612.0
Operating profit before tax ($mn)	5,180.0	5,628.0
Profit after tax ($mn)	3,779.0	3,955.0
Earnings per share (¢)	244.0	260.9
Dividend (¢)	147	163
Percentage franked	95	100
Non-interest income to total income (%)	39.2	42.4
Cost-to-income ratio (%)	50.1	51.4
Return on equity (%)	16.2	16.6
Return on assets (%)	1.0	1.0
Half-year to 31 March	**2003**	**2004**
Operating income ($mn)	6,259.0	6,496.0
Operating profit before tax ($mn)	2,563.0	2,909.0
Profit after tax ($mn)	1,877.0	2,102.0
Earnings per share (¢)	116.3	129.2
Dividend (¢)	80	83
Percentage franked	100	100
Net tangible assets per share ($)	14.92	15.78

NATIONAL FOODS LIMITED

Share price ($)	4.67	
12-month high ($)	4.79	
12-month low ($)	3.66	
Market capitalisation ($mn)	1,379.1	
Price-to-NTA-per-share ratio	4.8	
5-year share price return (% p.a.)	17.0	
Sector: Consumer staples	**Company**	**Sector**
Price-earnings ratio (times)	20.1	16.8
Dividend yield (%)	4.7	3.7

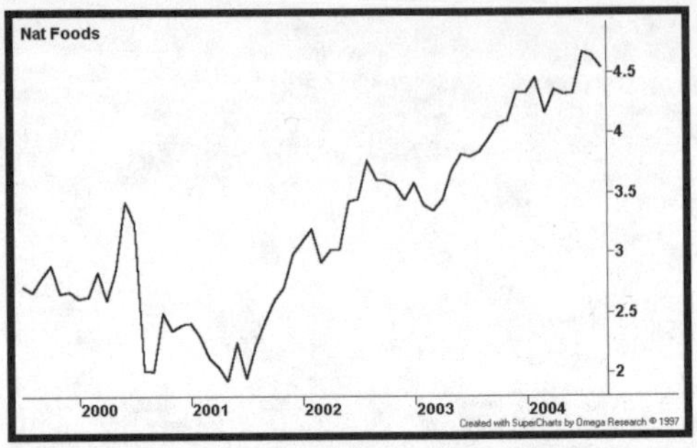

www.natfoods.com.au

National Foods, headquartered in Melbourne, was created in 1991 from the amalgamation of several dairy and food-related businesses, some with histories dating back to the 1880s. It is one of Australia's foodstuffs giants, specialising in milk and other dairy products. It is a market leader for many of its products, and Australia's only nationwide milk processor, with its Pura brand produced and marketed in all states. Other brands include Classic, Farmers Union, Masters, Big M, Yoplait, Fruche, Yogo, King Island Dairy and Timboon. It holds the Yoplait franchise for several Asian countries, and is also a major cheese exporter.

LATEST BUSINESS RESULTS (JUNE 2004, FULL YEAR)

The company posted a good result, with particularly good gains from the 'route trade' (non-grocery channels), such as coffee shop chains and milk bars. It was also the first year in which the company obtained the full benefit of its contract to supply house brand milk to Woolworths supermarkets nationally, with the additional scale that this contract delivered resulting in lower costs and improved processing efficiency. There was a continuing improvement in the King Island specialty cheese and gourmet foods business and a very good performance from the fresh dairy foods business in New Zealand, where sales and profits rose strongly.

OUTLOOK

High national market shares — 42% for milk and 36% for fresh dairy foods — protect National Foods' profits, and in June 2004 it won a new three-year contract to supply Woolworths with its home brand milk. However, margins are known to be slim, and for the company to achieve growth it must continually reduce costs. It has been exploring the possibility of entering into longer-term contracts with its dairy farmer suppliers, to provide them with greater certainty in their businesses and thus helping them to cut their own costs. The company had until recently been realising some good growth from the fresh dairy foods and cheese businesses, and in 2004-05 plans to release 80 new products — four times more than in a normal year — in hopes of stimulating these markets. National Foods is also actively seeking acquisitions, as another means of boosting growth.

NFD Year to 30 June	2003	2004
Revenues ($mn)	1,156.0	1,208.2
EBIT ($mn)	93.4	104.1
EBIT margin (%)	8.1	8.6
Gross margin (%)	38.3	38.8
Operating profit before tax ($mn)	86.0	98.6
Profit after tax ($mn)	60.1	68.7
Earnings per share (¢)	20.6	23.2
Cash flow per share (¢)	35.3	38.7
Dividend (¢)	19.5	22
Percentage franked	100	100
Net tangible assets per share ($)	0.87	0.97
Interest cover (times)	12.5	18.7
Return on equity (%)	14.4	15.1
Debt-to-equity ratio (%)	7.1	8.7
Current ratio	0.8	0.9

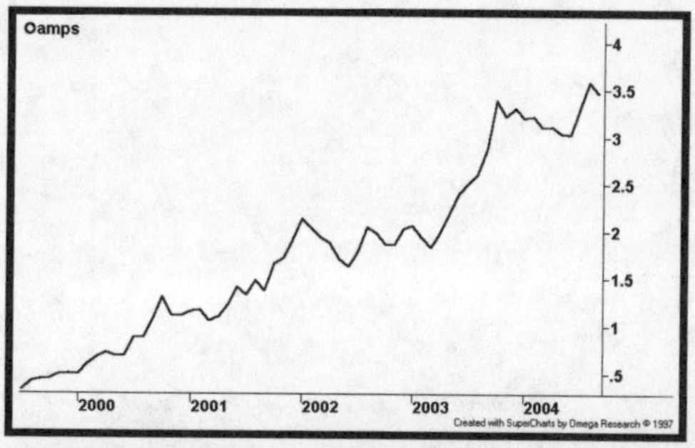

www.oamps.com.au

OAMPS LIMITED

Share price ($)	3.28	
12-month high ($)	4.08	
12-month low ($)	2.47	
Market capitalisation ($mn)	353.5	
Price-to-NTA-per-share ratio	9.7	
5-year share price return (% p.a.)	60.8	
Sector: Financials	**Company**	**Sector**
Price-earnings ratio (times)	13.6	12.9
Dividend yield (%)	4.9	5.2

Melbourne-based OAMPS, established in 1976 as the Oil Agents Mutual Provident Society, is one of Australia's largest insurance brokers and underwriters. It also operates in various other related businesses: its premium funding arm is a lending facility for clients, it has a funds management business, acts as trustee to superannuation funds and it provides clients with a range of other financial products, such as leasing facilities, warranty services and mortgage finance. It has a particular expertise in workers' compensation and occupational health and safety issues. It also operates an insurance broking and underwriting business in the United Kingdom, where it specialises in oil, tanker and hazardous goods risks. It has 27 offices in Australia, servicing more than 210,000 clients, and a further three offices in the UK.

LATEST BUSINESS RESULTS (JUNE 2004, FULL YEAR)

A buoyant insurance industry, organic growth and the company's continuing strategy of expansion by acquisition handed it another solid boost to revenues and profits. Both the broking and the underwriting operations achieved strong increases in profit, with a good contribution from the UK. However, the small financial services business fell into the red. The company benefited from new products and services and from an extension of its specialist underwriting activities, via two new acquisitions, Australian Home Warranty — an underwriting agent for builders warranty insurance — and Yourinsurancegroup — a marketer of insurance products for small retailers. There was a significant contribution from the acquisition of Chambers Gallop McMahon, one of Australia's leading corporate brokers.

OUTLOOK

Company management has already expressed confidence that OAMPS will boost EPS by at least a further 10% in the June 2005 year. It sees particular potential in the addition late in 2003 of Chambers Gallop McMahon, the largest single purchase by OAMPS since the start of its acquisition strategy in 1998. The integration of this business adds more than $100 million of insurance premium turnover, enhancing the company's position as a leading introducer of business to Australia's largest insurance underwriters. Other recent acquisitions include IEA (Brokers), which specialises in sports and leisure insurance operations, and Hadrill Insurance Brokers, one of Hobart's leading general insurance brokers.

OMP Year to 30 June	2003	2004
Revenues ($mn)	191.5	222.8
Underwriting (%)	60	56
Broking (%)	35	39
Financial services (%)	3	3
Premium funding (%)	2	2
EBIT ($mn)	23.5	32.2
EBIT margin (%)	12.3	14.5
Operating profit before tax ($mn)	27.4	36.8
Profit after tax ($mn)	18.1	24.6
Earnings per share (¢)	20.3*	24.1
Cash flow per share (¢)	26.0*	33.1
Dividend (¢)	13.6*	16
Percentage franked	100	100
Net tangible assets per share ($)	0.34*	0.34
Interest cover (times)	~	~
Return on equity (%)	19.5	19.3
Debt-to-equity ratio (%)	~	~
Current ratio	1.1	1.2

* Adjusted for a 1-for-4 bonus share issue

Orica Limited

	Company	Sector
Share price ($)	16.05	
12-month high ($)	16.14	
12-month low ($)	11.32	
Market capitalisation ($mn)	4,347.9	
Price-to-NTA-per-share ratio	5.1	
5-year share price return (% p.a.)	20.6	
Sector: Materials	**Company**	**Sector**
Price-earnings ratio (times)	16.5	14.3
Dividend yield (%)	3.2	2.6

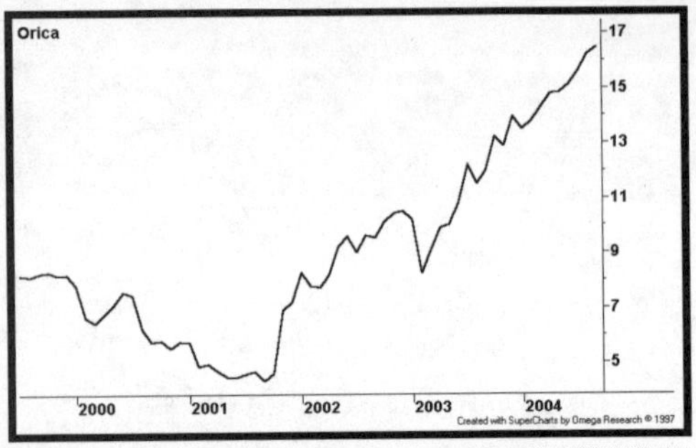

www.orica.com.au

Melbourne-based Orica, founded some 130 years ago as a supplier of explosives for the mining industry, is now a leading manufacturer of a range of industrial and consumer products. These include Australia's largest mining explosives business and largest chemicals business, as well as Dulux paints and Selleys home handyman and car care products. It also owns 70% of the equity of Incitec Pivot, Australia's leading producer of fertilisers.

Latest business results (March 2004, half-year)

A booming business environment, productivity gains and a series of new acquisitions combined to hand Orica a powerful lift in profits, with the company announcing that it expected the earnings momentum to continue at least through the second half. Strength in the resources industry led to record profits for the mining explosives division, while the continuing vigour of the home renovations business meant record profits for the company's consumer products division. The chemicals business recorded higher volumes, but profits were hurt by the stronger dollar. The fertiliser division — comprising the new Incitec Pivot merger — achieved a powerful boost to profits.

ORI Year to 30 September	2002	2003
Revenues ($mn)	4,085.2	3,958.6
EBIT ($mn)	406.3	439.5
EBIT margin (%)	9.9	11.1
Operating profit before tax ($mn)	346.8	378.8
Profit after tax ($mn)	239.1	270.3
Earnings per share (¢)	86.0	97.3
Cash flow per share (¢)	147.8	160.3
Dividend (¢)	44	52
Percentage franked	34	21
Interest cover (times)	6.8	7.2
Return on equity (%)	18.0	19.6
Half-year to 31 March	**2003**	**2004**
Revenues ($mn)	1,842.4	2,053.5
Mining services (%)	43	38
Chemicals (%)	24	23
Fertilisers (%)	13	20
Consumer products (%)	18	19
Operating profit before tax ($mn)	138.8	179.5
Profit after tax ($mn)	97.0	122.2
Earnings per share (¢)	34.8	44.2
Dividend (¢)	18	23
Percentage franked	25	30
Net tangible assets per share ($)	3.23	3.14
Debt-to-equity ratio (%)	74.8	67.1
Current ratio	1.3	1.3

Outlook

Despite operating in relatively mature markets, Orica has enjoyed an impressive recovery over several years, with new management restructuring operations to enable all four main business units to perform to their peak. The share price has surged in response. The challenge now for the company is to maintain that growth. The mining services business continues to expand globally, and has been seeing a pick-up in demand in the important North American market. The $110-million acquisition of the prominent specialty chemicals distributor Bronson and Jacobs is intended to boost Orica's chemicals business. The consumer products business has a 25% exposure to the new housing market and 75% to renovations, and the company does not expect to feel the impact of a housing slowdown before 2005, at which point its new Yates Consumer Lawn and Garden Care business should be contributing to the division's profit.

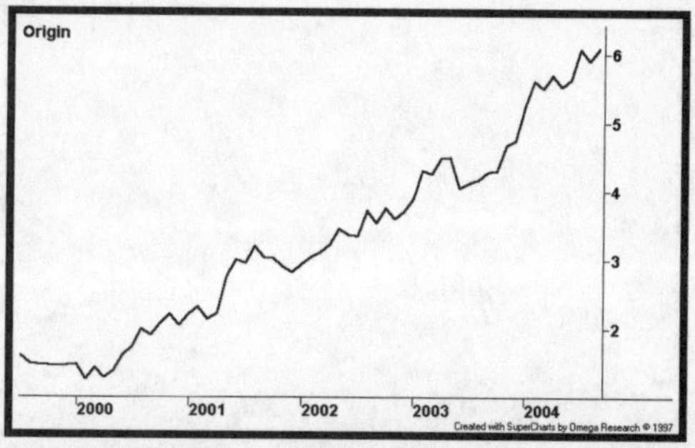

www.originenergy.com.au

Origin Energy Limited

Share price ($)	5.90	
12-month high ($)	6.24	
12-month low ($)	4.11	
Market capitalisation ($mn)	4,005.4	
Price-to-NTA-per-share ratio	3.5	
3-year share price return (% p.a.)	28.2	
Sector: Energy	**Company**	**Sector**
Price-earnings ratio (times)	19.1	18.4
Dividend yield (%)	2.2	2.4

Origin Energy, formerly the energy arm of the Boral group, was demerged in 2000. Today it is one of Australia's leading energy companies, supplying natural gas, electricity and liquefied petroleum gas to more than two million business and residential customers in Australia, New Zealand the Pacific. It operates under four core business units: exploration and production, retail, generation and networks. It owns 19% of the equity of the gas distributor Envestra.

Latest business results (June 2004, full year)

Origin's position at the heart of the booming energy business helped power it to a strong increase in profits, with all divisions strong. The best result came from the generation division, with EBIT up 59% to $42.2 million, thanks to a full-year contribution from the Mt Stuart power station in Queensland and a favourable tax adjustment. The networks division achieved a 24% rise in EBIT to $26.9 million, aided by a maiden contribution from the new SEA gas pipeline. The low-margin retail business — representing 85% of company revenues, but less than half of company profits — saw EBIT up 8% to $155.1 million, with tariff increases, colder winter weather and lower LPG purchasing costs more than offsetting increasing levels of customer churn and higher electricity purchasing costs. Increased oil sales from the Perth Basin and higher gas prices gave a 2% rise in EBIT to $105.1 million to the exploration and production business, and offset a significant disruption to production from a fire at the Moomba gas plant.

Outlook

Origin is one of Australia's leading energy companies, and at a time when investors are favouring the energy sector, its share price has been very strong. Its particular strength is that it operates across the entire energy supply chain, and it continues to expand. It has acquired the minority interests in Oil Company of Australia, and, in New Zealand, the remaining 50% of the Rockgas LPG business, an interest in the Kupe gas field and a conditional agreement to purchase 51.2% of Contact Energy, one of that country's leading energy suppliers. The company targets earnings growth of 10% to 15% annually for the medium term.

ORG Year to 30 June	2003	2004
Revenues ($mn)	3,326.5	3,521.8
EBIT ($mn)	295.3	329.2
EBIT margin (%)	8.9	9.3
Operating profit before tax ($mn)	246.6	283.8
Profit after tax ($mn)	162.0	204.9
Earnings per share (¢)	24.8	30.9
Cash flow per share (¢)	54.9	61.5
Dividend (¢)	10	13
Percentage franked	40	100
Net tangible assets per share ($)	1.48	1.68
Interest cover (times)	6.1	7.3
Return on equity (%)	9.7	11.1
Debt-to-equity ratio (%)	40.9	44.4
Current ratio	1.2	1.2

OrotonGroup Limited

Share price ($)	2.64	
12-month high ($)	3.30	
12-month low ($)	2.35	
Market capitalisation ($mn)	107.9	
Price-to-NTA-per-share ratio	3.9	
5-year share price return (% p.a.)	24.0	
Sector: Consumer discretionary	**Company**	**Sector**
Price-earnings ratio (times)	12.7	23.8
Dividend yield (%)	5.7	1.5

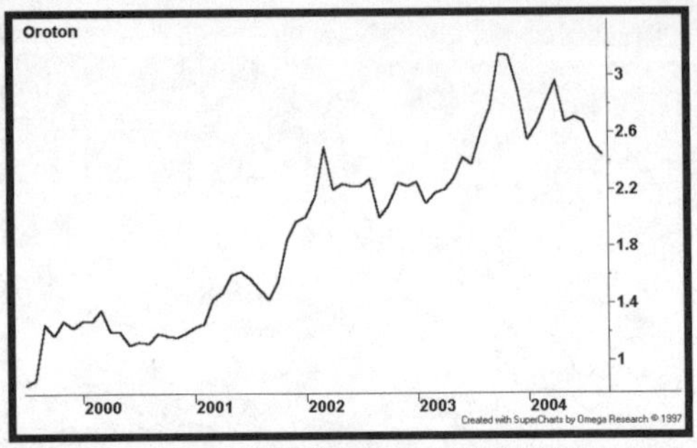

www.orotongroup.com.au

Sydney-based fashion company OrotonGroup was established in 1938. It operates through four premium brands — Polo Ralph Lauren, Oroton, Morrissey and Marcs — with a total of 87 stores. In 2004, it announced that it had acquired the licence to market the Aldo footwear brand. The company is still majority-owned by the founding Lane family.

Latest business results (July 2004, full year)

OrotonGroup rode the domestic retail boom to a healthy increase in sales. However, problems with its Marcs division — acquired for $21 million in 2002 — meant that profits were only marginally higher than in the previous year. There was a particularly strong performance from the core Oroton brand, with sales up 36% on a same-store basis. Morrissey products enjoyed a significant rise in sales, thanks to the opening of a number of new stores, as well as higher demand at existing stores. Polo Ralph Lauren products achieved just a modest improvement in sales.

Outlook

The company believes it is now on track for a period of strong growth, though much depends on the state of the domestic economy and consumer spending trends. Management have conceded that they handled badly the integration of Marcs into their company structure, and large amounts of inventory had to be sold cheaply. This process has now been largely completed and the company sees early indications of an improved performance from Marcs, thanks to its wholesale relationship with David Jones and new stores in Sydney, Melbourne and Brisbane. The company hopes to achieve growth with the Polo label through brand extensions such as Polo Kids. It is also moving the brand into the more contemporary and luxurious market segments. The Morrissey brand, acquired in 2000, continues to grow well, and the company is seeking further sites for new stores. OrotonGroup sees great potential for the Aldo footwear brand, and plans to open three or four Aldo stores each year, from late-2004 or early-2005, targeting the young, fashion-conscious consumer. It is also seeking further brands to add to its portfolio. In August 2004, the company introduced its new computerised inventory control system, and it expects this to improve efficiencies and enhance margins over a 12- to 18-month period.

ORL Year to 31 July*	2003	2004
Revenues ($mn)	118.3	143.6
EBIT ($mn)	12.6	13.6
EBIT margin (%)	10.7	9.5
Gross margin (%)	61.8	62.5
Operating profit before tax ($mn)	11.6	12.3
Profit after tax ($mn)	8.3	8.4
Earnings per share (c)	22.6	20.8
Cash flow per share (c)	35.0	36.4
Dividend (c)	11.5	15
Percentage franked	100	100
Net tangible assets per share ($)	0.31	0.67
Interest cover (times)	12.7	10.6
Return on equity (%)	34.1	23.5
Debt-to-equity ratio (%)	92.5	26.7
Current ratio	1.9	2.1

* 2 August 2003

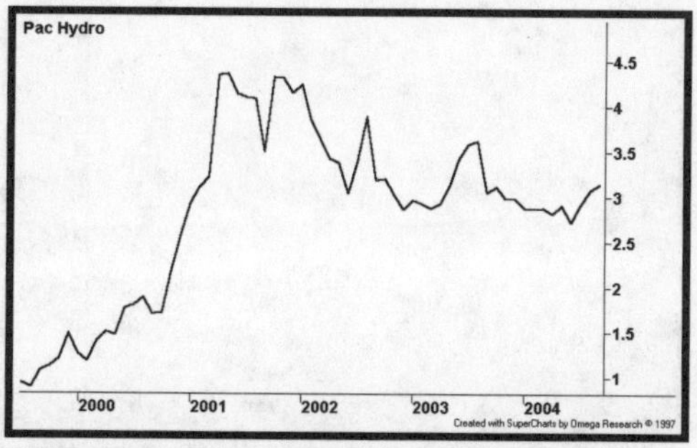

www.pacifichydro.com.au

PACIFIC HYDRO LIMITED

Share price ($)	2.96	
12-month high ($)	3.72	
12-month low ($)	2.60	
Market capitalisation ($mn)	463.1	
Price-to-NTA-per-share ratio	1.7	
5-year share price return (% p.a.)	29.5	
Sector: Utilities	**Company**	**Sector**
Price-earnings ratio (times)	13.1	17.1
Dividend yield (%)	1.7	4.9

Melbourne-based Pacific Hydro is a niche power producer dedicated to the development and operation of renewable energy generation projects. It has become a leader in hydro-electric power generation, and operates three facilities in Victoria and others in NSW and Western Australia. It also operates Australia's largest wind energy projects, at Challicum Hills and at Codrington, both in Victoria. It holds a 50% interest in the Bakun River hydro project in the Philippines, as well as interests in Chile and Fiji. American Electric Power, the largest generator of electricity in the United States, holds 19% of Pacific Hydro's equity.

LATEST BUSINESS RESULTS (JUNE 2004, FULL YEAR)

Profits rose 10%, after the exclusion of a large non-recurring gain arising from the transition to a new tax consolidation regime. Highlights included Pacific Hydro's first profits from the Challicum Hills wind farm operations, a maiden contribution from the Coya and Pangal hydro plants in Chile which were acquired in April 2004, higher generation revenues from the Victorian and NSW hydro projects and the completion and commencement of operation of the Wainikasou hydro plant, the company's first investment in Fiji. There was an improved performance from the Bakun hydro plant in the Philippines, although the benefits were largely offset by the impact of the higher dollar. The company's total installed generation capacity jumped by 139% during the year to 227 megawatts.

OUTLOOK

Pacific Hydro's steady growth and its status as a green energy company have been strong incentives for the shares. It has a string of new projects under development or in the planning stage, and the company's generating capacity has the potential to double within 18 to 24 months. In addition to Challicum Hills and Codrington, it has five other wind farm ventures around Australia, in the planning or construction stage, including the $270-million Portland project in Victoria, which will be one of the world's largest wind farm projects, and which is scheduled to start generating power by mid-2005. It sees Chile as offering great potential for future growth, and also plans further investment in the Philippines. As well, it is investigating possible renewable energy ventures in Europe, China and Canada.

PHY Year to 30 June	2003	2004
Revenues ($mn)	46.4	63.2
EBIT ($mn)	29.2	37.7
EBIT margin (%)	63.0	59.7
Operating profit before tax ($mn)	28.9	34.0
Profit after tax ($mn)	28.5	31.2
Earnings per share (¢)	22.0	22.7
Cash flow per share (¢)	25.6	27.8
Dividend (¢)	5	5
Percentage franked	0	0
Net tangible assets per share ($)	1.40	1.76
Interest cover (times)	84.9	10.2
Return on equity (%)	15.2	13.1
Debt-to-equity ratio (%)	15.5	39.5
Current ratio	0.9	3.8

Pacifica Group Limited

Share price ($)	3.72	
12-month high ($)	5.39	
12-month low ($)	3.68	
Market capitalisation ($mn)	506.0	
Price-to-NTA-per-share ratio	2.1	
5-year share price return (% p.a.)	–6.1	
Sector: Consumer discretionary	**Company**	**Sector**
Price-earnings ratio (times)	10.9	23.8
Dividend yield (%)	5.8	1.5

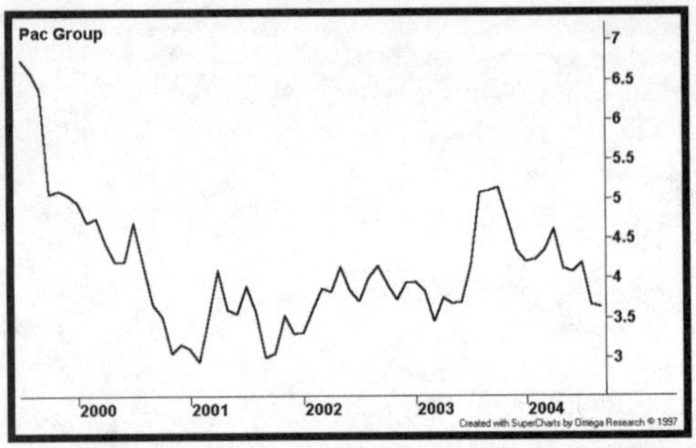

www.pacifica.com.au

Melbourne-based Pacifica is a major manufacturer of vehicle components, selling its innovative clutch and braking systems to top automobile makers around the world, and with overseas production facilities in America, Italy, Malaysia and Thailand. It also owns around half the equity of Friction Materials Pacific, a leading manufacturer in Australia and Asia of friction materials, disc brake pads, backing plates, clutch facings, truck blocks and drum brake linings. The company's small Melwire business manufactures woven wire, rubber and polyurethane products for mining, industrial and agricultural applications.

Latest business results (June 2004, half year)

Profits fell, though much of the decline came about because of the stronger dollar, which averaged US$0.74 for the period, compared to US$0.62 in the June 2003 half. Strength in the domestic and US markets was offset by the continuing decline of the Malaysian facility, which was only marginally profitable. AP Italia, the Italian business acquired in July 2003, had a strong first half, in line with expectations. The company won new contracts worth $117 million annually in revenues, and with an average contract life of five years.

PBB Year to 31 December	2002	2003
Revenues ($mn)	1,077.3	923.8
EBIT ($mn)	92.3	96.3
EBIT margin (%)	8.6	10.4
Gross margin (%)	15.9	15.4
Operating profit before tax ($mn)	77.0	83.9
Profit after tax ($mn)	44.3	46.7
Earnings per share (¢)	30.5	34.0
Cash flow per share (¢)	71.8	71.9
Dividend (¢)	20	21.5
Percentage franked	82	100
Interest cover (times)	6.0	7.8
Return on equity (%)	14.6	16.8
Half-year to 30 June	**2003**	**2004**
Revenues ($mn)	469.0	464.7
Operating profit before tax ($mn)	46.3	40.6
Profit after tax ($mn)	24.0	22.5
Earnings per share (¢)	17.3	16.5
Dividend (¢)	10	10.5
Percentage franked	100	100
Net tangible assets per share ($)	1.98	1.80
Debt-to-equity ratio (%)	33.1	50.5
Current ratio	1.3	1.7

Outlook

Pacifica's business is largely based on long-term contracts, and it can judge fairly well its profit outlook, although currency rate fluctuations introduce an element of uncertainty. The company sees little growth in 2004 and 2005, with the loss of some significant General Motors business in the US being largely offset by the continuing strength of the domestic market, new Ford business in the US and growth in Europe. However, based on contracts already negotiated, the company believes it can achieve 10% profit growth in 2006 and a further 15% in 2007. It plans a joint venture manufacturing business in China, supplying both overseas and Chinese auto firms, with production due to begin in mid-2005. It is reviewing options for its sagging Malaysian business, and is also known to be interested in selling its non-core Melwire subsidiary.

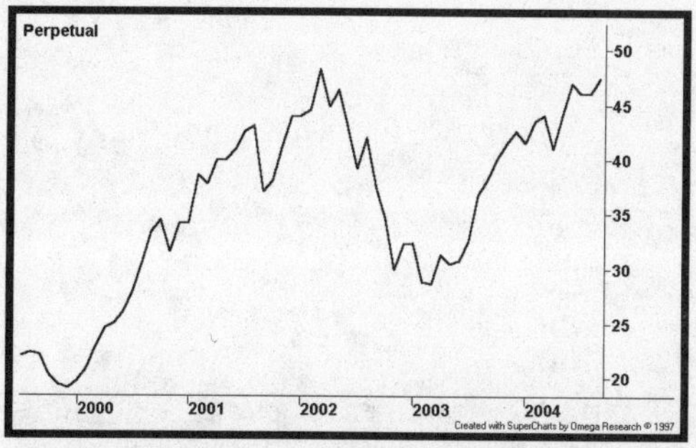

www.perpetual.com.au

Perpetual Trustees Australia Limited

Share price ($)	47.00	
12-month high ($)	48.50	
12-month low ($)	36.01	
Market capitalisation ($mn)	1,788.9	
Price-to-NTA-per-share ratio	6.8	
5-year share price return (% p.a.)	20.1	
Sector: Financials	**Company**	**Sector**
Price-earnings ratio (times)	19.8	12.9
Dividend yield (%)	3.2	5.2

Sydney-based Perpetual was established in 1885 and is now a dynamic financial services company. It is involved in trustee operations, funds management, estate administration, charitable planning, property management, financial planning and tax consulting. With the Australian Stock Exchange it operates the share registry business ASX Perpetual Registrars.

Latest business results (June 2004, full year)

Once again Perpetual delivered an impressive result, with profits up powerfully, thanks to the strength of its core businesses in wealth management and corporate trust, the improved profitability of ASX Perpetual Registrars, positive financial markets and enhanced investor confidence. Funds under management increased from $17.4 billion to $21.7 billion, and funds under advice and administration grew from $6 billion to $6.6 billion. The corporate trust division had another strong year with total securitisation funds under administration rising from $87.1 billion to $112.4 billion. Revenues in the securitisation business increased by 18%.

Outlook

Perpetual continues to go from strength to strength, which has been reflected in its surging share price. It has merged its personal financial services division and its Perpetual investments division to create the wealth management division, and sees this as a significant driver of future growth. It has already expressed confidence that it can achieve profit growth of at least 10% in the June 2005 year, depending on market conditions. The company is also working to lay the foundations for continuing long-term growth, including the expansion of its range of funds management products and its active participation in the ongoing consolidation of the trust industry. It is expanding its capabilities into new asset classes, including the addition of a strong fixed income capability in its wealth management division, and additional processing services for the lending and securitisation market. It has also created a new performance and remuneration system for staff, aimed at better rewarding strong results achieved within the company. Perpetual is reviewing its $2.5 billion global equity portfolio — currently invested through US-based Fidelity Investments — with the possibility of developing its own in-house global equity expertise. In order to enhance shareholder value, it has announced a generous new dividend policy.

PPT Year to 30 June	2003	2004
Revenues ($mn)	267.8	295.1
EBIT ($mn)	93.4	123.8
EBIT margin (%)	34.9	41.9
Operating profit before tax ($mn)	96.1	128.2
Profit after tax ($mn)	68.2	90.4
Earnings per share (¢)	180.6	237.8
Cash flow per share (¢)	217.8	282.5
Dividend (¢)	130	150
Percentage franked	100	100
Net tangible assets per share ($)	6.13	6.89
Interest cover (times)	~	~
Return on equity (%)	25.1	30.0
Debt-to-equity ratio (%)	~	~
Current ratio	2.0	2.5

Plaspak Group Limited

Share price ($)	0.99	
12-month high ($)	1.10	
12-month low ($)	0.89	
Market capitalisation ($mn)	66.2	
Price-to-NTA-per-share ratio	1.5	
5-year share price return (% p.a.)	25.1	
Sector: Materials	**Company**	**Sector**
Price-earnings ratio (times)	9.2	14.3
Dividend yield (%)	6.6	2.6

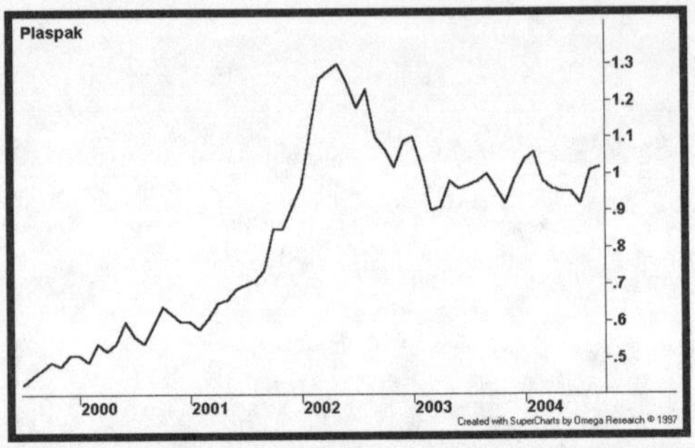

www.plaspak.com.au

Plaspak is the holding company for a group of manufacturing and distribution businesses centred on the rigid plastic packaging market. These produce a range of plastic bottles, containers, caps, closures, recyclable PET plastic products, and bottles for the transportation of dangerous goods such as petroleum and chemical products. It also imports from Japan disposable trigger spray devices under exclusive licence, and it holds the Australian and New Zealand rights to distribute and market the Pecap Aerosol System, a non-polluting, non-flammable, and non-toxic aerosol technology. Plaspak operates from sites in Queensland, NSW and Victoria.

Latest business results (June 2004, full year)

The continuing strength of the domestic economy, along with the rationalisation of under-performing businesses during the prior year and the implementation of further efficiency initiatives, resulted in a pleasing boost to company profits. The good result came despite unexpected and sustained plastic raw material price increases at various times during the year, and the closure of the company's loss-making Adelaide business in August 2003. The ending of that business was responsible for a decline in the company's sales revenues for the year. The after-tax profit got a substantial boost from a sharp reduction in the company's income tax expense as a result of the implementation of a tax consolidation scheme for the group.

Outlook

Plaspak occupies a strong position, with just limited competition, in various niche areas of the plastic packaging industry, and while the economy remains resilient this will support its business. Its 2002 acquisition of Peteron Plastics, a Melbourne manufacturer of blow-moulded plastic bottles, has boosted its exposure to the key Victorian market. The company supplies all the bottles for Cottees cordial, made by Cadbury Schweppes, and it is also a significant supplier to pharmaceutical companies such as CSL and Bayer. Operating in a mature industry, Plaspak continues to strive for growth through restructuring its businesses, including the mid-2004 sale of a surplus factory/warehouse premises at Mordialloc, Victoria, and the planned sale of a NSW facility. Thanks to a strengthened balance sheet, Plaspak is actively seeking further acquisitions, in the packaging or related businesses.

PPK Year to 30 June	2003	2004
Revenues ($mn)	84.1	73.8
EBIT ($mn)	8.1	8.9
EBIT margin (%)	9.6	12.1
Gross margin (%)	21.2	26.1
Operating profit before tax ($mn)	5.9	7.0
Profit after tax ($mn)	5.0	7.2
Earnings per share (¢)	7.5	10.7
Cash flow per share (¢)	19.2	19.3
Dividend (¢)	6	6.5
Percentage franked	100	100
Net tangible assets per share ($)	0.61	0.66
Interest cover (times)	3.7	4.5
Return on equity (%)	11.4	16.1
Debt-to-equity ratio (%)	75.7	63.0
Current ratio	1.7	1.6

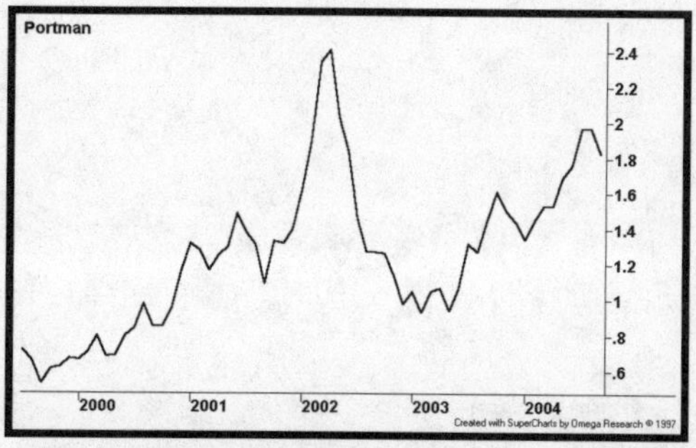

www.portman.com.au

Portman Limited

	Company	Sector
Share price ($)	1.96	
12-month high ($)	2.07	
12-month low ($)	1.19	
Market capitalisation ($mn)	348.5	
Price-to-NTA-per-share ratio	2.1	
5-year share price return (% p.a.)	35.4	
Sector: Materials	**Company**	**Sector**
Price-earnings ratio (times)	20.1	14.3
Dividend yield (%)	4.1	2.6

Perth-based mining company Portman was originally formed in 1925 as Sturts Meadows Prospecting Syndicate. Today it is Australia's third-largest iron ore producer, behind BHP Billiton and Rio Tinto. It owns the Koolyanobbing project, located between Perth and Kalgoorlie in Western Australia, and has a 50% interest in the Cockatoo Island project, in the north of the state. About 75% of its output is shipped to China, and the remainder to Japan.

Latest business results (June 2004, half-year)

Booming Chinese demand for iron ore handed Portman a record mid-year profit. Shipments from Koolyanobbing reached a record 2.7 million tonnes, up 17% from the June 2003 half. Shipments from Cockatoo Island totalled 298,500 tonnes, which was down 5%. Prices rose 18.6% from a year before, and the company was also helped by favourable foreign-exchange hedging.

Outlook

Its relatively small size and its high exposure to the boom in Chinese steel production have given rise to considerable market speculation that Portman could become a takeover target. A Hong Kong-listed investment company, China Online, has built up a 7.5% holding, with suggestions that this could be the start of a Chinese push to acquire a controlling stake in the company. Perth-based miner Consolidated Minerals has also taken a strategic holding. Portman is working to capitalise on the growing demand for its ore by ramping up production. A feasibility study will determine the viability of expanding production at Koolyanobbing from around five million tonnes per year to as high as eight million tonnes, and new support infrastructure has already been completed. Production at Cockatoo Island is being boosted to 1.2 million tonnes annually from late 2004, although problems with a new seawall could delay this. Portman sells directly to end users, rather than using agents or intermediaries, and regards its marketing ability as a valuable asset of the company. It has a marketing manager based in Asia, with offices in both Beijing and Tokyo, and has developed long-term relationships with customers.

PMM Year to 31 December	2002	2003
Revenues ($mn)	128.8	145.3
EBIT ($mn)	2.7	21.5
EBIT margin (%)	2.1	14.8
Gross margin (%)	43.2	35.6
Operating profit before tax ($mn)	5.8	24.1
Profit after tax ($mn)	3.3	16.9
Earnings per share (¢)	1.9	9.8
Cash flow per share (¢)	5.0	14.7
Dividend (¢)	8	8
Percentage franked	75	75
Interest cover (times)	~	~
Return on equity (%)	2.3	11.6
Half-year to 30 June	**2003**	**2004**
Revenues ($mn)	72.9	97.9
Operating profit before tax ($mn)	13.7	25.0
Profit after tax ($mn)	10.2	17.8
Earnings per share (¢)	5.9	10.3
Dividend (¢)	4	4.5
Percentage franked	50	100
Net tangible assets per share ($)	0.87	0.92
Debt-to-equity ratio (%)	~	~
Current ratio	2.0	1.9

Primary Health Care Limited

Share price ($)	5.92	
12-month high ($)	6.40	
12-month low ($)	4.00	
Market capitalisation ($mn)	604.1	
Price-to-NTA-per-share ratio	30.4	
5-year share price return (% p.a.)	14.6	
Sector: Health care	**Company**	**Sector**
Price-earnings ratio (times)	33.5	35.8
Dividend yield (%)	3.0	1.8

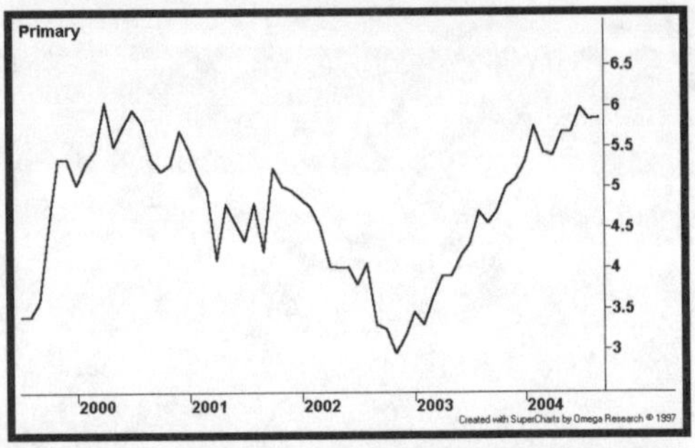

Website currently unavailable

Sydney-based Primary Health Care manages 21 medical centres, staffed by teams of general practitioners, in NSW and South Australia. It also operates a small pathology business.

Latest business results (June 2004, full year)

Profits accelerated as the company reaped the benefits of the rapid expansion of earlier years, and despite the continuing rises in medical operating costs. It was a year of consolidation for the company, with no new medical centres opened. There was a 24% increase in the year for GP patient attendances, and significant margin improvement across all areas of operation.

Outlook

Primary Health Care is a leading participant in the continuing consolidation of the private medical sector in Australia. It claims that its model of aggregating individual doctors' practices into large medical centres provides medical practitioners with capital from the sale of their business, along with a 30% increase in gross annual income in their first year of working in the company's centres. Because of the considerable cost savings derived from operating large medical centres, as opposed to individual practices, the company is able to offer very competitive pricing to patients. It is now seeking to expand further outside its NSW base, with its third Adelaide centre due to open in late 2004 and its first two in Melbourne planned for early 2005. It is also negotiating for further sites in NSW, South Australia and Victoria, and expects to be managing around 40 centres within several years. As the government struggles to contain fast-rising medical costs, it seems likely that it will place an increasing emphasis on promoting low-cost medical centres. In July 2004, Primary Health Care withdrew from the bidding to acquire rival Independent Practitioner Network, and sold much of its 20% stake in IPN to the other bidder, Sonic Healthcare, booking a $2-million profit. The company's pathology business has just a 2% national market share, well behind the leaders Sonic Healthcare, Mayne Group and Gribbles, and is less profitable than its medical centres. Nevertheless, this division is expanding firmly, with much of the growth being generated by the company's medical centres.

PRY Year to 30 June	2003	2004
Revenues ($mn)	126.8	150.4
Medical centres (%)	57	60
Pathology operations (%)	43	40
EBIT ($mn)	26.2	32.4
EBIT margin (%)	20.7	21.5
Operating profit before tax ($mn)	21.0	26.6
Profit after tax ($mn)	12.6	18.0
Earnings per share (¢)	12.6	17.7
Cash flow per share (¢)	30.8	38.6
Dividend (¢)	12.5	17.5
Percentage franked	100	100
Net tangible assets per share ($)	0.14	0.19
Interest cover (times)	5.0	5.6
Return on equity (%)	7.0	9.4
Debt-to-equity ratio (%)	50.4	46.6
Current ratio	1.3	1.4

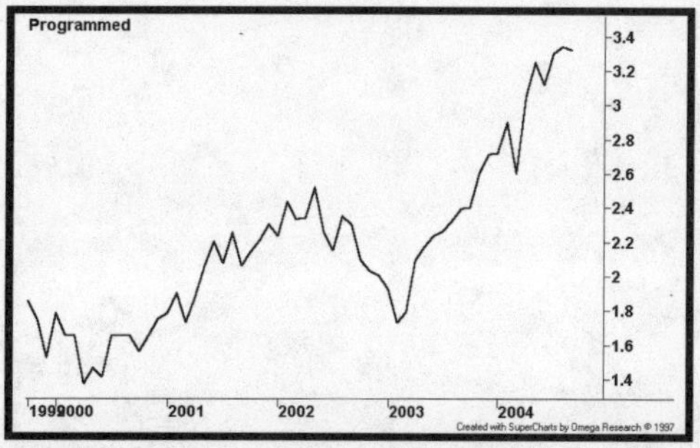

www.pmsltd.com.au

Programmed Maintenance Services Limited

Share price ($)	3.37	
12-month high ($)	3.44	
12-month low ($)	2.29	
Market capitalisation ($mn)	230.2	
Price-to-NTA-per-share ratio	2.3	
5-year share price return (% p.a.)	16.3	
Sector: Industrials	**Company**	**Sector**
Price-earnings ratio (times)	14.1	14.8
Dividend yield (%)	3.6	4.2

Melbourne-based Programmed Maintenance Services was established in 1951 to provide painting services to commercial clients. Today it has 5,500 clients on long-term contracts, covering 60,000 buildings and properties throughout Australia and New Zealand. Services have expanded from painting to a wide variety of building and property maintenance work. Its Barry Bros. Specialised Services subsidiary is involved in drain and sewer system maintenance work. The company has entered the UK market, with the acquisition in 2000 of the long-established Whittle Painting Group.

Latest business results (March 2004, full year)

For the sixth consecutive year, the company recorded growth in both revenues and profits of more than 10%. Domestically, the property maintenance business — about two-thirds of company revenues, and largely painting work — recorded 12% revenues growth and a 10% rise in profits. The Barry Bros. business saw profits more than double on an 11% revenues gain, thanks to a restructuring of its operations. New Zealand businesses achieved 11% sales growth and 7% profit expansion. Though New Zealand represents just 14% of company revenues, business there contributes nearly a third of total profit. British sales revenues — just 9% of the total — grew 4%, but with a large decline in profits.

Outlook

Programmed Maintenance Services has pioneered the concept of long-term commercial maintenance programs — initial refurbishment followed by regular preventative maintenance — offering building owners a cost-effective way to maintain the standard of buildings by spreading their costs over the life of a contract. Its steady profit growth is evidence of the success of this concept, and the company believes it can achieve further double-digit profit expansion in March 2005. The mid-2004 acquisition of servicing contracts from Serco Australia will boost non-painting revenues by approximately 40%, making a material contribution to earnings in the March 2006 year. Programmed Maintenance Services is making steady progress in introducing its business model to British clients, with 135 contracts worth $10.5 million signed by March 2004. However, earnings in the UK have been constrained by the costs of moving the business there from one-off painting jobs to long-term maintenance contracts.

PRG Year to 31 March	2003	2004
Revenues ($mn)	166.4	190.6
EBIT ($mn)	24.2	26.6
EBIT margin (%)	14.5	13.9
Operating profit before tax ($mn)	21.0	24.0
Profit after tax ($mn)	14.3	16.3
Earnings per share (¢)	21.8	23.9
Cash flow per share (¢)	31.9	33.9
Dividend (¢)	9	12
Percentage franked	41	50
Net tangible assets per share ($)	1.27	1.46
Interest cover (times)	7.7	10.4
Return on equity (%)	17.9	17.1
Debt-to-equity ratio (%)	53.5	40.7
Current ratio	3.3	3.1

Publishing and Broadcasting Limited

Share price ($)	13.65	
12-month high ($)	13.86	
12-month low ($)	10.18	
Market capitalisation ($mn)	9,028.2	
Price-to-NTA-per-share ratio	2.3	
5-year share price return (% p.a.)	10.2	
Sector: Consumer discretionary	**Company**	**Sector**
Price-earnings ratio (times)	18.7	23.8
Dividend yield (%)	3.2	1.5

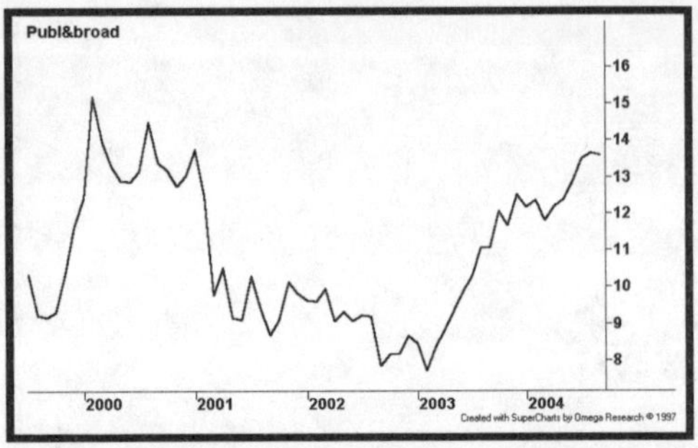

www.pbl.com.au

Publishing and Broadcasting (PBL), controlled by Kerry Packer and his family, operates television's Nine Network as well as Melbourne's Crown Casino. It also owns Australian Consolidated Press, which publishes many of Australia's best-known magazines, including the *Australian Women's Weekly*, *Woman's Day*, *Cleo* and *The Bulletin*. It owns the Ticketek ticketing agency, as well as 25% of Foxtel cable television, 50% of the Premier Media Group (formerly Fox Sports), 50% of the ninemsn internet service, 33.3% of Sky News Australia, 25% of AFIG (formerly Wizard Financial Services) and 25% of the SEEK online jobs service. It has acquired Perth's Burswood casino business.

Latest business results (June 2004, full year)

PBL posted an excellent result, with all its main businesses showing strong gains. A buoyant advertising environment helped the Nine Network to a 13% increase in revenues, with profits (before interest, tax, depreciation and amortisation) surging 29%. The magazines business was not far behind, achieving a 20% increase in profits on an 8% revenues rise. The casino business reported revenues up 5% and profits ahead 14%, though the company warned that this reflected above-average profits from high-roller gamblers, and that on a normalised basis a 3% rise in casino profits should have been expected. The ninemsn business moved out of the red and into profit. PBL classified as a significant item a $182-million after-tax distribution received from the New Regency television and movie production company.

PBL Year to 30 June	2003	2004
Revenues ($mn)	2,676.8	2,874.1
Gaming (%)	40	39
Television (%)	27	28
Magazines (%)	24	24
EBIT ($mn)	563.6	726.0
EBIT margin (%)	21.1	25.3
Gross margin (%)	8.9	7.6
Operating profit before tax ($mn)	451.2	620.4
Profit after tax ($mn)	331.9	484.0
Earnings per share (¢)	50.2	73.1
Cash flow per share (¢)	69.2	92.8
Dividend (¢)	25	43
Percentage franked	100	100
Net tangible assets per share ($)	5.20	5.95
Interest cover (times)	5.0	6.9
Return on equity (%)	9.2	12.2
Debt-to-equity ratio (%)	41.3	25.3
Current ratio	2.2	1.5

Outlook

The television business is able to leverage its high fixed costs into superb profit growth when advertising revenues are high, which has been happening for the Nine Network, thanks to its continuing leadership in viewer numbers. While the economy remains firm and consumer spending high, the boom could continue. The magazines operation is being helped by the same trends. The casino business is inherently volatile, though the Burswood acquisition will help spread risk. PBL plans a major investment in Burswood, and is sending senior Crown executives to take charge, aiming to boost profitability. The company's many other ventures have enormous potential, though remain a tiny part of business. Foxtel continues to lose money, with few signs of an imminent turnaround.

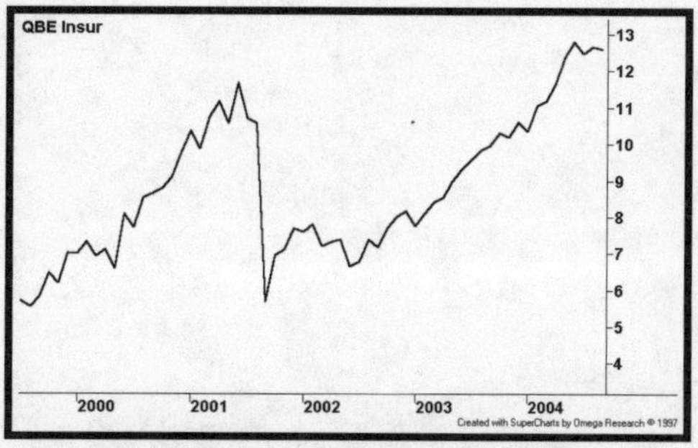

www.qbe.com.au

QBE Insurance Group Limited

Share price ($)	12.50	
12-month high ($)	13.06	
12-month low ($)	9.55	
Market capitalisation ($mn)	8,663.0	
Price-to-NTA-per-share ratio	3.2	
5-year share price return (% p.a.)	21.7	
Sector: Financials	**Company**	**Sector**
Price-earnings ratio (times)	14.0	12.9
Dividend yield (%)	3.4	5.2

Sydney-based QBE — founded as North Queensland Insurance Company in 1886 — is one of Australia's best-regarded insurance companies, specialising in general insurance and reinsurance. It has expanded globally, with operations in around 40 countries, and over three-quarters of business comes from abroad, with particular strength in Europe. It has become the largest underwriter at Lloyd's of London.

Latest business results (June 2004, half-year)

QBE unleashed another powerful rise in profits, thanks to higher premiums and several acquisitions. The insurance margin — profit as a percentage of insurance premium income — rose significantly from 8.4% to 13.1%. The company was a beneficiary of a global trend towards placing tougher terms and conditions on insurance policies, which has had the effect of reducing claims. It also benefited from a decline in natural disasters in the June 2004 half. Net investment income fell from $189 million to $120 million. On a geographical basis, Australia contributed 23% of gross earned premium, the Lloyd's of London division 27%, European company operations 28%, the Americas 16% and Asia-Pacific 6%.

Outlook

QBE has made a stunning recovery from the traumas of September 11, which forced the global insurance industry into a period of intense rationalisation. It has divested itself of under-performing businesses, bought out struggling rival insurers, raised premiums and tightened claim conditions. The question now is to what extent this expansion can continue. A series of acquisitions in mid-2004 has the potential to add around 7% to total gross written premium, as well as providing annual synergies of around $30 million by 2006. QBE continues to seek other acquisitions worldwide. It expects its insurance margin to remain at a high 12% to 13% throughout 2005. However, there are indications that the insurance cycle is at a peak, with growing competition starting to place pressure on premiums in some markets, including Australia.

QBE Year to 31 December	2002	2003
Net earned premium ($mn)	5,642.0	6,036.0
Operating profit before tax ($mn)	311.0	765.0
Profit after tax ($mn)	279.0	572.0
Earnings per share (¢)	46.6	89.5
Dividend (¢)	35	42
Percentage franked	12	23
Return on equity (%)	10.0	18.3
Half-year to 30 June	**2003**	**2004**
Net earned premium ($mn)	3,083.0	3,114.0
Operating profit before tax ($mn)	313.0	405.0
Profit after tax ($mn)	241.0	320.0
Earnings per share (¢)	37.3	47.2
Dividend (¢)	20	24
Percentage franked	15	50
Net tangible assets per share ($)	4.09	3.93
Debt-to-equity ratio (%)	14.8	8.8
Current ratio	1.4	1.2

Rebel Sport Limited

Share price ($)	2.85	
12-month high ($)	3.50	
12-month low ($)	2.44	
Market capitalisation ($mn)	220.5	
Price-to-NTA-per-share ratio	2.8	
5-year share price return (% p.a.)	35.0	
Sector: Consumer discretionary	**Company**	**Sector**
Price-earnings ratio (times)	12.0	23.8
Dividend yield (%)	3.5	1.5

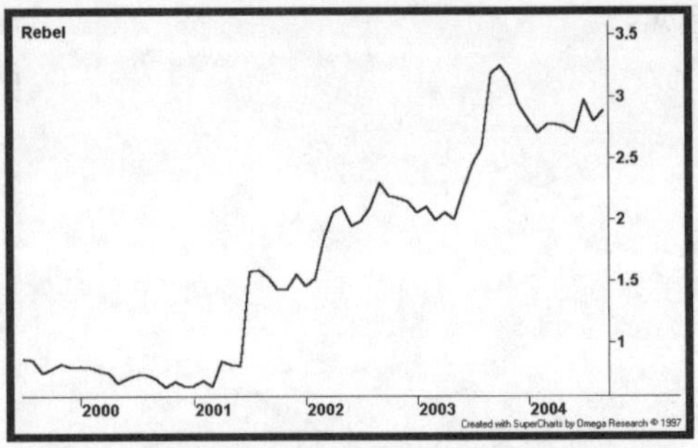

www.rebelsport.com.au

Rebel Sport, one of Australia's leading sporting goods retailers, began trading as a single store in Sydney's west in 1985. It has grown into a large chain of retail outlets across Australia and New Zealand. The New Zealand stores are operated as part of a master franchise agreement with the Briscoes retail housewares group. It has also bought the small Glue chain of 'athleisure' stores, which sell fashionable sporting and leisure wear. Following a takeover bid in 2001, Harvey Norman Holdings now owns a majority of Rebel Sport's equity.

Latest business results (July 2004, full year)

Rebel consolidated its powerful performance of the previous year — when profits more than doubled, as a result of a massive restructuring effort following the Harvey Norman takeover — with another firm rise in sales and earnings. Gains were fairly consistent across the company's product ranges, though with notable weakness in sporting footwear, due to high levels of competition. But sporting apparel sales were strong, aided by new home brand offers and enhanced advertising. The company also enjoyed particular success with its biggest promotion of the year, based on the rugby World Cup. During the year the company opened two new Rebel Sport stores, bringing the total to 52. It also opened two new Glue stores during the year, and two more in July and August 2004, bringing the total to eight.

Outlook

The company believes it can reap still further rewards from the restructuring of the previous two years. In particular, it is handing greater degrees of autonomy to store managers in product ordering and promotion, and believes this will further improve profits. It is also working on new advertising initiatives, including its first-ever women's catalogue and a dedicated exercise category catalogue, both of which have already delivered pleasing sales results. It is launching a new business, Rebel Direct, catering exclusively for the supply of sporting and leisure equipment and apparel to clubs, schools, resorts and corporate markets. It is also launching the Rebel Member Value Program, which is a loyalty scheme for schools and clubs. The company plans steady increases in store numbers for both Rebel Sport and Glue.

REB Year to 3 July*	2003	2004
Revenues ($mn)	276.9	305.4
EBIT ($mn)	23.5	24.5
EBIT margin (%)	8.5	8.0
Gross margin (%)	35.9	35.9
Operating profit before tax ($mn)	23.2	25.4
Profit after tax ($mn)	16.3	18.2
Earnings per share (¢)	21.8	23.7
Cash flow per share (¢)	35.1	36.0
Dividend (¢)	6	10
Percentage franked	100	100
Net tangible assets per share ($)	0.88	1.02
Interest cover (times)	77.4	~
Return on equity (%)	27.9	25.0
Debt-to-equity ratio (%)	~	~
Current ratio	1.9	2.2

* 28 June, 2003

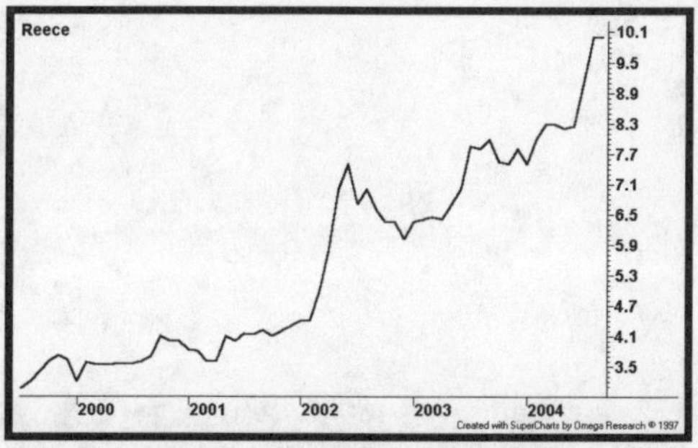

www.reece.com.au

Reece Australia Limited

Share price ($)	9.15	
12-month high ($)	9.35	
12-month low ($)	7.30	
Market capitalisation ($mn)	926.3	
Price-to-NTA-per-share ratio	3.2	
5-year share price return (% p.a.)	28.8	
Sector: Industrials	**Company**	**Sector**
Price-earnings ratio (times)	14.8	14.8
Dividend yield (%)	3.1	4.2

Melbourne-based hardware wholesaler Reece Australia traces its origins back to 1919, when Harold Reece started selling plumbing supplies from the back of a truck. It has gradually expanded from its Victorian roots, with notable growth coming from the acquisition of the Plumbing World and Bridglands chains. Today it is one of the country's leading suppliers of plumbing products, with more than 215 stores and showrooms nationwide, and it has also expanded into related fields. Its four operating divisions are plumbing and bathroom, Reece HVAC (heating, ventilation, air conditioning), industrial and irrigation. It operates a National Training Centre in Melbourne, for plumbers wishing to enhance their skills.

Latest business results (June 2004, full year)

The home construction boom and continuing strength in the home renovations sector delivered another substantial boost to Reece's profits. All four operating divisions saw increased profits. The company also benefited from continuing internally-generated efficiencies and from the opening of 21 new shops. This included Reece's first store in Tasmania. It now operates in every state and territory in Australia.

Outlook

Reece is a conservatively managed company that occupies a central position in the hardware supply business. It sells mainly to plumbers and builders, though does some retail business as well. Heavily geared to the housing cycle, it will be affected by any downturn, especially as its products are used quite early in the home construction phase. The company has said that it anticipates moderate but steady growth in the June 2005 year, though is reluctant to forecast profit trends, due to interest rate uncertainties, a softening of the domestic housing sector and continuing upward pressure on business costs. It expects to open around 20 new stores in the June 2005 year, and with no debt and more than $45 million in cash holdings it is also interested in growth by acquisition. It has launched a series of specialised stores and services to meet evolving needs, including Reece Irrigation for the landscape and agricultural supply industries, Reece Projects for larger residential developments, Reece Gas for customers working with domestic and commercial gas appliances and evaporative cooling systems, and Reecedesign for architects and interior designers.

REH Year to 30 June	2003	2004
Revenues ($mn)	740.2	871.8
EBIT ($mn)	66.6	88.1
EBIT margin (%)	9.0	10.1
Gross margin (%)	25.9	26.8
Operating profit before tax ($mn)	67.7	89.1
Profit after tax ($mn)	46.7	61.5
Earnings per share (¢)	46.9	61.8
Cash flow per share (¢)	56.2	72.3
Dividend (¢)	21	28
Percentage franked	100	100
Net tangible assets per share ($)	2.42	2.82
Interest cover (times)	~	~
Return on equity (%)	21.0	23.5
Debt-to-equity ratio (%)	~	~
Current ratio	2.0	1.9

Rio Tinto Limited

Share price ($)	36.27	
12-month high ($)	38.50	
12-month low ($)	31.98	
Market capitalisation ($mn)	18,168.6	
Price-to-NTA-per-share ratio	3.6	
5-year share price return (% p.a.)	10.2	
Sector: Materials	**Company**	**Sector**
Price-earnings ratio (times)	23.4	14.3
Dividend yield (%)	2.5	2.6

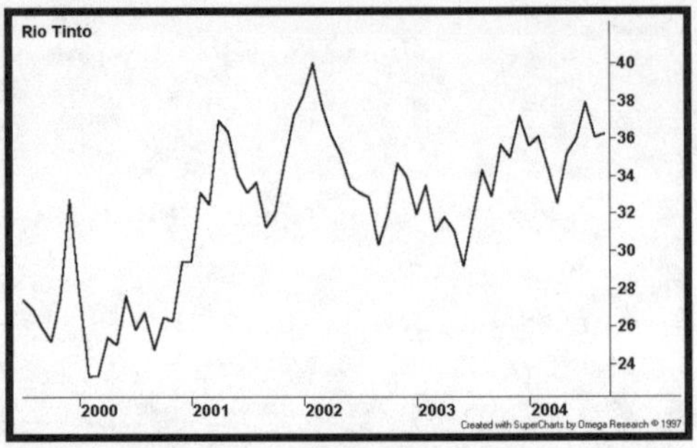

www.riotinto.com

British-based Rio Tinto, one of the world's largest mining companies, retains its ASX presence in a dual-listing structure, and continues to pay franked dividends to Australian shareholders. Australian subsidiaries include Coal and Allied Industries and Energy Resources of Australia, and it has a big stake in Papua New Guinea's Lihir Gold. Among its major products, it mines copper, gold, industrial minerals, iron ore, diamonds and coal and is a large aluminium producer.

Latest business results (June 2004, half-year)

A global resources recovery led to a surge in profits. The Chinese market was particularly strong, accounting for 9% of first-half sales. In addition, the Japanese, Korean and Taiwanese steel industries operated near capacity. Not only was demand higher, but prices too generally rose, especially for copper, aluminium and iron ore. Earnings also benefited from increased production from new projects at Diavik, Canada (diamonds), Eastern Range, Australia (iron ore), Hail Creek, Australia (coking coal) and Escondida, Chile (copper). However, a pit wall slip at the Grasberg copper/gold mine in Indonesia reduced earnings by around $224 million, and Western Australian iron ore operations were hurt badly by tropical cyclone Monty.

RIO Year to 31 December	2002	2003
Revenues ($mn)	19,945.0	18,143.0
EBIT ($mn)	4,331.0	3,251.8
EBIT margin (%)	21.7	17.9
Operating profit before tax ($mn)	4,034.0	3,038.0
Profit after tax ($mn)	2,818.0	2,133.0
Earnings per share (¢)	204.6	154.9
Cash flow per share (¢)	332.2	267.3
Dividend (¢)	105.93	89.7
Percentage franked	100	100
Interest cover (times)	14.6	15.2
Return on equity (%)	23.5	17.9
Half-year to 30 June	**2003**	**2004**
Revenues ($mn)	9,054.0	8,947.0
Operating profit before tax ($mn)	1,569.0	1,959.0
Profit after tax ($mn)	1,044.0	1,342.0
Earnings per share (¢)	75.8	97.3
Dividend (¢)	45.02	45.53
Percentage franked	100	100
Net tangible assets per share ($)	8.31	10.02
Debt-to-equity ratio (%)	66.1	42.0
Current ratio	1.0	1.4

Outlook

Rio Tinto is a prime beneficiary of the booming Chinese economy and that country's surging demand for raw materials. New long-term agreements with leading Chinese steel mills, signed in mid-2004, for the sale of an extra 40 million tonnes per year of iron ore, together with new Nippon Steel and Shanghai Baosteel arrangements, underpin Rio Tinto's major expansion of Western Australian port, rail and mine capacity that is on schedule for completion at the end of 2005. The Comalco Alumina Refinery remains on track for first shipments in early 2005. The Hail Creek hard coking coal mine has achieved its rated capacity of 5.5 million tonnes faster than expected and the company has already approved a $120-million expansion of capacity to 8 million tonnes a year.

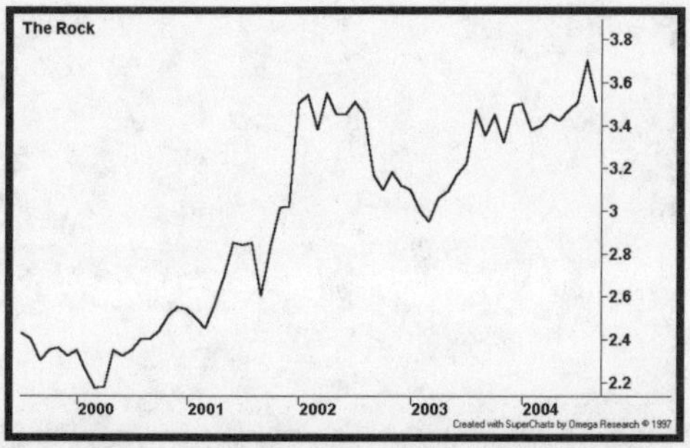

www.therock.com.au

The Rock Building Society Limited

Share price ($)	3.65	
12-month high ($)	3.72	
12-month low ($)	3.22	
Market capitalisation ($mn)	56.7	
Price-to-NTA-per-share ratio	2.1	
5-year share price return (% p.a.)	15.6	
Sector: Financials	**Company**	**Sector**
Price-earnings ratio (times)	14.4	12.9
Dividend yield (%)	5.6	5.2

The Rock Building Society was established in 1967 and is based in Rockhampton. Its main role has been to take retail deposits and provide housing finance for Queensland residents, and it is the leading home lender in central Queensland. It also has a strong presence in the south of the state and a growing business in NSW and Victoria.

Latest business results (June 2004, full year)

The company achieved a small profit increase, after excluding the $1.6 million after-tax profit realised from the sale of its holdings in Cashcard. The emphasis remained on home lending, and loan disbursements for the year rose 19% to $361 million, resulting in an increase in total loans under management of 11.5% to $978 million. Saving and fixed term deposits grew 13% to more than $50 million, with the cash management account continuing as the best-performing deposit product. Financial planning funds under management grew by 163% to $49 million, though this business remained in the red. Revenues from the company's small Rocksure insurance and broking business rose by 20%.

Outlook

The Rock is striving to diversify away from its heavy dependence on home lending, well aware that any sharp housing downturn would be damaging to its business. In particular, it has been working to build its financial planning operations, with an early emphasis on boosting funds under management, rather than profit. After three years of operations, it now believes it has established a sound platform for financial planning and expects to move into profit by June 2005. It is also seeking to expand its insurance revenues, while at the same time boosting the profitability of this business. With a new chief executive officer in place, The Rock is conducting a major strategic review of its operations, and it expects to announce major new growth initiatives during 2005. It plans to use its Cashcard profits to help fund these new initiatives. Because it remains very dependent on home lending, it is working to reduce its exposure to third-party mortgage originators. Loans sourced from outside Queensland now account for more than 50% of the company's loan book.

ROK Year to 30 June	2003	2004
Operating income ($mn)	20.2	25.4
Net interest income ($mn)	7.4	8.3
Operating expenses ($mn)	14.7	17.4
Operating profit before tax ($mn)	5.6	5.6
Profit after tax ($mn)	3.9	3.9
Earnings per share (¢)	24.9	25.3
Dividend (¢)	18.5	20.5
Percentage franked	100	100
Non-interest income to total income (%)	63.6	67.2
Net tangible assets per share ($)	1.51	1.71
Cost-to-income ratio (%)	72.7	68.4
Return on equity (%)	16.2	15.7
Return on assets (%)	1.0	0.9

Rural Press Limited

Share price ($)	8.08	
12-month high ($)	8.19	
12-month low ($)	6.20	
Market capitalisation ($mn)	949.2	
Price-to-NTA-per-share ratio	1.5	
5-year share price return (% p.a.)	16.3	
Sector: Consumer discretionary	**Company**	**Sector**
Price-earnings ratio (times)	10.3	23.8
Dividend yield (%)	4.8	1.5

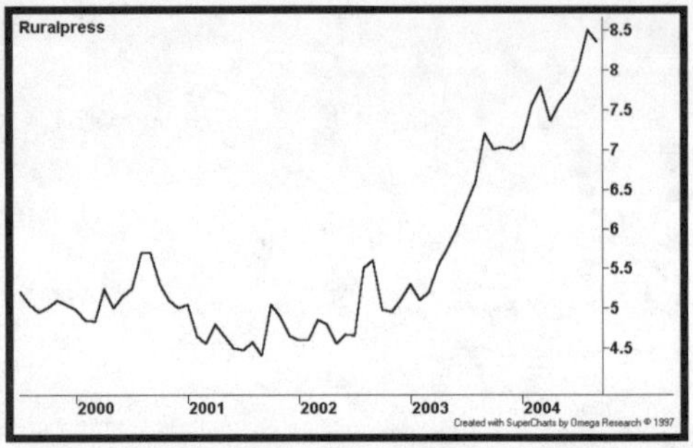

www.ruralpress.com.au

NSW-based Rural Press was established in 1911, and is today one of the world's leading agricultural publishers, with specialist newspapers and magazines in Australia, America and New Zealand. It also manages a string of regional newspapers — including *The Canberra Times* — throughout Australia. In addition, it operates major printing businesses in all Australian states, and it owns Star Broadcasting Network, which operates radio stations in South Australia and Queensland. The Fairfax family owns more than 50% of the equity.

Latest business results (June 2004, full year)

Rural Press was another beneficiary of the thriving advertising environment — along with the strength of much of the rural economy — notching up a record profit. Total advertising revenues were up 9%, even though some regions where the company operates remained affected by the drought. The core printing and publishing business saw revenues up 12%, with EBIT ahead more than 22%, with particular advertising gains in the property, national and classified sectors. US operations produced a solid profit turnaround in local currency, after several years of decline in a contracting agricultural advertising market, though in Australian dollar terms, profits were flat. New Zealand results were little changed from a year before, in a softer rural economy. The radio business boosted revenues, but remained in the red, though with a markedly lower loss than in the previous year.

Outlook

Rural Press, in common with other media companies, is being helped by the continuing strength of the Australian economy, and strong consumer spending levels, which have boosted advertising levels. This has helped it overcome the drought conditions which affected many of its markets. The company continues to expand. The most significant recent acquisition was an 85% interest in Harris & Company in Tasmania, publisher of The Advocate daily newspaper. Already Rural Press has boosted the paper's circulation and advertising levels. The company is also boosting its investment in printing technology, and plans a new greenfield press facility in Mandurah, Western Australia. It has appointed new management for its US business, and plans to launch a major new publishing strategy there that it believes will considerably enhance these operations.

RUP Year to 30 June	2003	2004
Revenues ($mn)	463.8	509.5
EBIT ($mn)	109.0	137.6
EBIT margin (%)	23.5	27.0
Operating profit before tax ($mn)	101.7	128.8
Profit after tax ($mn)	68.4	87.1
Earnings per share (¢)	58.9	78.3
Cash flow per share (¢)	71.7	95.2
Dividend (¢)	23.6	39
Percentage franked	100	100
Net tangible assets per share ($)	5.11	5.39
Interest cover (times)	14.8	15.8
Return on equity (%)	11.3	13.8
Debt-to-equity ratio (%)	19.5	22.2
Current ratio	1.3	1.2

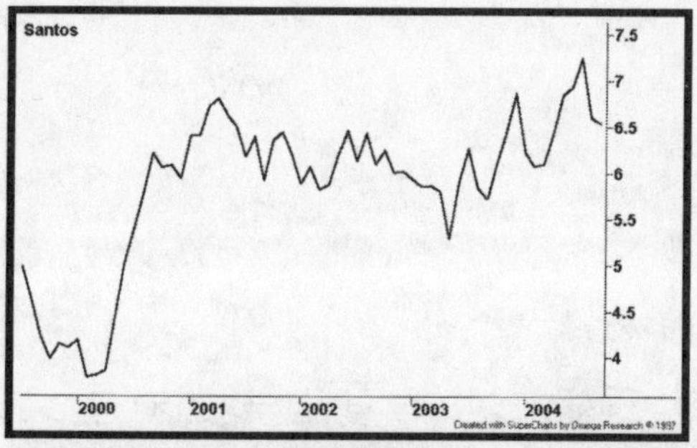

www.santos.com.au

Santos Limited

Share price ($)	7.26	
12-month high ($)	7.49	
12-month low ($)	5.54	
Market capitalisation ($mn)	4,205.6	
Price-to-NTA-per-share ratio	1.4	
5-year share price return (% p.a.)	15.7	
Sector: Energy	**Company**	**Sector**
Price-earnings ratio (times)	13.0	18.4
Dividend yield (%)	4.1	2.4

Adelaide-based Santos, established in 1954, is one of Australia's leading independent producers of oil and gas. Most of its output is from the Cooper/Eromanga Basins in central Australia, though it has additional interests in other parts of Australia, as well as in the US, Indonesia and Papua New Guinea. It is Australia's largest gas producer, supplying natural gas to all mainland states and territories.

Latest business results (June 2004, half-year)

Santos was hit by the loss of substantial production from a fire at its Moomba Gas Plant in January 2004. The company said that without the impact of that incident after-tax profit would have been approximately $62 million higher. The impact of the Moomba incident, combined with declining performance from producing fields in Western Australia and Victoria, resulted in total production of 21.2 million barrels of oil equivalent (boe), down from 26.8 million boe in the June 2003 half. The average realised oil price achieved of A$46.76 per barrel was only slightly higher than the A$45.91 of the June 2003 half, due to the strong dollar.

Outlook

At a time of robust energy prices, Santos has not been performing well, due principally to a lack of big new projects. However, it now has several ventures that offer the hope of a significant boost to production from 2005. This could have a major impact on the company's results, depending on trends in oil prices and the dollar. The two most important are in the Carnarvon Basin, offshore Western Australia. Santos is operator for one of these, the $480 million Mutineer-Exeter oil field development, and is also involved in the John Brookes gas project. Production at both is scheduled for mid-2005. At Bayu-Undan in the Timor Sea, Santos has a 10.6% interest in a world-class field, which has started producing at a higher rate than forecast, and it has also entered into an exploration venture in the Gulf of Suez.

STO Year to 31 December	2002	2003
Revenues ($mn)	1,478.4	1,465.0
EBIT ($mn)	535.5	463.0
EBIT margin (%)	36.2	31.6
Gross margin (%)	41.1	33.5
Operating profit before tax ($mn)	493.3	430.9
Profit after tax ($mn)	322.1	327.0
Earnings per share (¢)	55.5	56.0
Cash flow per share (¢)	136.2	146.7
Dividend (¢)	30	30
Percentage franked	100	100
Interest cover (times)	12.7	14.4
Return on equity (%)	11.5	11.0
Half-year to 30 June	**2003**	**2004**
Revenues ($mn)	716.0	590.5
Operating profit before tax ($mn)	252.0	158.7
Profit after tax ($mn)	170.0	116.6
Earnings per share (¢)	22.3	17.3
Dividend (¢)	15	15
Percentage franked	100	100
Net tangible assets per share ($)	5.10	5.25
Debt-to-equity ratio (%)	33.9	40.3
Current ratio	1.1	1.2

Schaffer Corporation Limited

Share price ($)	14.80	
12-month high ($)	15.35	
12-month low ($)	13.30	
Market capitalisation ($mn)	204.9	
Price-to-NTA-per-share ratio	3.7	
5-year share price return (% p.a.)	52.3	
Sector: Consumer discretionary	**Company**	**Sector**
Price-earnings ratio (times)	12.4	23.8
Dividend yield (%)	6.8	1.5

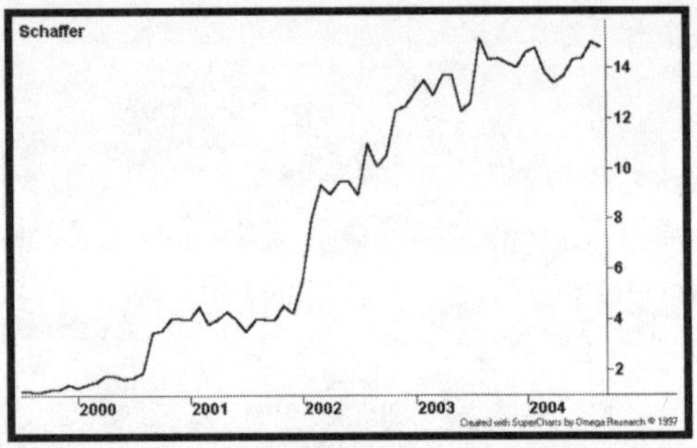

www.schaffer.com.au

Perth-based Schaffer Corporation has two main businesses — leather (about three-quarters of company revenues) and building products — along with extensive property investments. Its Australia Leather Holdings subsidiary comprises two divisions: Howe Leather manufactures leather for the global automobile industry, with some 90% of output exported, and with leading international auto makers among the customers; and Gosh Leather ('Gosh' stands for 'Great Oz Skins and Hides') is Australia's only specialist manufacturer of leather for the furniture industry. Schaffer's building products division consists of two wholly-owned subsidiaries — UrbanStone is a manufacturer of premium paving products, with a national distribution network, and Delta Corporation manufactures pre-cast and pre-stressed concrete floors, beams and wall products, predominantly for the Western Australian construction market.

Latest business results (June 2004, full year)

Schaffer is a significant exporter, and it was badly hurt by the strength of the dollar. After-tax profit on its core businesses fell 18% to $13.8 million, with the currency responsible for more than 90% of that decline. However, this was largely offset by a $2.8 million profit from property sales. Leather revenues fell 20% — affected by both the currency and a decline in sales volumes — with EBIT down 28%. Building products revenues and profits were largely in line with the previous year. At June 2004, Schaffer's property investment portfolio was worth approximately $21 million.

Outlook

In order to concentrate on its two core businesses, Schaffer is gradually disposing of its property investments, with the proceeds being used to pay down debt and provide shareholders with special dividends. The $6-billion global automotive leather market is growing steadily, particularly in Europe, where Howe Leather will expand its presence in 2005 with a new Eastern European cutting plant. It expects this, along with new leather programmes for Audi and Land Rover, to make a significant contribution from 2006, though start-up costs could have a negative impact on June 2005 results. The company is also considering opening a cutting plant in China. The construction environment remains firm, with continuing solid order inflow for the building products division, though the company has expressed concern that increasing competition in the paving market might hurt first-half earnings.

SFC Year to 30 June	2003	2004
Revenues ($mn)	222.3	183.6
EBIT ($mn)	31.1	28.5
EBIT margin (%)	14.0	15.5
Gross margin (%)	22.9	29.3
Operating profit before tax ($mn)	27.4	25.6
Profit after tax ($mn)	17.0	16.6
Earnings per share (¢)	125.2	119.8
Cash flow per share (¢)	162.2	155.8
Dividend (¢)	100	100
Percentage franked	100	100
Net tangible assets per share ($)	4.20	4.04
Interest cover (times)	8.3	9.9
Return on equity (%)	57.5	28.5
Debt-to-equity ratio (%)	67.3	42.2
Current ratio	3.1	3.1

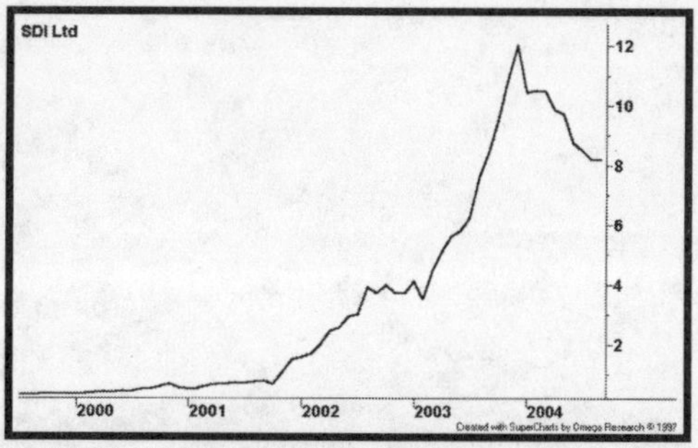

www.sdi.com.au

SDI LIMITED

Share price ($)	8.40	
12-month high ($)	12.30	
12-month low ($)	7.00	
Market capitalisation ($mn)	194.1	
Price-to-NTA-per-share ratio	10.1	
5-year share price return (% p.a.)	97.3	
Sector: Health care	**Company**	**Sector**
Price-earnings ratio (times)	24.5	35.8
Dividend yield (%)	1.0	1.8

Melbourne-based SDI (formerly Southern Dental Industries), founded in 1972, develops and manufactures specialist dental restorative materials. It has two major product groups: alloy materials for fillings; and aesthetic materials, such as composites, adhesives, sealants and tooth whitening systems. More than 90% of sales are overseas, mainly in Europe, North America and South America. All the company's manufacturing is done in Melbourne, and it has offices and warehouses in several countries.

LATEST BUSINESS RESULTS (JUNE 2004, FULL YEAR)

For the fifth straight year SDI recorded after-tax profit growth of more than 35%, with global demand continuing to swell for its products. Sales revenues were up nearly 16%, held back by the strong dollar. In local currencies, the company achieved sales growth of 26%. European sales rose 37% in local currencies and North America was up 12%. There was a combination of organic growth and a solid contribution from new products, particularly the Radii Light Emitting Diode curing device.

OUTLOOK

SDI has established a firm position in the Australian market for its products, and it is also among the top 10 worldwide. It has an estimated 60% of the Australian market for amalgams and 10% globally, and lesser shares for other products. It devotes a high percentage of revenues to research and development work, with over 15 scientists, and has been releasing a steady stream of new products. It expects strong returns in the June 2005 year from three new products introduced in 2003–04 — Rok (posterior alternative for amalgam), Ice (anterior and posterior nano-technology composite restorative) and Riva SC (glass ionomer cement). It has seven new products under development, with plans to release some of them at the International Dental Show in Germany in April 2005. With sales now in over 100 countries, SDI is moving to employ its own salaried staff in key markets, rather than using local agents. In August 2004, it opened a branch in Japan — the world's second-largest dental market — with a sales office, testing laboratory and warehouse, and believes this will lead to greatly enhanced sales. Company management has set a target of 24% EPS growth in the June 2005 year.

SDI Year to 30 June	2003	2004
Revenues ($mn)	36.7	42.5
EBIT ($mn)	8.1	11.3
EBIT margin (%)	22.0	26.7
Gross margin (%)	65.9	67.2
Operating profit before tax ($mn)	7.8	10.9
Profit after tax ($mn)	5.5	8.0
Earnings per share (¢)	23.3	34.3
Cash flow per share (¢)	29.5	41.9
Dividend (¢)	7.5	8.5
Percentage franked	100	100
Net tangible assets per share ($)	0.69	0.84
Interest cover (times)	34.0	24.0
Return on equity (%)	27.5	32.0
Debt-to-equity ratio (%)	14.7	34.1
Current ratio	2.8	3.2

Select Harvests Limited

Share price ($)	7.10	
12-month high ($)	7.60	
12-month low ($)	4.80	
Market capitalisation ($mn)	279.4	
Price-to-NTA-per-share ratio	5.3	
5-year share price return (% p.a.)	57.7	
Sector: Consumer staples	**Company**	**Sector**
Price-earnings ratio (times)	17.8	16.8
Dividend yield (%)	3.7	3.7

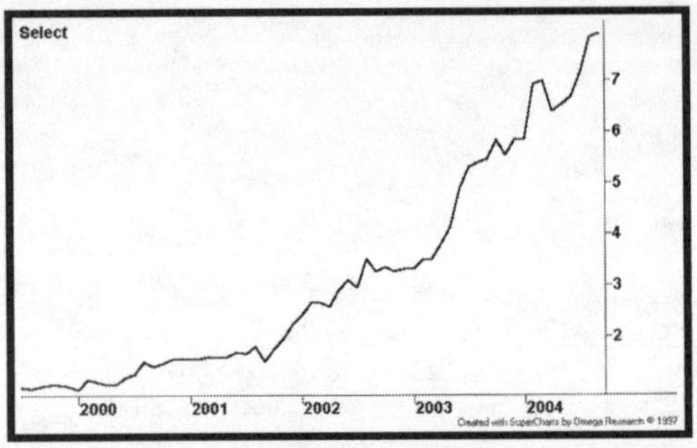

www.selectharvests.com.au

Melbourne-based Select Harvests is Australia's biggest almond grower and processor, and one of the five largest growers in the world. As well as its own almond orchards, in Victoria's Sunraysia district, it has a thriving business managing orchards owned by external investors. In addition, it operates the Lucky Candy and Munch Nuts businesses, which involves the processing, packing and marketing of edible nuts, dried fruits and seeds, as well as the Meriram group of health food companies. It also manufactures a range of pesticides.

Latest business results (June 2004, full year)

Select Harvest continued its spectacular growth. Its food products division saw sales up 73% to $88 million — with pre-tax profits surging 94% — thanks to the mid-2003 acquisition of the Meriram companies and continuing demand for almond products. Revenues were flat for the almond orchards business, though profits rose 23%. There was a big 58% jump in revenues from the company's business providing management services to almond orchard investors, with profits up 55%. Sales and profits were down for the company's small pesticides business.

Outlook

Select Harvests has achieved outstanding success in transforming itself from a tiny grower into a global force in the almond business, and the share price has responded powerfully. The development of an additional 4,000 acres of new almond orchards in 2004 increased the total area under Select Harvests' management to approximately 14,000 acres, with a further 3,500 acres planned for 2005. Almond production continues to rise, with economies of scale bringing lower costs. At the same time, the health benefits of almonds are leading to a strong rise in global demand and prices have reached seven-year highs. There are some forecasts that the US — responsible for 80% of global almond output — has reached a plateau in its production. The Meriram acquisition has helped Select Harvests increase its product range and branding, and has extended its distribution to more retailers. The pesticide business is small, but highly profitable, and the company is working to cut costs and boost its marketing, in order to revive sales. With little debt, the company is also seeking further acquisitions.

SHV Year to 30 June	2003	2004
Revenues ($mn)	81.0	127.4
Food products (%)	63	69
Management services (%)	20	20
Almond orchards (%)	11	7
Pesticide products (%)	5	3
EBIT ($mn)	17.4	23.8
EBIT margin (%)	21.5	18.7
Gross margin (%)	14.8	10.1
Operating profit before tax ($mn)	16.1	22.6
Profit after tax ($mn)	11.0	15.2
Earnings per share (¢)	31.3	40.0
Cash flow per share (¢)	42.6	51.4
Dividend (¢)	18.5	26
Percentage franked	100	100
Net tangible assets per share ($)	1.08	1.35
Interest cover (times)	13.3	19.1
Return on equity (%)	20.1	21.9
Debt-to-equity ratio (%)	14.5	9.6
Current ratio	1.6	1.7

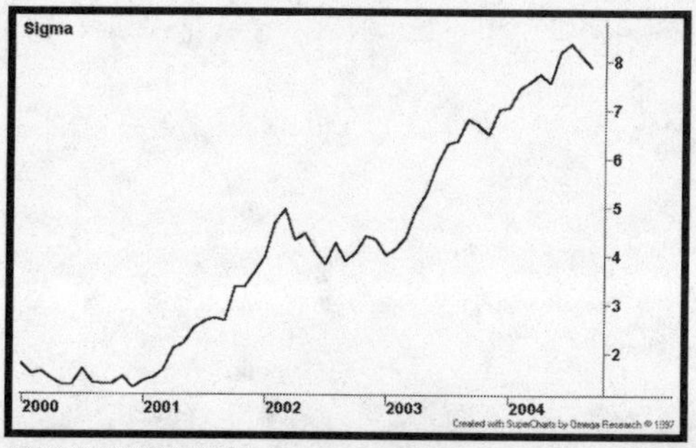

www.sigmaco.com.au

Sigma Company Limited

Share price ($)	7.75	
12-month high ($)	8.55	
12-month low ($)	5.95	
Market capitalisation ($mn)	1,114.5	
Price-to-NTA-per-share ratio	9.8	
3-year share price return (% p.a.)	49.7	
Sector: Health care	**Company**	**Sector**
Price-earnings ratio (times)	24.7	35.8
Dividend yield (%)	2.6	1.8

Melbourne-based Sigma, founded in 1912, is Australia's largest pharmaceuticals company. It manufactures more than 500 drugs and medicines, and distributes its products to around 3,500 pharmacies nationwide, including to Guardian and Amcal stores. In mid-2003 it acquired the iconic Herron Group pharmaceuticals business.

Latest business results (July 2004, half-year)

Sigma reported another powerful increase in profits, driven by strong performances in both its pharmaceutical and healthcare divisions. The high-margin pharmaceuticals division — responsible for drugs manufacture — saw sales rise 18%, with a 26% surge in EBIT, with a good contribution from the Herron acquisition. The profit figure would have been higher but for an increase in compliance costs of approximately $2.5 million for the period. The pharmaceuticals division, though just 15% of total company revenues, contributes nearly 60% of company profit. The healthcare division, which is responsible for drugs distribution, saw sales up 13%, while EBIT jumped 55%.

Outlook

Sigma's impressive growth has led to a powerful share price performance. However, the rapid expansion has also led to reports that the company has quietly been forced to recall some of its products, due to safety concerns about their efficacy. The company itself is forecasting further profit growth of at least 20% in the January 2005 year. Part of this will derive from the successful integration of the Herron Group acquisition. It had been forecast that this business would break even in its first year as part of Sigma, but in fact it contributed $4 million in after-tax profit in the January 2004 year, even after absorbing integration costs and the interest cost of the acquisition. The company continues to look for further acquisitions, and is also striving for continued organic growth. It is working to streamline its healthcare division, in order to improve stock management and enhance supplier relationships. Thanks to a growing level of business from the company's Amcal and Guardian members, Sigma is significantly increasing its investment to support these stores.

SIG Year to 31 January	2003	2004
Revenues ($mn)	1,733.4	1,908.6
EBIT ($mn)	57.2	83.6
EBIT margin (%)	3.3	4.4
Gross margin (%)	10.1	11.5
Operating profit before tax ($mn)	47.0	67.3
Profit after tax ($mn)	31.0	44.2
Earnings per share (¢)	22.4	31.4
Cash flow per share (¢)	34.7	44.0
Dividend (¢)	15.5	20
Percentage franked	100	100
Interest cover (times)	5.6	5.1
Return on equity (%)	11.5	14.7
Half-year to 31 July	**2003**	**2004**
Revenues ($mn)	904.0	1,021.8
Operating profit before tax ($mn)	26.5	37.2
Profit after tax ($mn)	17.5	25.0
Earnings per share (¢)	12.5	17.7
Dividend (¢)	7.5	10.5
Percentage franked	100	100
Net tangible assets per share ($)	0.62	0.79
Debt-to-equity ratio (%)	50.8	46.5
Current ratio	1.2	1.2

Sims Group Limited

Share price ($)	11.86	
12-month high ($)	12.55	
12-month low ($)	9.55	
Market capitalisation ($mn)	1,083.9	
Price-to-NTA-per-share ratio	2.9	
5-year share price return (% p.a.)	24.1	
Sector: Materials	**Company**	**Sector**
Price-earnings ratio (times)	9.7	14.3
Dividend yield (%)	5.6	2.6

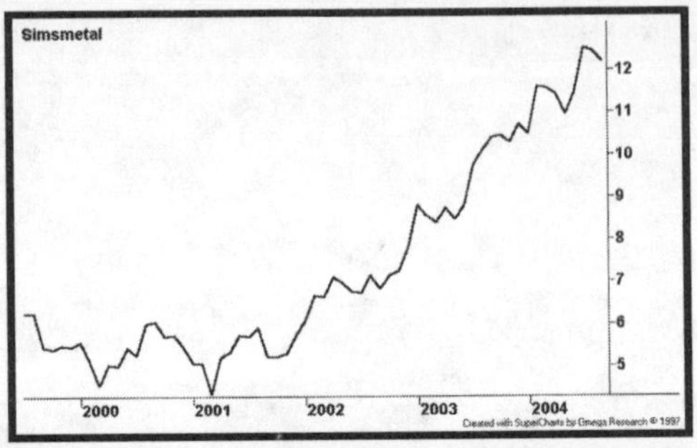

www.simsmetal.com.au

Sydney-based Sims, formerly called Simsmetal, was founded in 1917, and is today Australia's largest metals recycler. It has become the world's largest producer of ferrous scrap metal, used in steel making, and a leading producer of non-ferrous scrap, particularly copper and aluminium. Some 60% of revenues and profits come from overseas operations, primarily in America, Britain and New Zealand.

Latest business results (June 2004, full year)

The Chinese economic boom lay behind another powerful profit rise for Sims — thanks to surging ferrous prices — and more than offsetting the impact of the stronger dollar and higher freight rates. Much of the gain came in the third quarter, when prices reached their peak, leading many Chinese buyers to suspend purchases, and forcing prices down. All the company's global business units produced record results, with the North American operation the standout performer, trebling EBIT in US dollar terms. The company also enjoyed improvements in its secondary aluminium business, following a successful rationalisation in 2003 and a strong performance by ARA, the secondary lead joint venture with Zinifex. The company's Sims Recycling Solutions also made considerable progress during the year in refrigerator recycling. In the UK over 360,000 refrigerators were processed, up nearly 130%, following the commissioning of the division's second recycling plant.

Outlook

As another Australian beneficiary of the Chinese boom, Sims now sees its immediate fortunes tied in large part to that country's economy. With extreme volatility now evident in the ferrous metals market, the company must also be astute in the timing of sales. It reported that early indications at the start of the June 2005 year were that price strength was being maintained. Sims is making strong moves into the recycling business, which is growing in importance. It is boosting capacity at its new UK refrigerator recycling plant, and domestically has acquired Tyrecycle, Australia's largest collector and processor of used vehicle tyres. In the US the company has consolidated its strategic position on the East Coast with the acquisition of another shredder and an important export facility, and expects this to provide the platform for a second phase of strong growth.

SMS Year to 30 June	2003	2004
Revenues ($mn)	1,579.7	1,873.9
EBIT ($mn)	114.2	168.4
EBIT margin (%)	7.2	9.0
Operating profit before tax ($mn)	112.0	166.6
Profit after tax ($mn)	75.0	112.5
Earnings per share (¢)	82.2	122.6
Cash flow per share (¢)	122.5	155.5
Dividend (¢)	54	66
Percentage franked	73	52
Net tangible assets per share ($)	3.69	4.12
Interest cover (times)	51.9	91.2
Return on equity (%)	20.4	26.6
Debt-to-equity ratio (%)	~	4.0
Current ratio	1.9	1.6

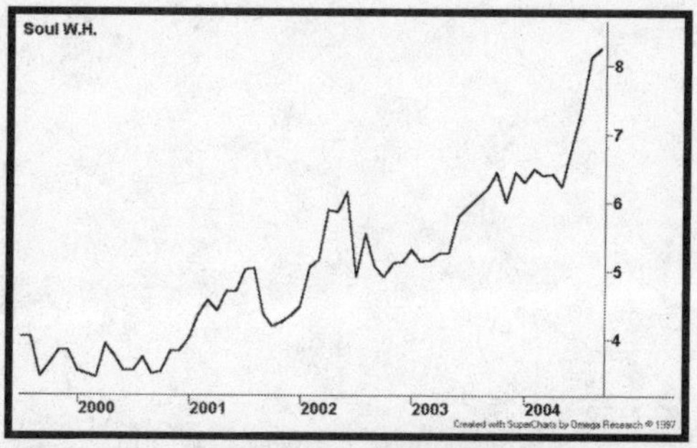

www.whsp.com.au

Soul Pattinson & Company Limited, Washington H.

Share price ($)	7.75	
12-month high ($)	7.83	
12-month low ($)	5.85	
Market capitalisation ($mn)	1,845.8	
Price-to-NTA-per-share ratio	2.6	
5-year share price return (% p.a.)	22.5	
Sector: Financials	**Company**	**Sector**
Price-earnings ratio (times)	20.9	12.9
Dividend yield (%)	2.2	5.2

With its origins as a Sydney pharmacy store opened in 1872, and publicly listed for more than 100 years, Washington H. Soul Pattinson is today a diversified group operating in many businesses — New Hope Corporation (64% owned, and now publicly listed) has coal mining operations in Queensland and Indonesia; SP Telecommunications (53% owned, also publicly listed) provides telecommunications services to the Hunter Valley region; and Keith Harris (84% owned, also publicly listed) manufactures juices and fragrances. In addition, the company retains ownership of nine Sydney pharmacies, and it owns 23% of the equity in Australian Pharmaceutical Industries and 29% of nutritional supplement maker Clover Corporation. In a cross-shareholding arrangement designed to forestall takeovers, it owns nearly 50% of the equity of Brickworks, which in turn owns 43% of Soul Pattinson.

Latest business results (January 2004, half-year)

The company saw a big surge in profits, though much of this was attributable to the company's equity-accounted share of a special profit realised by Brickworks on the sale of its investment portfolio. Excluding this and some other, smaller, non-regular items, the after-tax profit actually dipped 1% from the January 2003 half, to $40.4 million. Coal profits rose, though largely due to a special profit from the settlement of a handling contract with a customer. Brickworks made a major contribution, thanks to the strong housing market and its acquisition of Bristile. Profits from the now-sold NBN Television rose sharply, thanks to a buoyant advertising environment.

Outlook

With the listing in September 2003 of its New Hope subsidiary, Soul Pattinson has largely transformed itself into an investment company. It has also sold, in mid-2004, its wholly owned NBN Television business to its subsidiary SP Telecommunications. Much of its fortunes are now tied to its large stake in Brickworks, with a housing downturn clouding the outlook for this business. It will also be greatly influenced by trends in the coal market.

SOL Year to 31 July	2002	2003
Revenues ($mn)	334.3	340.6
EBIT ($mn)	118.0	133.6
EBIT margin (%)	35.3	39.2
Operating profit before tax ($mn)	114.1	128.8
Profit after tax ($mn)	72.7	88.3
Earnings per share (¢)	30.5	37.0
Cash flow per share (¢)	41.8	49.8
Dividend (¢)	14	17
Percentage franked	100	100
Interest cover (times)	30.3	27.6
Return on equity (%)	11.1	12.6
Half-year to 31 January	**2003**	**2004**
Revenues ($mn)	179.8	175.5
Coal mining (%)	46	53
Media (%)	18	14
Investment (%)	8	12
Pharmaceutical (%)	10	6
Operating profit before tax ($mn)	68.0	147.7
Profit after tax ($mn)	45.4	98.0
Earnings per share (¢)	19.0	41.1
Dividend (¢)	7	8
Percentage franked	100	100
Net tangible assets per share ($)	2.66	3.03
Debt-to-equity ratio (%)	21.7	11.5
Current ratio	1.4	1.5

St George Bank Limited

	Company	Sector
Share price ($)	20.85	
12-month high ($)	22.69	
12-month low ($)	19.13	
Market capitalisation ($mn)	10,804.8	
Price-to-NTA-per-share ratio	3.6	
5-year share price return (% p.a.)	21.3	
Sector: Financials	**Company**	**Sector**
Price-earnings ratio (times)	15.9	12.9
Dividend yield (%)	4.6	5.2

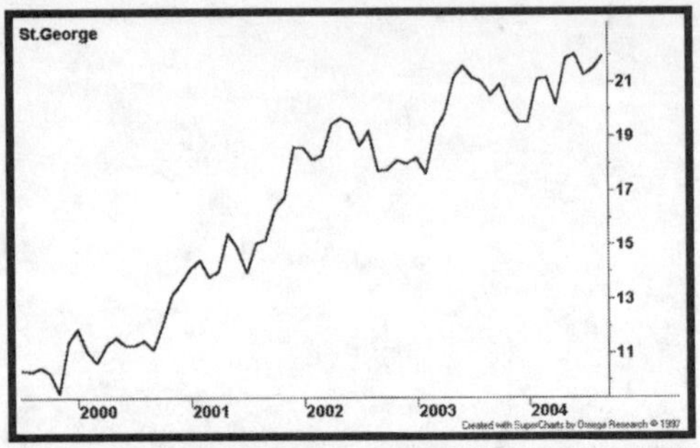

www.stgeorge.com.au

Sydney-based St George has grown from a series of mergers and acquisitions to become Australia's fifth-largest retail bank. It has its business centred in South Australia (where it is Number One, thanks to its acquisition of BankSA) and in NSW. It also owns the master trust business Sealcorp.

Latest business results (March 2004, half-year)

Effective cost containment helped St George to a healthy gain in profits. Net interest income rose by nearly 12%, though contracting interest margins limited earnings growth for lending activities. Home mortgages grew by 15% to $46 billion. Non-interest income growth was restricted to 6%, due to the impact of credit and debit card interchange fee changes and higher home loan broker commissions. Managed funds under management increased by 28% to more than $22 billion. A particularly strong result came from BankSA, with booming lending activity and a sharp reduction in the cost-to-income ratio.

Outlook

St George has embarked on an organic growth strategy, which it believes offers less risk than growth through acquisition. It maintains a particular focus on customer service, which could hamper its drive to reduce costs. It is achieving strong growth in private banking for high-net-worth individuals, with customer numbers up 57% since 2002. It is also seeing success in boosting its business banking activities, and claims a 5.8% national market share in business banking, up from 4.2% in 2001. It believes that it can achieve continued growth, above the national average, in both commercial and home lending, and expects double-digit EPS growth in both the September 2004 and 2005 years, even with a housing downturn. St George is working to expand outside its bases in NSW and South Australia, and is targeting strong growth in Victoria, where it plans a series of new branches and ATMs. It is often seen as a takeover target, and this has supported the share price, although in early 2004 the National Australia Bank sold its strategic equity stake in St George.

SGB Year to 30 September	2002	2003
Operating income ($mn)	2,185.0	2,361.0
Net interest income ($mn)	1,333.0	1,451.0
Operating expenses ($mn)	1,247.0	1,170.0
Operating profit before tax ($mn)	834.0	978.0
Profit after tax ($mn)	563.0	658.0
Earnings per share (¢)	114.2	131.0
Dividend (¢)	80	95
Percentage franked	100	100
Non-interest income to total income (%)	39.0	38.5
Cost-to-income ratio (%)	57.1	49.6
Return on equity (%)	16.6	17.5
Return on assets (%)	1.1	1.1
Half-year to 31 March	**2003**	**2004**
Operating income ($mn)	1,159.0	1,269.0
Operating profit before tax ($mn)	484.0	556.0
Profit after tax ($mn)	325.0	377.0
Earnings per share (¢)	59.5	69.7
Dividend (¢)	45	60
Percentage franked	100	100
Net tangible assets per share ($)	5.03	5.81

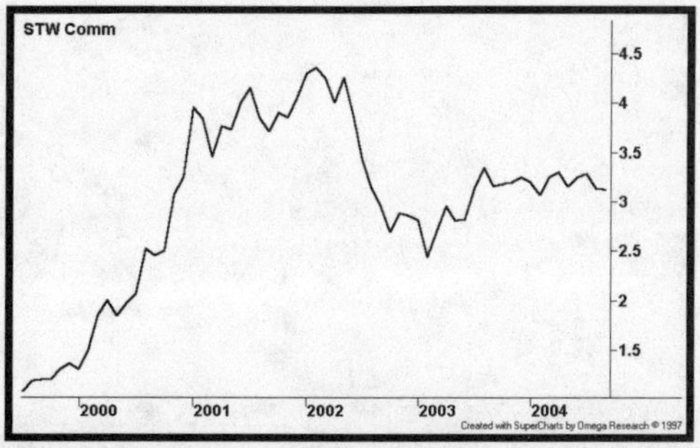

www.stwgroup.com.au

STW Communications Group Limited

Share price ($)	3.28	
12-month high ($)	3.44	
12-month low ($)	3.02	
Market capitalisation ($mn)	564.1	
Price-to-NTA-per-share ratio	2.9	
5-year share price return (% p.a.)	23.9	
Sector: Consumer discretionary	**Company**	**Sector**
Price-earnings ratio (times)	19.3	23.8
Dividend yield (%)	4.1	1.5

Sydney-based STW Communications Group, formerly called Singleton Group, was founded by entrepreneur John Singleton, who is the largest shareholder. It is a holding company, owning two-thirds of Singleton Ogilvy & Mather Holdings, as well as a 49% interest in the Australian and New Zealand operations of the advertising company J. Walter Thompson and a 20% stake in Indonesia's third-largest television network, PT Surya Citra Television, known as SCTV. It also owns over 60 smaller businesses in such fields as internet design and marketing, ethnic advertising, public relations and direct marketing.

Latest business results (June 2004, half-year)

STW presents its financial results in varying ways, and it can be difficult sometimes to make valid comparisons. Growth continued, thanks to a buoyant advertising environment and the company's management strengths. Advertising business — about two-thirds of profit — saw earnings up 29%, while the company's diversified marketing and communications businesses realised a 73% jump in earnings. There was a 29% decline in profits from the Indonesian television holding.

Outlook

STW retains a string of blue-chip domestic and international clients, and this underpins its business. Thanks to its holding company structure, it is able to attract rival corporations, such as Telstra and Vodaphone, as clients, each dealing with different arms of the company. It continues to expand, with a rising number of acquired companies providing numerous synergies and cross-selling opportunities. Management have said they expect growth will increasingly be driven by gaining a larger slice of clients' total marketing budgets, and they forecast EPS growth in December 2004 of 10% to 15%, and an even higher rate in 2005. STW expects a restructuring of New Zealand operations to provide greater growth there. The company has conceded that its Indonesian acquisition was a mistake, and it plans to sell it. Longer term, major shareholder John Singleton has discussed joining STW with his private radio station company, Macquarie Media, to create a giant media organisation.

SGN Year to 31 December	2002	2003
Revenues ($mn)	122.5	129.2
EBIT ($mn)	25.6	26.2
EBIT margin (%)	20.9	20.3
Operating profit before tax ($mn)	25.5	25.6
Profit after tax ($mn)	25.3	26.0
Earnings per share (¢)	16.8	17.0
Cash flow per share (¢)	16.8	17.2
Dividend (¢)	12.5	13.4
Percentage franked	100	100
Interest cover (times)	399.9	46.0
Return on equity (%)	19.0	13.2
Half-year to 30 June	**2003**	**2004**
Revenues ($mn)	60.8	69.2
Operating profit before tax ($mn)	16.4	17.8
Profit after tax ($mn)	11.0	11.3
Earnings per share (¢)	7.2	6.8
Dividend (¢)	4.3	4.3
Percentage franked	100	100
Net tangible assets per share ($)	1.14	1.15
Debt-to-equity ratio (%)	~	8.5
Current ratio	1.7	6.5

Suncorp-Metway Limited

Share price ($)	14.13	
12-month high ($)	14.60	
12-month low ($)	11.65	
Market capitalisation ($mn)	7,598.7	
Price-to-NTA-per-share ratio	2.5	
5-year share price return (% p.a.)	18.8	
Sector: Financials	**Company**	**Sector**
Price-earnings ratio (times)	12.2	12.9
Dividend yield (%)	5.0	5.2

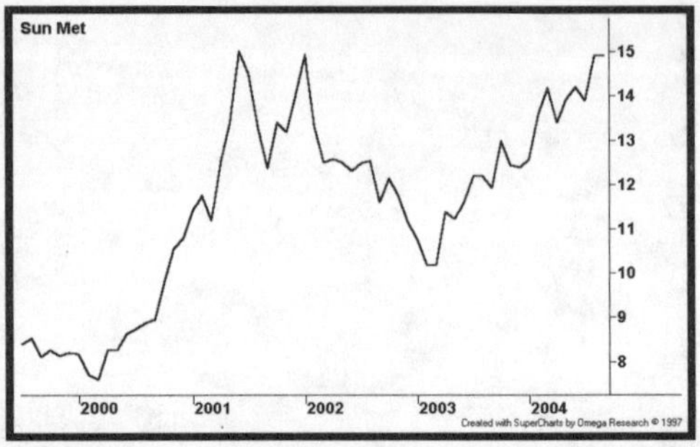

www.suncorp.com.au

Brisbane-based Suncorp-Metway, Queensland's largest company, was formed from the merger of Metway Bank, the Queensland Industry Development Corporation and the insurance company Suncorp. It divides its businesses into three core areas — banking, insurance and wealth management. It is Australia's sixth-largest bank and second-largest general insurance company — the latter under the GIO brand — with some 3.8 million customers.

Latest business results (June 2004, full year)

Suncorp-Metway delivered a superb result, with a big jump in profits and strength across all its businesses. The company's general insurance business was the best performer, with profits nearly doubling. In large part, this was due to increased investment returns. However, the business also benefited from higher prices, increased revenues and a tighter claims environment, based on legislative reforms, which have reined in escalating claims costs. Banking profits were up 17%, with large increases in home loans, business lending and retail deposits, which all grew well ahead of national averages. The bank managed to maintain its lending margins — the difference between interest paid on deposits and interest received on loans — unlike many of the other banks. The company's third main business — wealth management — achieved a 61% increase in profits. Again, this was in large part due to stronger investment returns, though it also reflected a solid improvement in the underlying business performance.

Outlook

Suncorp-Metway now has all its businesses in excellent shape, and it believes it can continue to grow, including through the cross-selling of products to its large customer base. Despite a housing slowdown, it actually managed to boost home lending by 22% in the June 2004 second half, and expects at least 10% growth in the June 2005 year. It also plans a major interstate expansion of its branch network, bringing the number of branches outside Queensland from about 40 at present to around 100 over five years. It also plans a major nationwide push of its GIO insurance business, and believes that — barring no unusual claim event — it can lift profitability, as well as gain market share from competitors. It also expects a further double-digit increase in profits for its wealth management business, as long as equity markets remain firm.

SUN Year to 30 June	2003	2004
Operating income ($mn)	4,022.0	4,594.0
Net interest income ($mn)	592.0	656.0
Operating expenses ($mn)	3,361.0	3,514.0
Operating profit before tax ($mn)	550.0	971.0
Profit after tax ($mn)	384.0	618.0
Earnings per share (¢)	72.7	115.8
Dividend (¢)	56	70
Percentage franked	100	100
Non-interest income to total income (%)	85.3	85.7
Net tangible assets per share ($)	4.90	5.61
Cost-to-income ratio (%)	83.6	76.5
Return on equity (%)	11.0	16.2
Return on assets (%)	1.0	1.5

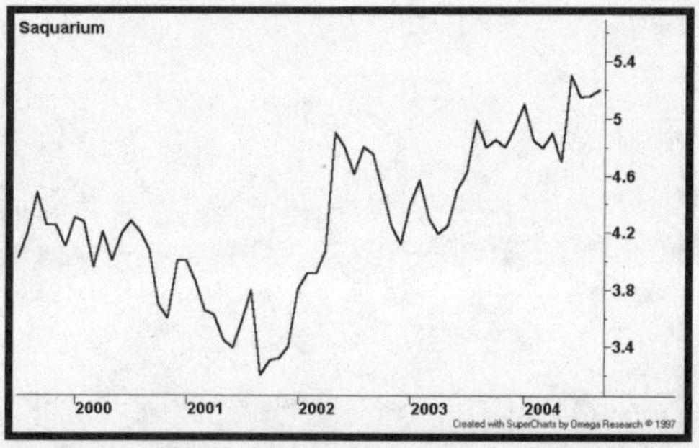

www.sydneyaquarium.com.au

Sydney Aquarium Limited

Share price ($)	5.13	
12-month high ($)	5.60	
12-month low ($)	4.62	
Market capitalisation ($mn)	113.2	
Price-to-NTA-per-share ratio	5.5	
5-year share price return (% p.a.)	9.1	
Sector: Consumer discretionary	**Company**	**Sector**
Price-earnings ratio (times)	17.0	23.8
Dividend yield (%)	5.5	1.5

The Sydney Aquarium at Darling Harbour is one of Australia's most popular tourist attractions, and includes the $14 million Great Barrier Reef Oceanarium and the Shark Bite cafe. The company also owns and operates the long-established Oceanworld Manly, and in mid-2004 it announced the $9-million acquisition of Sydney Tower Observatory, the company which operates the popular Skytour tourist attraction at Sydney Tower.

Latest business results (June 2004, full year)

Profits recovered well after the battering they received in the previous year when global tourism fell into a slump. The second half of the year saw particularly significant growth in both international and domestic tourist activity in Sydney. Total attendance at Sydney Aquarium was up by 9.1% to 1,296,000. Overseas visitors — 57% of the total — increased by 8.6%, thanks to the rugby World Cup and an easing of SARS concerns, which meant that more Asian residents chose to travel abroad. NSW visitor numbers rose 7.3% and a big marketing effort led to a 19.1% jump in interstate visitors. The average revenue per visitor went up 5.6%, thanks especially to higher admission prices and the popularity of the gift shop, which has become one of the highest volume souvenir shops in Sydney. Oceanworld Manly, which contributes about 7% of total company revenues, saw its small profit rise, thanks to the continuing success of its shark dive attraction.

Outlook

Sydney Aquarium is a key attraction for international visitors to Australia, and it is quite dependent on global tourism trends. As long as Australia remains popular with overseas tourists it can expect good business. However, it necessitates a continuing stream of new attractions, such as the recently opened Seal Oceanarium and a novel series of 'behind the scenes' tours. The company has begun work on a major new attraction, the $45-million Australia's Animal World, which is expected to open in mid-2006. The company also sees great potential in its Sydney Tower Observatory acquisition, and is planning the addition of a $5-million SkyWalk attraction, allowing Sydney Tower visitors to view Sydney from a specially constructed turret walkway. This new addition is due to open in April 2005.

SAQ Year to 30 June	2003	2004
Revenues ($mn)	23.6	27.2
EBIT ($mn)	9.1	10.0
EBIT margin (%)	38.5	36.7
Gross margin (%)	58.6	59.9
Operating profit before tax ($mn)	8.4	9.2
Profit after tax ($mn)	6.0	6.6
Earnings per share (¢)	27.8	30.1
Cash flow per share (¢)	36.8	41.9
Dividend (¢)	27	28
Percentage franked	100	100
Net tangible assets per share ($)	0.89	0.93
Interest cover (times)	14.0	13.4
Return on equity (%)	34.0	33.1
Debt-to-equity ratio (%)	47.0	46.0
Current ratio	0.4	0.6

Tasmanian Perpetual Trustees Limited

Share price ($)	14.75	
12-month high ($)	16.95	
12-month low ($)	10.61	
Market capitalisation ($mn)	79.8	
Price-to-NTA-per-share ratio	5.7	
5-year share price return (% p.a.)	15.2	
Sector: Financials	**Company**	**Sector**
Price-earnings ratio (times)	18.5	12.9
Dividend yield (%)	4.4	5.2

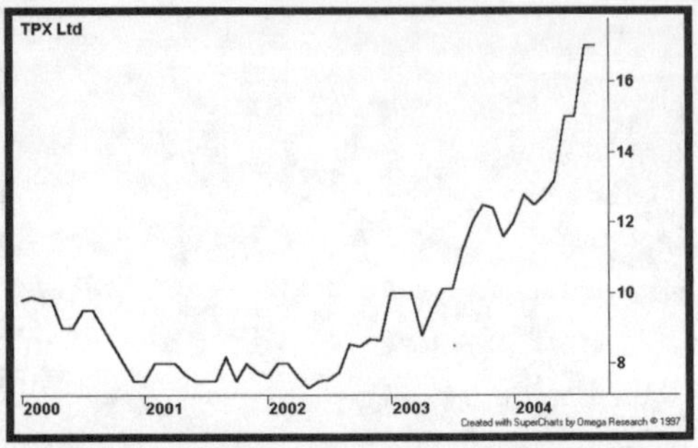

www.tasmanianperpetual.com.au

Tasmanian Perpetual Trustees, with its headquarters in Launceston, was formed from the merger in December 2001 of Tasmanian Trustees and Perpetual Trustees Tasmania. Both companies had been founded in 1887. It engages in traditional trustee services, such as estate planning, will preparation, estate management and powers of attorney, and also offers a range of financial planning and wealth management services. In addition it runs managed funds and it jointly owns Tasmanian Banking Services, in a 50-50 partnership with Bendigo Bank.

Latest business results (June 2004, full year)

Tasmanian Perpetual enjoyed a strong boost to profits, ahead of expectations, as benefits continued to flow from the second full year of the merger. Total funds under management increased by $77 million to $1.2 billion, and during the year $117 million in additional lending to Tasmanian businesses and individuals was approved. There was a $405,000 profit contribution from Tasmanian Banking Services, which experienced strong demand and growth throughout the year.

Outlook

Tasmanian Perpetual Trustees enjoys a strong reputation in its home state, and together with its Tasmanian Banking Services joint venture it is a powerful force in Tasmanian finance, with seven branch offices. It services a quarter of all adult Tasmanian residents, and it has more than 5,000 business and community clients. It is seen as having particular strength in rural services. Since the merger, it has been working to implement the first stages of a growth program, aiming at EPS expansion of at least 8% annually, and it has also been streamlining its internal processes. Thanks to its unique standing in Tasmania, it stands to be a particular beneficiary of the continuing growth in the managed fund and superannuation industries. It has enjoyed particular success with its Axis Retirement Solutions Fund, which provides contributors with a choice of investment strategy. The joint venture Tasmanian Banking Services is showing excellent growth, and as well as making a strong contribution to Tasmanian Perpetual's profits, it also provides considerable synergies, including shared branch offices and the ability to gain new clients. Tasmanian Perpetual management is concerned about the lack of liquidity of the company's shares, and has proposed a share split.

TPX Year to 30 June	2003	2004
Revenues ($mn)	13.6	15.5
EBIT ($mn)	4.3	6.0
EBIT margin (%)	31.2	38.4
Operating profit before tax ($mn)	4.5	6.4
Profit after tax ($mn)	2.8	4.3
Earnings per share (¢)	52.1	79.6
Cash flow per share (¢)	75.4	101.4
Dividend (¢)	45	65
Percentage franked	100	100
Net tangible assets per share ($)	2.09	2.57
Interest cover (times)	~	~
Return on equity (%)	10.8	15.9
Debt-to-equity ratio (%)	~	~
Current ratio	3.6	3.8

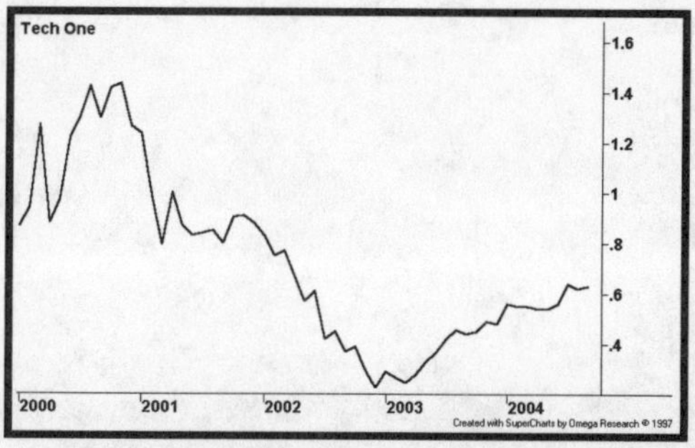

www.technologyonecorp.com

Technology One Limited

Share price ($)	0.63	
12-month high ($)	0.67	
12-month low ($)	0.41	
Market capitalisation ($mn)	191.2	
Price-to-NTA-per-share ratio	6.9	
3-year share price return (% p.a.)	-4.1	
Sector: Information technology	**Company**	**Sector**
Price-earnings ratio (times)	19.8	28.7
Dividend yield (%)	4.5	2.5

Brisbane-based Technology One, founded in 1987, designs, develops, implements and supports financial management and accounting software. It has gained success with its Finance One software product, and enjoys particular strength in local government. Its Student One software is used by many colleges and universities. The company also has a thriving business developing custom software for clients. It operates in Australia, Malaysia and New Zealand.

Latest business results (June 2004, full year)

The company enjoyed an excellent result, with a 7% rise in sales revenues translating into a 35% jump in after-tax profit. The core Finance One financial management product continued to perform strongly, with new licence fee revenue up 54%, and the company gained 74 new clients. The New Zealand office did well, signing 12 new clients. Research and development expenditure of $9.55 million was up 3% from the previous year, and represented 19% of company revenues.

Outlook

Technology One is one of the high-tech companies that listed on the ASX late in 1999, near the height of the dot-com boom. However, unlike virtually all the others, it not only has prospered but has managed a record of five consecutive years of good profits and dividend payouts. It is a conservatively managed company. It devotes considerable amounts towards R&D, and this money is fully expensed as it is incurred, — thus providing a realistic picture of its financial position — rather than being capitalised, as is common among many companies. It has built up a strong balance sheet, and maintains high dividend payouts to its shareholders. Thanks to its continuing innovations, along with a record of good customer support, it has built up a strong position in the highly competitive market for financial software, in both Australia and New Zealand. It believes it can obtain a product leadership position over rivals with its next-generation product, the Connected Intelligence series, due for general distribution from early 2005. The company also plans further international expansion, with the possibility of developing markets in South Africa, China and the UK. It also plans a scaled-down version of its financial management software, Biz One, aimed at smaller and medium-sized enterprises.

TNE Year to 30 June	2003	2004
Revenues ($mn)	47.0	50.5
Service delivery (%)	62	69
Software engineering (%)	33	27
EBIT ($mn)	9.3	12.2
EBIT margin (%)	19.7	24.1
Operating profit before tax ($mn)	10.1	13.1
Profit after tax ($mn)	7.0	9.5
Earnings per share (¢)	2.3	3.2
Cash flow per share (¢)	2.8	3.7
Dividend (¢)	2.5	2.85
Percentage franked	100	100
Net tangible assets per share ($)	0.08	0.09
Interest cover (times)	~	~
Return on equity (%)	19.4	26.1
Debt-to-equity ratio (%)	~	~
Current ratio	3.6	3.4

Timbercorp Limited

Share price ($)	1.60	
12-month high ($)	1.69	
12-month low ($)	1.08	
Market capitalisation ($mn)	352.2	
Price-to-NTA-per-share ratio	1.8	
5-year share price return (% p.a.)	1.8	
Sector: Materials	**Company**	**Sector**
Price-earnings ratio (times)	12.4	14.3
Dividend yield (%)	2.2	2.6

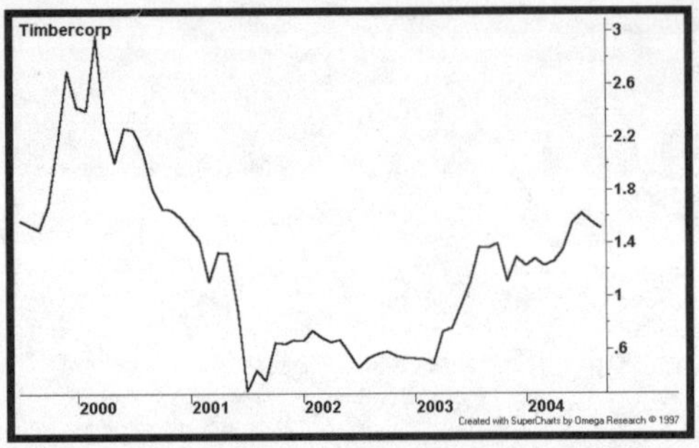

www.timbercorp.com.au

Melbourne-based Timbercorp, established in 1992, is a prominent agribusiness company. It promotes plantation projects for outside investors, provides finance and manages the properties, receiving recurring annuity-style income — including licence fees, rent and management fees — for its services. The investments are intended for long-term investors, and offer the promise of substantial tax benefits, along with potentially high returns. The company's primary plantations are 74,000 hectares of blue gums in the Green Triangle region of Victoria-South Australia and in Western Australia. It also manages a 2,700-hectare olive tree plantation — one of the largest in the world — in central Victoria. With Select Harvests it has moved into the almond orchard business, with plantings of more than 3,600 hectares. In 2004 it expanded into grape and citrus plantings. It is a substantial shareholder in Select Harvests and in the listed olive oil marketer Piquant Blue.

Latest business results (March 2004, half-year)

Timbercorp recorded another good result, driven by a growing stream of annuity-style income, which rose 24% from the March 2003 half to nearly $39 million, with an EBIT contribution of $16.4 million, which was up 15%. New business revenue for the period grew 13% to $5.1 million. There was a particularly strong contribution from the company's recent moves into almond cultivation, and timber plantations also provided good growth.

TIM Year to 30 September*	2002	2003
Revenues ($mn)	100.5	108.7
Forestry (%)	38	37
Almonds (%)	29	32
Olives (%)	25	24
EBIT ($mn)	44.9	48.6
EBIT margin (%)	44.7	44.7
Operating profit before tax ($mn)	38.0	44.1
Profit after tax ($mn)	23.2	27.1
Earnings per share (¢)	9.0**	12.9
Cash flow per share (¢)	11.0**	15.6
Dividend (¢)	2.5	3.5
Percentage franked	100	100
Interest cover (times)	6.5	11.0
Return on equity (%)	11.4**	12.9

* 15 months to September 2002

** annualised figure

Half-year to 31 March	2003	2004
Revenues ($mn)	41.0	52.8
Operating profit before tax ($mn)	8.2	8.8
Profit after tax ($mn)	5.1	5.6
Earnings per share (¢)	1.5	1.7
Dividend (¢)	0	0
Percentage franked	~	~
Net tangible assets per share ($)	0.88	0.88
Debt-to-equity ratio (%)	54.2	53.1
Current ratio	1.0	1.2

Outlook

Timbercorp's shares have been strong performers in recent years as the company's business model starts to provide evidence of great future potential. In July 2004 it announced that its September 2004 full-year after-tax profit would be more than $40 million, or 50% higher than in the previous year. It expected revenues to be up by around 45%, to at least $162 million. This would include a 30% jump in annuity-style revenue to at least $85 million and new sales revenue of $77 million. The new sales would contribute to further growth in annuity-style revenue to more than $110 million in September 2005.

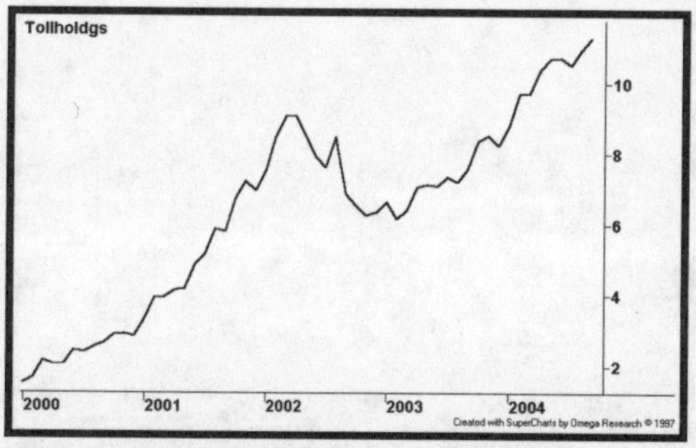

www.toll.com.au

Toll Holdings Limited

Share price ($)	10.42	
12-month high ($)	11.20	
12-month low ($)	6.75	
Market capitalisation ($mn)	3,422.2	
Price-to-NTA-per-share ratio	3.5	
5-year share price return (% p.a.)	57.4	
Sector: Industrials	**Company**	**Sector**
Price-earnings ratio (times)	19.6	14.8
Dividend yield (%)	2.0	4.2

Melbourne-based Toll Holdings was founded in Newcastle in 1888. It is today a giant transportation, warehousing and freight logistics company. It has one million square metres of warehouse space, it manages the ports of Geelong and Hastings and it has moved into rail freight, with the Pacific National joint venture with Patrick Corporation. It has also bought New Zealand's Tranz Rail.

Latest business results (June 2004, full year)

Toll Holdings' continuing expansion powered it to another surge in sales and profits, with solid contributions from all main businesses of the company. Toll derives over 40% of its income from the food, beverage and retail sectors, and thanks to the strength of the Australian economy, these businesses continued to deliver excellent returns. There was also strong demand for Toll's services from the automotive sector, which represents a further 10% of revenues. The company's margins continued to improve, thanks to significant investment in new depot and warehouse facilities, technology development and integration benefits from past acquisitions. There was a maiden contribution from Tranz Rail, acquired in October 2003, of $415 million in revenues and EBIT of $42 million. Pacific National contributed after-tax equity earnings of $42 million for the year, up from $28 million in the previous year, thanks in particular to increased coal transportation.

Outlook

Toll has become a transportation and logistics powerhouse, with rapidly growing businesses and a surging share price. It has already forecast another record profit for the June 2005 year. It is working to transform the transportation of goods in Australia, through integrated high-tech road, rail, port and warehousing services. It views Australia's vast rail freight infrastructure as inefficient and under-utilised and desires to create a modern network, based on its acquisition of Pacific National, formerly the rail freight operations of the federal and NSW governments. In August 2004, Pacific National paid $285 million for Freight Australia, Victoria's rail freight operator and track owner. Toll sees considerable potential in working with large retail chains in achieving long-term cost reductions through greater supply chain efficiencies. It is working to restructure its new rail business in New Zealand.

TOL Year to 30 June	2003	2004
Revenues ($mn)	2,569.8	3,271.9
Networks (%)	48	48
Logistics (%)	36	35
Toll North (%)	18	17
EBIT ($mn)	156.7	235.2
EBIT margin (%)	6.1	7.2
Operating profit before tax ($mn)	137.4	212.1
Profit after tax ($mn)	106.1	168.6
Earnings per share (¢)	35.9	53.3
Cash flow per share (¢)	61.9	89.4
Dividend (¢)	14.5	20.5
Percentage franked	100	100
Net tangible assets per share ($)	1.69	2.97
Interest cover (times)	8.1	10.2
Return on equity (%)	20.6	20.0
Debt-to-equity ratio (%)	41.7	29.0
Current ratio	1.0	1.1

Troy Resources NL

Share price ($)	2.63	
12-month high ($)	3.33	
12-month low ($)	1.58	
Market capitalisation ($mn)	130.9	
Price-to-NTA-per-share ratio	3.9	
5-year share price return (% p.a.)	61.7	
Sector: Materials	**Company**	**Sector**
Price-earnings ratio (times)	10.2	14.3
Dividend yield (%)	2.3	2.6

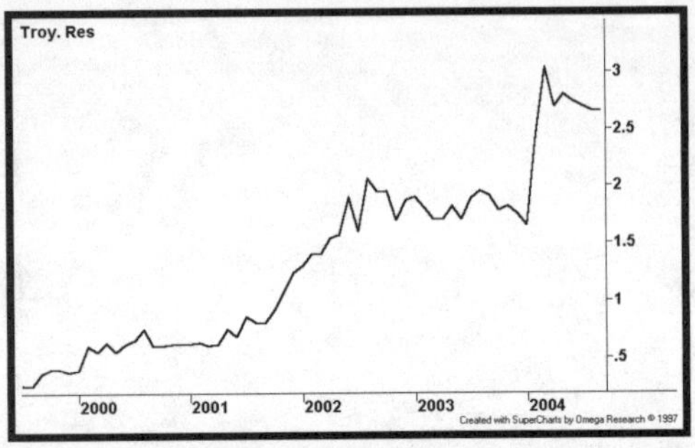

www.try.com.au

Perth-based Troy Resources, founded in 1984, is among the 10 largest Australian-owned gold mining companies. It operates from three mines. It owns the Bulchina mine in the Sandstone region of Western Australia, and has a 49% stake with partners Sons of Gwalia in the Cornishman mine in the Southern Cross area of Western Australia. Its third resource is a 70% holding in the Sertão mine in the state of Goiás in central Brazil, which was officially opened in 2003.

Latest business results (June 2004, full year)

Higher gold prices and increased production were behind a big jump in Troy's sales and profits. It was the company's fifth consecutive record profit. The Bulchina mine produced a total of 34,123 ounces for the year, which was 20% less than in the June 2003 year, due to the cessation of mining during April and lower-grade ore. Troy's share of production of the Cornishman mine was 27,973 ounces, a 70% rise on the previous year. Production costs rose at both mines. The Sertão mine began production only in April 2003. In the year to June 2004 Troy's share of its production was 59,752 ounces, with an average cost of just $64 per ounce. Some analysts believe Sertão might be the lowest-cost gold mine in the world.

Outlook

Troy's immediate outlook is for a decline in production. Mining finished at the Cornishman mine in February 2004, with treatment of stockpiled ore due to be completed during 2004. The company says the financial problems of its partner in the mine, Sons of Gwalia, will have minimal impact. Mining work has also largely been suspended at Bulchina, though will be replaced by mining at two recent discoveries nearby, the Lord Henry and Lord Nelson deposits. The company is fast-tracking development of these, and expects mining to begin early in 2005. In Brazil, the company will continue test drilling at numerous sites within the Sertão project area, hoping to find extensions to the Sertão deposit, or new deposits. With no debt, and more than $24 million in cash holdings, the company maintains an active exploration policy, and is also ready to expand by acquisition.

TRY Year to 30 June	2003	2004
Revenues ($mn)	40.8	85.1
EBIT ($mn)	9.4	22.0
EBIT margin (%)	23.1	25.9
Gross margin (%)	41.5	38.5
Operating profit before tax ($mn)	9.5	22.8
Profit after tax ($mn)	5.6	14.1
Earnings per share (¢)	10.5	25.7
Cash flow per share (¢)	19.1	46.5
Dividend (¢)	5.5	6
Percentage franked	100	100
Net tangible assets per share ($)	0.55	0.67
Interest cover (times)	~	~
Return on equity (%)	24.2	43.8
Debt-to-equity ratio (%)	~	~
Current ratio	1.9	6.8

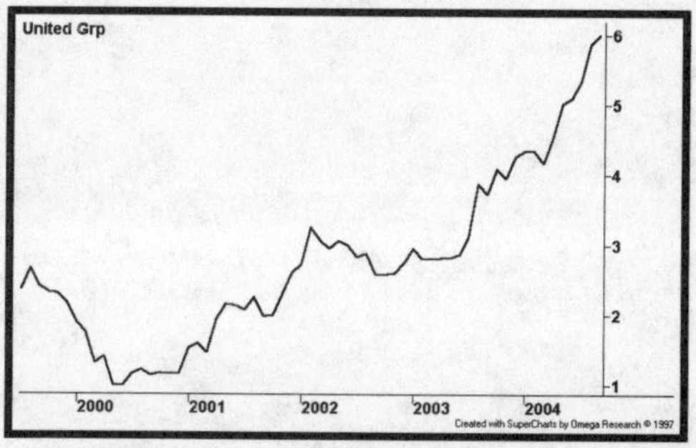

www.unitedgroup.com.au

United Group Limited

Share price ($)	5.63	
12-month high ($)	5.80	
12-month low ($)	3.38	
Market capitalisation ($mn)	563.0	
Price-to-NTA-per-share ratio	6.0	
5-year share price return (% p.a.)	26.0	
Sector: Industrials	**Company**	**Sector**
Price-earnings ratio (times)	19.3	14.8
Dividend yield (%)	3.2	4.2

Sydney-based United Group is one of Australia's leading engineering companies, with specialties in power supply, water and waste management, defence, resources engineering, telecommunications and heavy haulage railways. It groups its activities into four businesses: United Goninan is a leader in railway manufacturing, maintenance and engineering; United KG is engaged in engineering, construction, facilities management and industrial maintenance businesses; United KFPW provides corporate property services; and United Gooder is a New Zealand engineering and construction business.

Latest business results (June 2004, full year)

The company achieved its third successive year of profit growth exceeding 30%. The United Goninan division was the key, recording 34% profit growth, with revenues up 10%, thanks to increased rail infrastructure spending in NSW, growing demand for rolling stock in Australia's resources sector, and a stronger presence in Asia. The buoyant resources environment helped United KG boost revenues 41%. However, profits fell, with the division unable to maintain the high margins of the previous year. The relatively small United KFPW division achieved 40% growth in revenues, and profits up 37%, with important business from government departments and from major corporations such as Telstra and the National Australia Bank. A turnaround in New Zealand operations handed the United Gooder division a 19% rise in revenues, with profits soaring eightfold. United Group's order book remained steady at $2.3 billion, with over 70% of this amount in long-term contracts.

Outlook

For several years United Group has been working to lay the groundwork for sustainable long-term expansion, and its medium-term target is earnings growth of 10% to 15% each year, though it believes it can again exceed this in the June 2005 year. It is working to boost its presence in Asia, and has acquired from Thames Water a series of projects in Australia, Singapore and Malaysia. It plans to use these businesses as a platform for expansion into other sectors. It is also actively seeking further acquisitions. In addition, it is working to give itself a competitive advantage in its projects by forming a series of partnerships with global leaders, such as Siemens, GE Transportation Systems and Balfour Beatty.

UGL Year to 30 June	2003	2004
Revenues ($mn)	855.2	1,076.9
Construction & fabrication (%)	40	47
Service & maintenance (%)	49	42
Property management (%)	5	7
Facilities management (%)	5	4
EBIT ($mn)	37.0	43.9
EBIT margin (%)	4.3	4.1
Operating profit before tax ($mn)	31.0	38.5
Profit after tax ($mn)	21.9	29.1
Earnings per share (¢)	24.0	29.1
Cash flow per share (¢)	39.6	45.6
Dividend (¢)	14	18
Percentage franked	100	100
Net tangible assets per share ($)	0.69	0.93
Interest cover (times)	6.1	8.1
Return on equity (%)	15.1	17.4
Debt-to-equity ratio (%)	26.1	22.5
Current ratio	1.3	1.3

Volante Group Limited

Share price ($)	1.34	
12-month high ($)	1.55	
12-month low ($)	1.01	
Market capitalisation ($mn)	172.8	
Price-to-NTA-per-share ratio	4.8	
3-year share price return (% p.a.)	15.1	
Sector: Information technology	**Company**	**Sector**
Price-earnings ratio (times)	15.4	28.7
Dividend yield (%)	6.3	2.5

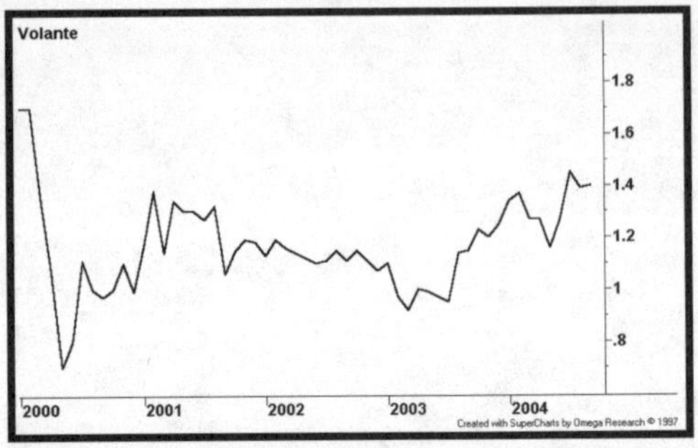

www.volante.com.au

Sydney company Volante Group is an IT procurement and services specialist, working with corporations and government departments through five divisions: Volante Systems provides a huge range of procurement and technical services to a large customer base; Volante Solutions is a provider of a large range of IT products and services; Affinity IT Recruitment specialises in providing permanent and contracting recruitment services to the IT industry; Global Remarketing is Australia's largest refurbisher and supplier of second-hand IT products; and Ipex Manufacturing, acquired in February 2004, designs, manufactures and installs IT systems to corporate and government clients, and provides support services.

Latest business results (June 2004, full year)

The Ipex acquisition — included in Volante's accounts from February 2004 — helped the company to a big leap in sales and revenues, though even without the acquisition there was a 20% increase in earnings. The results were helped by a string of big contracts, and a major restructuring of the company that followed the Ipex deal.

Outlook

Volante is one of just a handful of high-tech companies listed near the height of the dot-com boom late in 1999 that has flourished to the extent that it has been able to report five consecutive years of profits and dividend payouts. It has been transformed by the acquisition of Ipex, which has become its biggest division, and it now believes that it has the scale to compete against the giant multi-national computer companies for major corporate and government IT contracts. It hopes to benefit from a trend — especially among government departments — to favour local companies for IT services. Recent new deals include renewal of a $40-million-per-year contract to supply government agencies with computer services until 2009; a $6.7-million contract to maintain and support the Department of Finance and Administration's IT infrastructure for three years; and a $16-million, four-year contract to provide IT services to the Department of Transport and Regional Services. The company believes it can win a significant amount of new work from South Australian government departments, and has 100 staff members there for this purpose. It is also interested in expansion to New Zealand, but has ruled out entering other offshore markets.

VGL Year to 30 June	2003	2004
Revenues ($mn)	324.5	345.4
EBIT ($mn)	6.7	12.0
EBIT margin (%)	2.1	3.5
Operating profit before tax ($mn)	6.4	11.4
Profit after tax ($mn)	4.1	7.6
Earnings per share (¢)	6.1	8.7
Cash flow per share (¢)	11.6	21.9
Dividend (¢)	8	8.5
Percentage franked	100	100
Net tangible assets per share ($)	0.28	0.28
Interest cover (times)	20.6	21.7
Return on equity (%)	10.1	9.1
Debt-to-equity ratio (%)	~	~
Current ratio	1.6	1.2

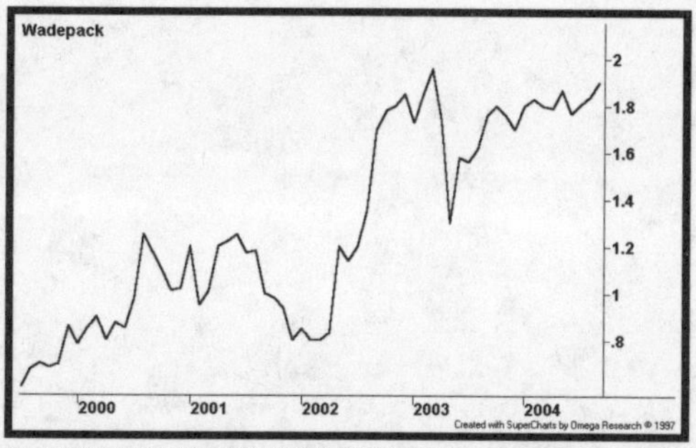

www.wadepack.com.au

Wadepack Limited

Share price ($)	1.83	
12-month high ($)	1.90	
12-month low ($)	1.60	
Market capitalisation ($mn)	57.5	
Price-to-NTA-per-share ratio	1.8	
5-year share price return (% p.a.)	26.8	
Sector: Industrials	**Company**	**Sector**
Price-earnings ratio (times)	10.8	14.8
Dividend yield (%)	4.1	4.2

Sydney-based Wadepack is a small, specialist printing and packaging company that was founded in 1947, and has grown through a series of mergers and acquisitions. Today it has activities in Sydney and Melbourne. Its product range includes individual cartons, beverage baskets, display cartons, tissue boxes, window-faced cartons, blister cards and box and lid sets. Among its activities, it supplies 80% of Australia's pharmaceutical companies with part of their packaging, it is a major supplier of CD packaging and promotional printing for the music industry, it prints around 80% of Australian takeaway popcorn packaging and it is a significant supplier of printed packaging for takeaway food supplier KFC.

Latest business results (June 2004, half-year)

The company's half-year profits rebounded, after a sharp fall in the June 2003 half. However, the rise was only modest, despite buoyant economic conditions, with intense competition in the packaging business a continuing negative for the company. Lower borrowing costs — following the repayment of some debt — helped the result, and the company also has been achieving increases in efficiency from the commissioning of its Roland 706 printing press and from the closure late in 2003 of its Brisbane facility.

Outlook

Wadepack operates in a competitive business that is dominated by giant and highly efficient companies such as Amcor and Visy. As a result, it must be nimble to get business and maintain growth, and the company's profit record and share price performance have been volatile, although the long-term average performance has been sound. It has had success in various niche areas of the market, and offers specialist in-house skills in fields like foil stamping, embossing, heat seal coating and carton and form design. Among its achievements, it has worked with brand names like Libra and Macleans on holographic foil packs that help their products stand out, it has helped Cadbury Schweppes to design innovative new Easter egg packaging and it has worked with pharmaceuticals companies to incorporate Braille lettering onto packaging.

WDP Year to 31 December	2002	2003
Revenues ($mn)	84.9	79.0
EBIT ($mn)	13.0	8.0
EBIT margin (%)	15.3	10.2
Gross margin (%)	25.3	21.4
Operating profit before tax ($mn)	11.1	6.7
Profit after tax ($mn)	7.6	5.3
Earnings per share (¢)	24.1	17.0
Cash flow per share (¢)	33.7	28.2
Dividend (¢)	5	7.5
Percentage franked	100	100
Interest cover (times)	7.0	5.8
Return on equity (%)	24.9	15.1
Half-year to 30 June	**2003**	**2004**
Revenues ($mn)	36.8	38.9
Operating profit before tax ($mn)	2.9	3.1
Profit after tax ($mn)	2.0	2.0
Earnings per share (¢)	6.3	6.5
Dividend (¢)	3.5	5
Percentage franked	100	100
Net tangible assets per share ($)	0.94	1.04
Debt-to-equity ratio (%)	55.0	39.8
Current ratio	1.4	1.4

Wesfarmers Limited

Share price ($)	29.00	
12-month high ($)	30.50	
12-month low ($)	24.45	
Market capitalisation ($mn)	10,997.1	
Price-to-NTA-per-share ratio	5.9	
5-year share price return (% p.a.)	25.8	
Sector: Industrials	**Company**	**Sector**
Price-earnings ratio (times)	19.1	14.8
Dividend yield (%)	4.8	4.2

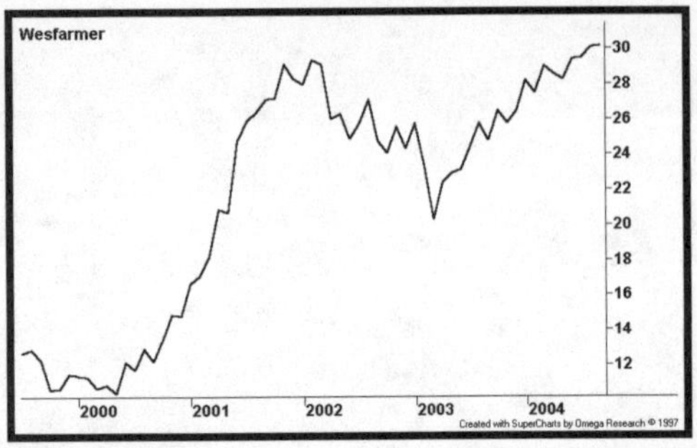

www.wesfarmers.com.au

Perth-based Wesfarmers, founded in 1914 as a farmers' cooperative, is a major force in rural business. It manufactures fertilisers and agricultural chemicals, and it operates the Bunnings and Hardwarehouse chains of hardware stores. It has forestry interests, is a coal miner and a supplier of liquefied petroleum gas (LPG). It is also engaged in numerous businesses related to livestock, wool, real estate, insurance and finance. In August 2003, it sold its Landmark rural services business.

Latest business results (June 2004, full year)

Wesfarmers continued to power ahead, with another strong profit result. The Bunnings hardware business was again the star, with a double-digit boost to sales and profits, despite a marked slowdown in the June quarter. The high-margin energy business recorded a sharp decline in profits, though much of this reflected the sale in the previous year of the Girrah coal deposit. However, the division was also hurt by higher costs, lower coking coal prices and by the dollar's appreciation. The industrial and safety products business achieved higher sales, but profits edged down, due mainly to problems at one business unit. The new insurance division achieved excellent results, thanks to a buoyant insurance environment and an eight-and-a-half month contribution from an acquisition. The chemicals and fertilisers business was also strong, and the company received a $304 million after-tax profit from the sale of its Landmark rural services business, recorded as a significant item.

WES Year to 30 June	2003	2004
Revenues ($mn)	7,425.8	7,451.5
Hardware (%)	45	46
Industrial & safety distribution (%)	14	14
Energy (%)	14	12
Insurance (%)	3	10
Chemicals & fertilisers (%)	6	6
Rural services (%)	17	3
EBIT ($mn)	779.3	886.9
EBIT margin (%)	10.5	11.9
Gross margin (%)	28.5	30.3
Operating profit before tax ($mn)	708.1	832.4
Profit after tax ($mn)	481.9	569.2
Earnings per share (¢)	127.9	151.5
Cash flow per share (¢)	205.5	225.8
Dividend (¢)	127	140
Percentage franked	100	100
Net tangible assets per share ($)	5.95	4.94
Interest cover (times)	11.0	16.3
Return on equity (%)	13.5	16.1
Debt-to-equity ratio (%)	23.5	45.3
Current ratio	1.4	1.5

Outlook

Wesfarmers has been a stock market powerhouse, with surging revenues, profits and share price over many years. However, there is now concern that the company has reached the top of the cycle for some of its businesses. The Bunnings warehouse operation has been a huge beneficiary of the boom in housing and home renovations, but it is now facing growing competition at a time when the housing market seems to have entered a downturn. Many analysts believe the insurance business too is near the top of its cycle. However, the prospects appear strong for the energy operations. In addition, Wesfarmers continues to actively seek out business ventures or acquisitions that offer the potential for new streams of growth.

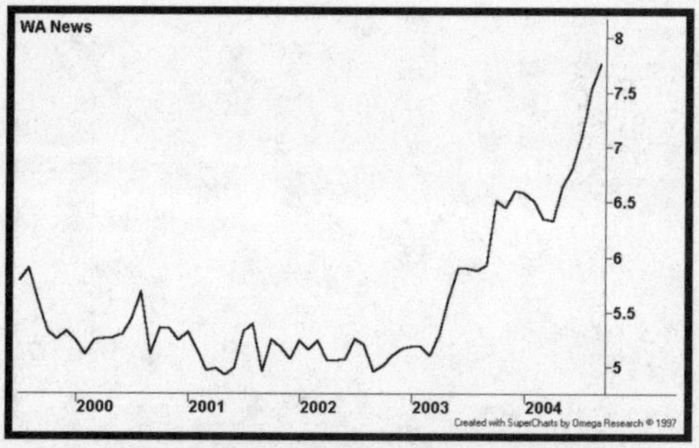

www.thewest.com.au

West Australian Newspapers Holdings Limited

Share price ($)	7.40	
12-month high ($)	7.50	
12-month low ($)	5.80	
Market capitalisation ($mn)	1,567.3	
Price-to-NTA-per-share ratio	18.1	
5-year share price return (% p.a.)	12.7	
Sector: Consumer discretionary	**Company**	**Sector**
Price-earnings ratio (times)	19.5	23.8
Dividend yield (%)	5.1	1.5

West Australian Newspapers Holdings is the publisher of *The West Australian*, founded in 1833, and one of Australia's leading regional daily newspapers. The company also publishes *The West Magazine*, the weekly farming periodical *Countryman*, the classified advertising weekly *Quokka* and a string of country newspapers. It also operates a flourishing commercial printing business and it owns Redwave Media, which manages radio stations.

Latest business results (June 2004, full year)

The buoyant Western Australian economy gave the company a large boost to its profits. *The West Australian* newspaper — representing nearly 80% of company revenues and 90% of profits — saw advertising revenue up 6.4% and circulation revenue up 3.5%. There was particularly strong growth in real estate and employment advertising. Actual circulation figures were little changed, but circulation revenues were boosted by the rise in the cover price of the popular Saturday edition. Operating costs for the newspaper edged up just 0.6%, thanks to a 3.7% decline in newsprint expenditure. Increased advertising revenues and stringent cost controls led to higher profits at *The West Magazine*, the *Countryman*, *Quokka* and at the company's regional newspapers. Commercial printing profits soared fourfold, reflecting the introduction of commercial charges for inter-company printing work and the benefits of a major overhaul of the plant. Redwave Media, acquired in July 2003, provided an initial contribution to profits.

Outlook

The company occupies a prominent position within Western Australia, and its fortunes are to a large degree linked to trends in the state's economy. Like other newspaper companies, it has high fixed costs, meaning that its profits can soar when times are good and then drop sharply when the economy turns down. With consumer demand and employment levels remaining high in Western Australia, the near-term outlook looks positive. However, the company has been struggling to find means of achieving new channels of growth. Its foray into commercial radio is one step, and it has also launched a commercial website. The share price has been supported by continual speculation that West Australian Newspapers could be acquired by one of the major media groups.

WAN Year to 30 June	2003	2004
Revenues ($mn)	317.4	347.2
EBIT ($mn)	98.7	119.8
EBIT margin (%)	31.1	34.5
Operating profit before tax ($mn)	90.9	111.7
Profit after tax ($mn)	64.0	79.5
Earnings per share (¢)	30.7	38.0
Cash flow per share (¢)	38.9	46.1
Dividend (¢)	30	38
Percentage franked	100	100
Net tangible assets per share ($)	0.39	0.41
Interest cover (times)	12.6	14.7
Return on equity (%)	42.0	43.6
Debt-to-equity ratio (%)	81.7	68.2
Current ratio	1.8	1.8

Westpac Banking Corporation

Share price ($)	16.26	
12-month high ($)	18.28	
12-month low ($)	15.00	
Market capitalisation ($mn)	29,064.6	
Price-to-NTA-per-share ratio	2.5	
5-year share price return (% p.a.)	17.6	
Sector: Financials	**Company**	**Sector**
Price-earnings ratio (times)	13.6	12.9
Dividend yield (%)	4.8	5.2

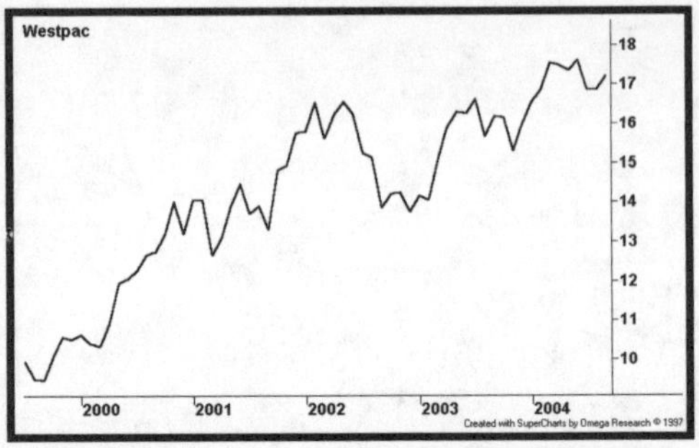

www.westpac.com.au

Westpac, which began trading in 1817 as the Bank of New South Wales, is the smallest of Australia's big four banks, with interests in most areas of financial services. Around 15% of revenues and profit come from New Zealand, where Westpac Trust is one of that country's leading banks. It has moved strongly into wealth management, with the acquisition of BT Financial Group, Rothschild Australia Asset Management and Hastings Funds Management.

Latest business results (March 2004, half-year)

The company saw another excellent result, with a strong performance by all business units. The increase in profit was driven by resilient household credit growth and a particularly strong increase in deposits, as well as non-interest income growth from the wealth management businesses. Operating expense growth was contained to 4%, despite increases in several compliance costs, higher superannuation expenses and rising personnel costs. Bad debt charges of $207 million were down from the prior corresponding period. There was a pleasing resumption of profit growth in New Zealand.

Outlook

With its focus on Australia and New Zealand, Westpac is now working to boost efficiency across all areas of its operations. Its particular goal is to be able to offer the best customer service of all the banks by September 2005. Despite initial fund outflows following the BT acquisition, the bank is now achieving significant synergies as it integrates this business with its other wealth management operations. It has been reducing its exposure to investor housing lending, in order to lessen risk in the event of any sharp housing downturn. It is also working to gain market share in the small business sector, where it lags its rivals, and has been achieving success with its revitalised business banking operations. It also hopes to boost its insurance business, and there has been speculation that it might seek a merger with AMP. It is realising particularly robust growth from its operations in New Zealand, where it has been gaining market share in several sectors.

WBC Year to 30 September	2002	2003
Operating income ($mn)	7,263.0	7,330.0
Net interest income ($mn)	4,285.0	4,344.0
Operating expenses ($mn)	3,995.0	3,926.0
Operating profit before tax ($mn)	2,807.0	2,919.0
Profit after tax ($mn)	2,192.0	2,183.0
Earnings per share (¢)	121.0	119.7
Dividend (¢)	70	78
Percentage franked	100	100
Non-interest income to total income (%)	41.0	40.7
Cost-to-income ratio (%)	55.0	53.6
Return on equity (%)	21.8	17.9
Return on assets (%)	1.2	1.1
Half-year to 31 March	**2003**	**2004**
Operating income ($mn)	3,537.0	3,878.0
Operating profit before tax ($mn)	1,388.0	1,662.0
Profit after tax ($mn)	1,051.0	1,225.0
Earnings per share (¢)	56.0	62.1
Dividend (¢)	38	42
Percentage franked	100	100
Net tangible assets per share ($)	5.46	6.43

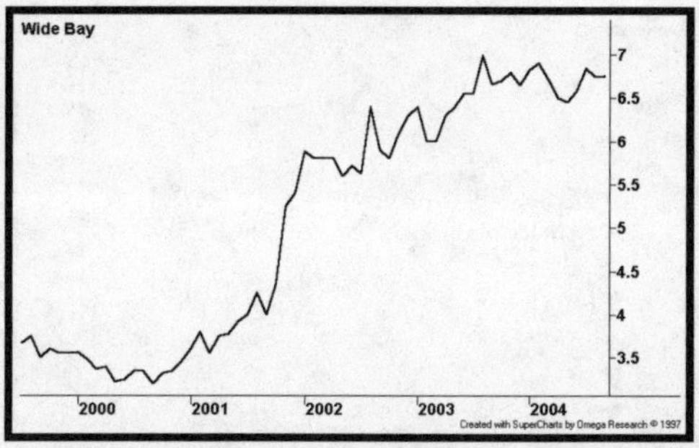

www.widebaycap.com.au

Wide Bay Australia Limited

Share price ($)	6.87	
12-month high ($)	7.25	
12-month low ($)	6.40	
Market capitalisation ($mn)	139.7	
Price-to-NTA-per-share ratio	1.7	
5-year share price return (% p.a.)	20.1	
Sector: Financials	**Company**	**Sector**
Price-earnings ratio (times)	14.1	12.9
Dividend yield (%)	4.9	5.2

Based in Bundaberg in Queensland, Wide Bay Australia — formerly known as Wide Bay Capricorn Building Society — was founded in 1979 from the merger of two smaller building societies. It is a leading provider of financial services in south-east and central Queensland, with a network of 30 branches and 80,000 customers, and is one of Queensland's largest non-bank deposit-taking institutions. It operates a financial planning joint venture with Financial Technologies Securities. A 44%-owned subsidiary, Fincom, is marketing automatic telling machine technology and software in Australia and abroad.

Latest business results (June 2004, full year)

Income and profits edged up. Lending for the year totalled $485.4 million, up more than 28% from the previous year. Outstanding loans, including loans under management, rose 15% to $1.17 billion. This reflected not only the increased lending but also a slowing in the churning of loans, particularly in the southern capital cities. Profits would have been higher but for the application of an accounting standard that reduced the reportable profit from Wide Bay Australia's wholly owned mortgage insurance business, Mortgage Risk Management, from an anticipated $1.2 million to $432,000.

Outlook

Wide Bay Australia will likely be hurt by any slowdown in the housing market, although it could be protected to a degree by the buoyancy of the Queensland economy. It has lending activities in NSW, Victoria and South Australia, using mortgage brokers and specialist loan introducers, and is working to bolster this business through the opening in August 2004 of its first interstate branch, in Sydney. It believes the branch will lift its profile in NSW, and attract additional direct business, including for non-lending products such as deposits, insurance and banking services. The company expects significant cost savings from its new mortgage documentation electronic processing system, which was due to be fully operational by the end of October 2004, and which will also enable Wide Bay to expand its lending program at minimal cost. There has been widespread speculation that Wide Bay might be acquired by one of the banks, or could seek a merger with another large building society, and it is believed that Wide Bay and The Rock Building Society have held merger discussions.

WBB Year to 30 June	2003	2004
Operating income ($mn)	33.8	37.5
Net interest income ($mn)	24.8	26.9
Operating expenses ($mn)	20.5	23.5
Operating profit before tax ($mn)	13.3	14.0
Profit after tax ($mn)	9.2	9.9
Earnings per share (¢)	45.5	48.7
Dividend (¢)	32	34
Percentage franked	100	100
Non-interest income to total income (%)	26.8	28.1
Net tangible assets per share ($)	3.96	3.94
Cost-to-income ratio (%)	60.7	62.7
Return on equity (%)	11.7	12.3
Return on assets (%)	1.3	1.2

Woodside Petroleum Limited

	Company	Sector
Share price ($)	18.37	
12-month high ($)	19.13	
12-month low ($)	12.92	
Market capitalisation ($mn)	12,300.0	
Price-to-NTA-per-share ratio	4.1	
5-year share price return (% p.a.)	14.7	
Sector: Energy	**Company**	**Sector**
Price-earnings ratio (times)	23.3	18.4
Dividend yield (%)	2.5	2.4

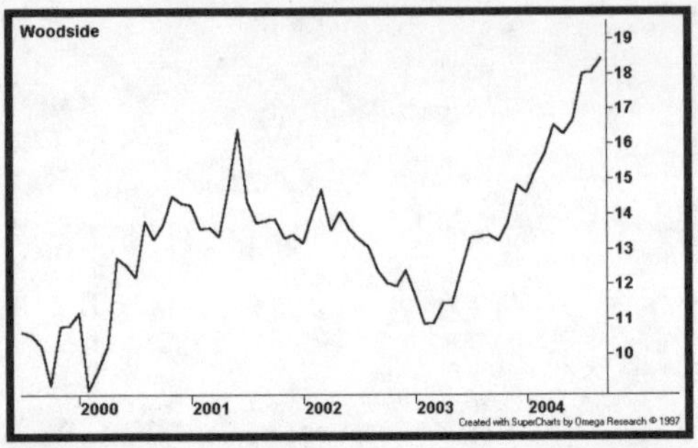

www.woodside.com.au

Perth-based Woodside, founded in 1954, is Australia's largest listed specialist energy company. Its major interest is the North West Shelf project off Western Australia, which supplies liquefied natural gas for Asia, natural gas for the domestic market and liquefied petroleum gas, crude oil and condensate for international markets. It also has major exploration and development interests in Western Australia. It is operator of oil and gas discoveries in offshore Mauritania, is a partner in gas and condensate production in Algeria and has exploration interests in the US, Libya, Kenya, Sierra Leone and the Canary Islands. Shell Australia owns 34% of Woodside's equity.

Latest business results (June 2004, half-year)

Strong energy prices helped Woodside to a solid rise in profits. The company also made a large $373.6 million after-tax profit on the sale of its 40% equity in the Enfield oil development, which it reported as a significant item. Production of 28 million barrels of oil equivalent (boe) was down from 29.9 million in the June 2003 half. Sales volumes were down 9.6%. During the period the average oil price increased 22%, but a 19% increase in the average A$/US$ exchange rate partially offset this. There was also a solid contribution to profits from unrealised foreign-exchange gains.

WPL Year to 31 December	2002	2003
Revenues ($mn)	2,240.6	2,059.3
EBIT ($mn)	1,109.1	854.2
EBIT margin (%)	49.5	41.5
Gross margin (%)	57.7	61.2
Operating profit before tax ($mn)	1,063.1	827.9
Profit after tax ($mn)	729.4	526.7
Earnings per share (¢)	109.4	79.0
Cash flow per share (¢)	150.8	114.0
Dividend (¢)	39	46
Percentage franked	100	100
Interest cover (times)	24.1	32.5
Return on equity (%)	29.9	22.2
Half-year to 30 June	**2003**	**2004**
Revenues ($mn)	1,118.6	994.4
Operating profit before tax ($mn)	436.8	541.2
Profit after tax ($mn)	272.2	351.0
Earnings per share (¢)	40.8	52.6
Dividend (¢)	21	27
Percentage franked	100	100
Net tangible assets per share ($)	3.00	4.49
Debt-to-equity ratio (%)	61.9	13.3
Current ratio	1.1	2.3

Outlook

Woodside has a 20-year supply agreement, starting from 1989, with eight Japanese electric power and gas companies to supply 7.5 million tonnes annually of LNG, and this underpins profits. Its business will receive a boost from a $25 billion contract to supply China's Guangdong Province with three million tonnes of North West Shelf LNG annually for 25 years from 2005 to 2006. The company's target is to raise its total output from 58 million boe in 2004 to 80 million in 2007. It sees enormous potential in its Mauritania oil ventures, and believes these will provide 12% of company revenues from 2006.

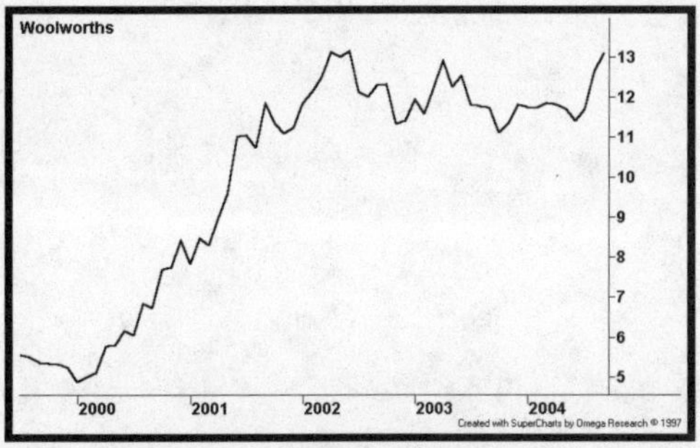

www.woolworths.com.au

Woolworths Limited

Share price ($)	11.73	
12-month high ($)	12.22	
12-month low ($)	10.73	
Market capitalisation ($mn)	12,243.2	
Price-to-NTA-per-share ratio	8.1	
5-year share price return (% p.a.)	24.4	
Sector: Consumer staples	**Company**	**Sector**
Price-earnings ratio (times)	16.4	16.8
Dividend yield (%)	3.8	3.7

Woolworths, founded in Sydney in 1924, is one of Australia's retail giants, with around 10% of the total retail market and an estimated 28% of all grocery sales. Its 1,400 Australian stores include Safeway, Big W, Dick Smith Electronics, Tandy, Dan Murphy Liquor, MGW Hotels (50% owned) and Plus Petrol. It also owns 33 Dick Smith Electronics stores in New Zealand.

Latest business results (June 2004, full year)

Woolworths overcame increasing competitive pressures from Coles Myer and other rivals, to post another strong profit gain. Supermarket sales rose 6.3%, though a part of this rise came through the company's moves into discounted petrol. Food and liquor sales were up 4.6% for the year. Supermarket EBIT grew faster than sales, up 12.3%, thanks to the company's continuing moves to cut costs. Woolworths opened 18 new supermarkets during the year, bringing the total number to 708. Big W sales were up 8.7%, with particular strength in home entertainment equipment, and EBIT rose 12.1%. The Dick Smith consumer electronics division enjoyed strong demand for television sets and DVD equipment, and saw sales growth of 12%, with EBIT up 19.2%.

Outlook

Woolworths continues to grow, though its main rival Coles Myer is now growing at a faster pace, and there are concerns that deep-discount specialists like the Aldi chain are continuing to pick up market share. In response, Woolworths continues to work to drive down costs. It claims that its Project Refresh initiative has delivered cumulative savings of $2.5 billion over five years, and it is ahead of schedule in the introduction of its StockSmart automated store stock program. It is also enhancing its emphasis on home-brand products. It continues to boost the number of liquor outlets, where it sees strong growth potential, with six to 12 new Dan Murphy stores anticipated annually. It is part of a group that has made a $1-billion takeover bid for the hotel group Australian Leisure and Hospitality. However, its attempts to move into the pharmacy business have been thwarted by the government. Its petrol station alliance with Caltex has grown to 407 outlets, with the company aiming for a total of around 470.

WOW Year to 27 June*	2003	2004
Revenues ($mn)	26,321.4	27,933.9
Supermarkets (%)	86	87
Big W (%)	9	10
Consumer electronics (%)	3	3
EBIT ($mn)	945.7	1,065.1
EBIT margin (%)	3.6	3.8
Gross margin (%)	23.3	23.0
Operating profit before tax ($mn)	906.0	1,017.8
Profit after tax ($mn)	650.6	730.7
Earnings per share (¢)	62.0	71.6
Cash flow per share (¢)	100.0	111.5
Dividend (¢)	39	45
Percentage franked	100	100
Net tangible assets per share ($)	1.20	1.45
Interest cover (times)	23.8	22.5
Return on equity (%)	35.8	37.8
Debt-to-equity ratio (%)	19.7	8.0
Current ratio	0.8	0.9

* June 29, 2003

PART II

Tables index

Table A

Market capitalisation

A company's market capitalisation is determined by multiplying the share price by the number of shares. To be included in this book, a company must be in the All Ordinaries Index, which comprises the 500 largest companies by market capitalisation.

	$mn
BHP Billiton	49,430.2
National Australia Bank	40,932.3
Commonwealth Bank of Australia	36,853.1
Australia & New Zealand Banking	32,533.1
Westpac Banking	29,064.6
Rio Tinto	18,168.6
Woodside Petroleum	12,300.0
Woolworths	12,243.2
Wesfarmers	10,997.1
Coles Myer	10,857.8
St George Bank	10,804.8
Foster's Group	9,268.2
Publishing & Broadcasting	9,028.2
QBE Insurance	8,663.0
Suncorp-Metway	7,598.7
Macquarie Bank	7,058.6
AXA Asia Pacific	6,785.5
Amcor	6,181.1
Australian Gas Light	5,780.3
Orica	4,347.9
Santos	4,205.6
Boral	4,007.6
Origin Energy	4,005.4
Toll Holdings	3,422.2
Fairfax (John) Holdings	3,400.7
Harvey Norman	3,128.2
Leighton Holdings	2,451.5
CSR	2,086.1
Foodland	1,953.6
Flight Centre	1,891.7
Washington H Soul Pattison	1,845.8
Computershare	1,822.5
Perpetual Trustees	1,788.9
West Australian Newspapers	1,567.3
Australian Stock Exchange	1,510.7
National Foods	1,379.1
Australand	1,378.9
Brickworks	1,369.9
Bendigo Bank	1,309.5
Gunns	1,151.0
Sigma	1,114.5
Incitec Pivot	1,107.3
Sims Group	1,083.9
Iluka Resources	1,043.0
Cochlear	1,029.1
Corporate Express Australia	991.0
Rural Press	949.2
Reece Australia	926.3
Macquarie Goodman Management	920.9
Downer EDI	904.2
Bank of Queensland	870.9
GWA International	860.0
Adelaide Bank	831.1
Coates Hire	798.9
Great Southern Plantations	757.4
GUD	615.2
Primary Health Care	604.1
Hills Industries	574.2
STW Communications	564.1
United Group	563.0
Crane Group	546.3
McGuigan Simeon Wines	535.1
Pacifica	506.0
Alesco	499.7
Colorado Group	494.5
Pacific Hydro	463.1
ION	423.7
Cabcharge Australia	411.9
FKP	382.9
AV Jennings Homes	381.0
Fleetwood	379.0
Fantastic Holdings	369.4
OAMPS	353.5
Timbercorp	352.2
Portman	348.5
Miller's Retail	340.3
Campbell Brothers	284.4
Select Harvests	279.4
Housewares International	269.8
McPherson's	254.3
Programmed Maintenance Services	230.2
ARB	224.4
Rebel Sport	220.5
Equigold	215.4
Brazin	214.0
Coventry Group	207.0
Schaffer Corporation	204.9
Auspine	203.4
SDI	194.1
Technology One	191.2
Central Equity	180.2
Volante Group	172.8
Blackmores	170.4
Gazal	162.6
K & S Corporation	154.7
Integrated Group	153.1
Wide Bay Australia	139.7
Troy Resources	130.9
Monadelphous Group	118.7
Sydney Aquarium	113.2
Cedar Woods Properties	109.1
OrotonGroup	107.9
Institute of Drug Technology	100.6
Angus & Coote	95.0
HGL	94.3
Danks Holdings	80.6
Tasmanian Perpetual Trustees	79.8
Coffey International	79.4
AJ Lucas	77.4
Adcorp Australia	70.8
Candle Australia	69.2
Cellnet	67.7
Plaspak Group	66.2
Wadepack	57.5
Rock Building Society	56.7

Table B

Revenues

This list ranks the companies in the book according to their most recent full-year revenues figures (operating income for the banks). The figures include revenues from sales and services, but other revenues — such as interest receipts and investment income — are not generally included.

	$mn
Coles Myer	32,266.8
BHP Billiton	31,876.0
Woolworths	27,933.9
Rio Tinto	18,143.0
National Australia Bank	12,873.0
Commonwealth Bank of Australia	10,491.0
Amcor	10,405.9
Wesfarmers	7,451.5
Westpac Banking	7,330.0
Australia & New Zealand Banking	7,013.0
QBE Insurance	6,036.0
Foodland	6,026.5
Leighton Holdings	4,834.4
AXA Asia Pacific	4,761.0
Suncorp-Metway	4,594.0
Australian Gas Light	4,153.8
Boral	4,149.8
Orica	3,958.6
Foster's Group	3,908.1
Origin Energy	3,521.8
Toll Holdings	3,271.9
Downer EDI	3,112.3
Publishing & Broadcasting	2,874.1
Macquarie Bank	2,465.0
St George Bank	2,361.0
Crane Group	2,087.7
Woodside Petroleum	2,059.3
CSR	1,970.8
Sigma	1,908.6
Sims Group	1,873.9
Fairfax (John) Holdings	1,765.9
Harvey Norman	1,751.7
Santos	1,465.0
Australand	1,405.4
National Foods	1,208.2
Miller's Retail	1,109.9
United Group	1,076.9
Pacifica	923.8
Corporate Express Australia	896.3
Reece Australia	871.8
Computershare	871.2
Iluka Resources	786.0
Flight Centre	774.3
Hills Industries	713.6
Incitec Pivot	686.3
Cabcharge Australia	681.1
ION	671.2
GWA International	667.9
Gunns	649.7
AV Jennings Homes	550.0
Danks Holdings	527.9
Rural Press	509.5
Brickworks	485.7
Alesco	481.5
Housewares International	457.6
Coates Hire	456.9
Cellnet	446.6
Colorado Group	440.8
Coventry Group	433.9
Brazin	421.3
Bendigo Bank	411.1
GUD	393.8
Campbell Brothers	390.3
West Australian Newspapers	347.2
Volante Group	345.4
Washington H Soul Pattinson	340.6
Integrated Group	331.2
McPherson's	329.0
McGuigan Simeon Wines	305.7
Rebel Sport	305.4
K & S Corporation	295.7
Perpetual Trustees	295.1
Central Equity	281.7
FKP	263.7
Cochlear	252.5
Australian Stock Exchange	241.2
Angus & Coote	239.0
Adelaide Bank	234.9
Fleetwood	231.1
OAMPS	222.8
Monadelphous Group	220.8
Bank of Queensland	214.3
Great Southern Plantations	204.2
Auspine	203.7
Gazal	193.0
Programmed Maintenance Services	190.6
Schaffer Corporation	183.6
Adcorp Australia	183.2
Fantastic Holdings	183.0
Candle Australia	179.2
Primary Health Care	150.4
Portman	145.3
OrotonGroup	143.6
Coffey International	131.0
STW Communications	129.2
Select Harvests	127.4
AJ Lucas	116.8
HGL	116.2
Blackmores	115.7
Timbercorp	108.7
ARB	100.7
Equigold	93.0
Troy Resources	85.1
Wadepack	79.0
Macquarie Goodman Management	78.8
Plaspak Group	73.8
Pacific Hydro	63.2
Cedar Woods Properties	57.0
Technology One	50.5
SDI	42.5
Wide Bay Australia	37.5
Sydney Aquarium	27.2
Rock Building Society	25.4
Institute of Drug Technology	25.2
Tasmanian Perpetual Trustees	15.5

Table C

Year-on-year revenues growth

Companies generally strive for growth, though profit growth is usually of far more significance than a boost in revenues. In fact, it is possible for a company to increase its revenues by all kinds of means — including cutting profit margins or acquiring other companies — and YOY revenues growth is of little relevance if other ratios are not also improving.

	%
Brickworks	170.5
Great Southern Plantations	113.3
Troy Resources	108.4
Macquarie Goodman Management	104.8
AXA Asia Pacific	74.8
Select Harvests	57.3
Cedar Woods Properties	54.6
Fairfax (John) Holdings	46.1
Cellnet	40.3
Fantastic Holdings	36.3
BHP Billiton	36.2
Pacific Hydro	36.2
Timbercorp	35.2
McPherson's	32.3
Macquarie Bank	30.4
Flight Centre	27.8
Toll Holdings	27.3
Harvey Norman	26.8
United Group	25.9
Rock Building Society	25.6
Central Equity	25.5
Computershare	25.4
Equigold	23.5
Australand	23.4
Bank of Queensland	23.3
Alesco	22.8
Fleetwood	22.6
Blackmores	22.3
OrotonGroup	21.4
Downer EDI	20.9
Coates Hire	20.7
Coles Myer	19.4
Bendigo Bank	18.6
Coffey International	18.6
Primary Health Care	18.6
Sims Group	18.6
Corporate Express Australia	18.3
Reece Australia	17.8
Adcorp Australia	17.6
Danks Holdings	17.5
Adelaide Bank	16.8
Australian Stock Exchange	16.6
OAMPS	16.4
SDI	15.7
Sydney Aquarium	15.3
Programmed Maintenance Services	14.6
ARB	14.4
Suncorp-Metway	14.2
Tasmanian Perpetual Trustees	14.0
Incitec Pivot	13.6
Portman	12.8
Commonwealth Bank of Australia	11.6
Candle Australia	10.7
Wide Bay Australia	10.7
Rebel Sport	10.3
Perpetual Trustees	10.2
Sigma	10.1
Rural Press	9.9
Angus & Coote	9.7
West Australian Newspapers	9.4
Crane Group	9.2
Campbell Brothers	8.6
National Australia Bank	8.4
Boral	8.3
St George Bank	8.1
Hills Industries	8.0
McGuigan Simeon Wines	7.9
Cabcharge Australia	7.5
Publishing & Broadcasting	7.4
Technology One	7.4
Australian Gas Light	7.3
Gunns	7.3
QBE Insurance	7.0
Volante Group	6.4
Integrated Group	6.2
Woolworths	6.1
Origin Energy	5.9
GUD	5.8
Miller's Retail	5.7
STW Communications	5.5
AV Jennings Homes	4.6
National Foods	4.5
Coventry Group	4.4
ION	2.6
Washington H Soul Pattinson	1.9
HGL	1.4
GWA International	1.3
Westpac Banking	0.9
K & S Corporation	0.8
Australia & New Zealand Banking	0.4
Colorado Group	0.4
Housewares International	0.4
Wesfarmers	0.3
Leighton Holdings	–0.3
Gazal	–0.9
Santos	–0.9
Institute of Drug Technology	–1.2
Amcor	–2.8
Orica	–3.1
CSR	–3.9
Foodland	–5.6
Wadepack	–6.9
Woodside Petroleum	–8.1
Rio Tinto	–9.0
Monadelphous Group	–9.4
Auspine	–10.2
FKP	–10.3
Iluka Resources	–12.1
Plaspak Group	–12.2
Cochlear	–12.5
Pacifica	–14.2
Foster's Group	–15.7
Schaffer Corporation	–17.4
Brazin	–21.9
AJ Lucas	–22.8

Table D

EBIT margin

A company's earnings before interest and taxation (EBIT) is sometimes regarded as a better measure of its profitability than the straight pre-tax or post-tax profit figure. EBIT is derived by adding net interest payments (that is, interest payments minus interest receipts) to the pre-tax profit. Different companies choose different methods of financing their operations; by adding back interest payments to their profits we can help minimise these differences and make comparisons between companies more valid.

The EBIT margin is the EBIT figure as a percentage of annual sales. Clearly a high figure is to be desired, though of course this can be achieved artificially by inflating borrowings (and hence interest payments). And it is noteworthy that efficient companies like some of the giant retailers can operate most satisfactorily on low margins.

The EBIT margin figure has little relevance for banks — whose high interest payments to their customers mean they have virtually no EBIT — and they have been excluded, as have the insurance companies.

	%				
Macquarie Goodman Management	69.7	Coates Hire	17.2	AJ Lucas	8.6
Great Southern Plantations	64.2	Harvey Norman	16.9	Incitec Pivot	8.6
Pacific Hydro	59.7	Australian Gas Light	16.6	National Foods	8.6
Australian Stock Exchange	45.3	Central Equity	16.4	Housewares International	8.5
Timbercorp	44.7	GUD	15.9	Coffey International	8.2
Brickworks	44.2	Schaffer Corporation	15.5	Hills Industries	8.2
Perpetual Trustees	41.9	Flight Centre	15.2	Rebel Sport	8.0
Woodside Petroleum	41.5	GWA International	14.9	Campbell Brothers	7.7
Washington H Soul Pattinson	39.2	Portman	14.8	Corporate Express Australia	7.7
Tasmanian Perpetual Trustees	38.4	OAMPS	14.5	Toll Holdings	7.2
Sydney Aquarium	36.7	Boral	14.4	Alesco	7.0
West Australian Newspapers	34.5	Auspine	14.0	Amcor	6.8
BHP Billiton	31.9	Programmed Maintenance Services	13.9	K & S Corporation	6.8
Santos	31.6	Fleetwood	13.5	Angus & Coote	5.4
Cedar Woods Properties	27.9	Iluka Resources	13.4	Monadelphous Group	5.4
Rural Press	27.0	Computershare	13.3	Coventry Group	5.3
Gunns	26.8	CSR	13.3	Integrated Group	5.3
SDI	26.7	HGL	13.1	Brazin	4.8
Troy Resources	25.9	ION	12.7	Cabcharge Australia	4.5
Publishing & Broadcasting	25.3	Blackmores	12.2	Downer EDI	4.5
Equigold	25.0	Plaspak Group	12.1	Sigma	4.4
Technology One	24.1	Fantastic Holdings	12.0	Crane Group	4.3
Institute of Drug Technology	23.9	Wesfarmers	11.9	Foodland	4.3
FKP	22.4	Australand	11.1	United Group	4.1
Primary Health Care	21.5	Orica	11.1	Adcorp Australia	3.9
Fairfax (John) Holdings	20.9	Pacifica	10.4	Candle Australia	3.9
STW Communications	20.3	Wadepack	10.2	Miller's Retail	3.9
McGuigan Simeon Wines	20.1	Reece Australia	10.1	Woolworths	3.8
Foster's Group	20.0	Colorado Group	9.6	Volante Group	3.5
Select Harvests	18.7	Gazal	9.5	Leighton Holdings	3.4
Cochlear	18.0	OrotonGroup	9.5	Cellnet	3.3
Rio Tinto	17.9	McPherson's	9.4	Coles Myer	2.8
AV Jennings Homes	17.8	Origin Energy	9.3	Danks Holdings	1.7
ARB	17.2	Sims Group	9.0		

Table E

Year-on-year EBIT margin growth

The EBIT (earnings before interest and taxation) margin is one of the measures of a company's efficiency. So a rising margin is much to be desired, as it suggests that a company is achieving success in cutting its costs. This table does not include banks or insurance companies.

	%
Portman	598.7
Brazin	107.1
Volante Group	67.2
FKP	65.4
Coates Hire	51.0
Fleetwood	36.2
Computershare	33.6
GUD	33.5
Sigma	32.6
Monadelphous Group	30.2
AJ Lucas	25.7
Plaspak Group	25.3
Fairfax (John) Holdings	25.2
Auspine	24.8
Gunns	24.7
Macquarie Goodman Management	24.7
Sims Group	24.3
Tasmanian Perpetual Trustees	23.0
Colorado Group	22.8
Technology One	22.0
Pacifica	21.7
SDI	21.2
Perpetual Trustees	20.2
Publishing & Broadcasting	20.0
Alesco	18.7
Australian Stock Exchange	18.4
Coventry Group	18.1
Toll Holdings	17.9
OAMPS	17.7
Cellnet	17.2
AV Jennings Homes	16.1
Boral	15.9
Gazal	15.4
Rural Press	14.8
Candle Australia	14.4
Incitec Pivot	14.4
Blackmores	13.7
McPherson's	13.4
Wesfarmers	13.4
Angus & Coote	12.6
Reece Australia	12.3
Troy Resources	12.2
Coffey International	11.6
Orica	11.6
K & S Corporation	11.4
Washington H Soul Pattinson	11.2
Campbell Brothers	11.1
Schaffer Corporation	10.9
West Australian Newspapers	10.9
Coles Myer	9.3
Housewares International	8.7
Cabcharge Australia	8.4
Fantastic Holdings	8.0
GWA International	8.0
Foodland	7.6
National Foods	6.6
Woolworths	6.1
Great Southern Plantations	5.4
Origin Energy	5.3
Primary Health Care	4.0
HGL	3.1
BHP Billiton	2.9
ARB	2.8
ION	2.6
McGuigan Simeon Wines	2.3
Integrated Group	2.0
Institute of Drug Technology	1.7
Brickworks	0.8
Hills Industries	0.0
Timbercorp	–0.1
CSR	–0.6
Amcor	–0.9
STW Communications	–3.1
Australand	–3.9
Programmed Maintenance Services	–4.1
Flight Centre	–4.6
Foster's Group	–4.7
Sydney Aquarium	–4.7
Australian Gas Light	–5.2
Equigold	–5.2
Pacific Hydro	–5.2
Rebel Sport	–5.6
United Group	–6.0
Downer EDI	–6.3
Iluka Resources	–6.6
Cedar Woods Properties	–7.1
Corporate Express Australia	–8.1
Adcorp Australia	–8.8
Harvey Norman	–8.9
OrotonGroup	–11.2
Santos	–12.7
Select Harvests	–13.0
Danks Holdings	–13.3
Crane Group	–13.7
Woodside Petroleum	–16.2
Rio Tinto	–17.5
Central Equity	–22.8
Leighton Holdings	–25.7
Miller's Retail	–26.8
Wadepack	–33.6
Cochlear	–35.2

Table F
After-tax profit

This table ranks all the companies according to their most recent full-year after-tax profit.

	$mn
BHP Billiton	4,682.5
National Australia Bank	3,955.0
Commonwealth Bank of Australia	2,572.0
Australia & New Zealand Banking	2,348.0
Westpac Banking	2,183.0
Rio Tinto	2,133.0
Woolworths	730.7
St George Bank	658.0
Suncorp-Metway	618.0
Coles Myer	616.5
QBE Insurance	572.0
Wesfarmers	569.2
AXA Asia Pacific	547.0
Woodside Petroleum	526.7
Macquarie Bank	494.0
Publishing & Broadcasting	484.0
Foster's Group	469.4
Amcor	440.3
Boral	369.8
Australian Gas Light	349.5
Santos	327.0
Orica	270.3
Fairfax (John) Holdings	207.6
Origin Energy	204.9
Harvey Norman	176.1
Toll Holdings	168.6
CSR	160.2
Brickworks	157.4
Foodland	142.7
Sims Group	112.5
Leighton Holdings	110.0
Gunns	105.3
Australand	95.2
Great Southern Plantations	93.2
Perpetual Trustees	90.4
Washington H Soul Pattinson	88.3
Rural Press	87.1
Iluka Resources	85.2
Australian Stock Exchange	82.7
Flight Centre	81.9
Downer EDI	81.5
West Australian Newspapers	79.5
Computershare	77.8
Bendigo Bank	73.2
National Foods	68.7
AV Jennings Homes	68.5
Adelaide Bank	65.1
GWA International	62.1
Reece Australia	61.5
ION	55.2
Coates Hire	52.1
Pacifica	46.7
Corporate Express Australia	45.7
Bank of Queensland	44.7
Sigma	44.2
GUD	41.7
McGuigan Simeon Wines	40.2
Macquarie Goodman Management	37.0
Cochlear	36.8
FKP	36.7
Crane Group	35.9
Incitec Pivot	35.1
Central Equity	33.6
Pacific Hydro	31.2
Hills Industries	31.1
United Group	29.1
Auspine	28.9
Colorado Group	28.8
Timbercorp	27.1
STW Communications	26.0
OAMPS	24.6
Cabcharge Australia	23.1
Housewares International	22.9
Miller's Retail	21.3
Fleetwood	20.2
Alesco	19.8
Rebel Sport	18.2
Primary Health Care	18.0
Portman	16.9
McPherson's	16.8
Brazin	16.7
Equigold	16.7
Schaffer Corporation	16.6
Programmed Maintenance Services	16.3
Fantastic Holdings	15.7
Select Harvests	15.2
Coventry Group	14.8
Campbell Brothers	14.6
Troy Resources	14.1
K & S Corporation	12.2
ARB	12.1
Integrated Group	11.8
Gazal	10.8
Cedar Woods Properties	10.3
AJ Lucas	10.0
HGL	9.9
Wide Bay Australia	9.9
Technology One	9.5
Blackmores	9.3
Cellnet	9.1
Monadelphous Group	8.5
OrotonGroup	8.4
Angus & Coote	8.1
SDI	8.0
Volante Group	7.6
Plaspak Group	7.2
Coffey International	7.0
Sydney Aquarium	6.6
Danks Holdings	5.3
Wadepack	5.3
Adcorp Australia	4.9
Candle Australia	4.6
Institute of Drug Technology	4.3
Tasmanian Perpetual Trustees	4.3
Rock Building Society	3.9

TABLE G

YEAR-ON-YEAR EARNINGS PER SHARE GROWTH

The earnings-per-share (EPS) figure is a crucial one. It tells you — the shareholder — what your part is of the company's profits, for each of your shares. So investors invariably look for EPS growth in a stock. The YOY EPS growth figure is often one of the first ratios that investors look to when evaluating a stock.

	%
Portman	404.2
Troy Resources	144.8
Brickworks	116.5
Great Southern Plantations	113.1
Macquarie Goodman Management	104.4
Auspine	94.0
QBE Insurance	92.2
AXA Asia Pacific	74.8
Cellnet	72.2
Computershare	69.1
BHP Billiton	67.7
Suncorp-Metway	59.2
Fleetwood	54.1
Coates Hire	53.3
Tasmanian Perpetual Trustees	52.9
GUD	52.5
Brazin	52.2
Sims Group	49.1
Toll Holdings	48.4
Fantastic Holdings	47.9
SDI	47.1
Publishing & Broadcasting	45.8
Blackmores	44.7
Angus & Coote	43.7
Timbercorp	43.3
Volante Group	42.6
Plaspak Group	42.3
Macquarie Bank	41.4
Fairfax (John) Holdings	41.1
Primary Health Care	40.9
Coles Myer	40.7
Sigma	40.2
Bank of Queensland	40.1
Cedar Woods Properties	39.2
Technology One	38.2
Gunns	36.6
Coventry Group	35.0
Australian Stock Exchange	34.9
Rural Press	33.0
Coffey International	32.6
Perpetual Trustees	31.7
Reece Australia	31.6
FKP	30.7
Boral	29.9
Equigold	29.5
Select Harvests	27.9
Commonwealth Bank of Australia	27.5
Adelaide Bank	27.1
Candle Australia	25.1
Colorado Group	25.0
Alesco	24.9
Origin Energy	24.5
West Australian Newspapers	23.8
HGL	23.0
Washington H Soul Pattinson	21.4
United Group	21.2
Campbell Brothers	20.8
AV Jennings Homes	20.6
OAMPS	18.7
Wesfarmers	18.4
Foodland	18.1
Bendigo Bank	17.9
ARB	17.4
Harvey Norman	16.4
Monadelphous Group	16.4
Woolworths	15.5
St George Bank	14.7
McGuigan Simeon Wines	14.5
Cabcharge Australia	14.1
Flight Centre	13.6
Orica	13.1
National Foods	12.8
GWA International	12.7
Pacifica	11.4
Gazal	11.0
K & S Corporation	10.3
AJ Lucas	10.0
Programmed Maintenance Services	9.7
Rebel Sport	8.9
Adcorp Australia	8.7
Hills Industries	8.5
Sydney Aquarium	8.5
Downer EDI	7.6
Wide Bay Australia	7.1
National Australia Bank	6.9
Housewares International	6.2
Corporate Express Australia	5.3
Australian Gas Light	5.0
McPherson's	3.8
Pacific Hydro	2.8
Australand	2.7
Central Equity	2.5
Integrated Group	2.4
Danks Holdings	2.3
Rock Building Society	1.6
Institute of Drug Technology	1.1
Santos	1.1
STW Communications	1.0
Australia & New Zealand Banking	0.0
Westpac Banking	–1.1
Amcor	–1.7
ION	–3.2
Schaffer Corporation	–4.3
CSR	–6.6
Incitec Pivot	–6.9
OrotonGroup	–8.3
Foster's Group	–17.6
Leighton Holdings	–21.4
Rio Tinto	–24.3
Iluka Resources	–24.6
Crane Group	–25.7
Woodside Petroleum	–27.8
Wadepack	–29.5
Miller's Retail	–31.8
Cochlear	–38.0

Table H

Return on equity

Shareholder's equity is the company's assets minus its liabilities. It is, in theory, the amount owned by the shareholders of the company. Return on equity is the after-tax profit expressed as a percentage of that equity. Thus, it is the amount of profit that the company managers made for you — the shareholder — from your assets. For many investors it is one of the most important gauges of how well a company is doing. It is one of the requirements for inclusion in this book that all companies have a return on equity of at least 9% in their latest financial year.

	%
Fantastic Holdings	56.8
Troy Resources	43.8
West Australian Newspapers	43.6
Australian Stock Exchange	38.3
Woolworths	37.8
Blackmores	37.0
Macquarie Goodman Management	35.2
Sydney Aquarium	33.1
Coffey International	32.5
SDI	32.0
GUD	31.0
Perpetual Trustees	30.0
ARB	29.3
Colorado Group	29.3
Schaffer Corporation	28.5
Cochlear	28.4
Corporate Express Australia	28.4
AV Jennings Homes	27.9
Great Southern Plantations	27.6
Sims Group	26.6
BHP Billiton	26.4
Gunns	26.4
Technology One	26.1
AJ Lucas	25.6
Rebel Sport	25.0
Cedar Woods Properties	24.2
Integrated Group	24.0
OrotonGroup	23.5
Reece Australia	23.5
Brazin	23.3
Equigold	23.3
Monadelphous Group	23.2
Fleetwood	22.9
Woodside Petroleum	22.2
Select Harvests	21.9
Brickworks	21.0
ION	20.9
Flight Centre	20.7
Adcorp Australia	20.3
Toll Holdings	20.0
Macquarie Bank	19.8
McPherson's	19.8
Orica	19.6
HGL	19.5
K & S Corporation	19.5
OAMPS	19.3
Cabcharge Australia	18.7
Australia & New Zealand Banking	18.6
QBE Insurance	18.3
Rio Tinto	17.9
Westpac Banking	17.9
FKP	17.5
St George Bank	17.5
United Group	17.4
Central Equity	17.2
Programmed Maintenance Services	17.1
Pacifica	16.8
Cellnet	16.7
Harvey Norman	16.6
Hills Industries	16.6
National Australia Bank	16.6
Boral	16.5
AXA Asia Pacific	16.2
Suncorp-Metway	16.2
Plaspak Group	16.1
Wesfarmers	16.1
Coates Hire	15.9
CSR	15.9
Tasmanian Perpetual Trustees	15.9
Coles Myer	15.7
Institute of Drug Technology	15.7
Rock Building Society	15.7
Housewares International	15.2
National Foods	15.1
Wadepack	15.1
Angus & Coote	14.8
GWA International	14.7
Sigma	14.7
Foodland	14.4
Adelaide Bank	14.0
Bank of Queensland	14.0
Rural Press	13.8
McGuigan Simeon Wines	13.3
Computershare	13.2
STW Communications	13.2
Pacific Hydro	13.1
Leighton Holdings	12.9
Timbercorp	12.9
Auspine	12.7
Washington H Soul Pattinson	12.6
Wide Bay Australia	12.3
Publishing & Broadcasting	12.2
Commonwealth Bank of Australia	12.1
Bendigo Bank	11.9
Gazal	11.9
Australian Gas Light	11.8
Portman	11.6
Campbell Brothers	11.2
Origin Energy	11.1
Alesco	11.0
Santos	11.0
Australand	10.8
Fairfax (John) Holdings	10.8
Foster's Group	10.4
Downer EDI	10.3
Candle Australia	10.2
Danks Holdings	10.0
Iluka Resources	10.0
Miller's Retail	10.0
Amcor	9.7
Incitec Pivot	9.7
Primary Health Care	9.4
Coventry Group	9.1
Volante Group	9.1
Crane Group	9.0

TABLE I

YEAR-ON-YEAR RETURN ON EQUITY GROWTH

Company managers have a variety of strategies they can use to boost profits. It is much harder to lift the return on equity (ROE). Find a company with a high ROE figure, and one that is growing year by year, and the chances are that you have found a real growth stock.

	%
Portman	403.4
QBE Insurance	82.3
Troy Resources	81.0
Computershare	77.5
BHP Billiton	71.4
Auspine	67.9
Brickworks	66.0
Cellnet	57.8
AXA Asia Pacific	55.8
Brazin	55.4
Suncorp-Metway	47.5
Tasmanian Perpetual Trustees	46.4
Macquarie Goodman Management	45.2
ARB	41.5
Coates Hire	41.1
Plaspak Group	40.8
GUD	40.3
Great Southern Plantations	38.6
Technology One	34.9
Angus & Coote	34.4
Fairfax (John) Holdings	34.4
Primary Health Care	33.8
Publishing & Broadcasting	32.0
Fleetwood	31.6
Coventry Group	30.7
Sims Group	30.5
Coles Myer	29.4
Australian Stock Exchange	28.1
Sigma	27.6
Macquarie Bank	24.8
Blackmores	23.8
Rural Press	22.0
Campbell Brothers	19.7
Perpetual Trustees	19.6
Candle Australia	19.2
Wesfarmers	19.2
Boral	18.7
Commonwealth Bank of Australia	17.7
SDI	16.6
Pacifica	15.2
United Group	15.0
Origin Energy	14.9
Bank of Queensland	14.5
Washington H Soul Pattinson	13.9
Downer EDI	13.2
Timbercorp	13.2
Reece Australia	11.9
Cedar Woods Properties	11.7
Alesco	10.5
HGL	10.5
Equigold	10.0
Foodland	9.2
Select Harvests	9.0
Orica	8.9
Fantastic Holdings	8.2
FKP	8.1
GWA International	7.4
Bendigo Bank	5.7
Woolworths	5.7
St George Bank	5.6
Wide Bay Australia	5.5
National Foods	4.8
West Australian Newspapers	4.0
Cabcharge Australia	3.7
McGuigan Simeon Wines	2.9
National Australia Bank	2.6
Gunns	2.2
Monadelphous Group	1.8
Coffey International	1.4
Gazal	1.1
Colorado Group	0.7
Amcor	–0.4
Adelaide Bank	–1.1
OAMPS	–1.3
Adcorp Australia	–1.8
Housewares International	–2.4
Sydney Aquarium	–2.5
Harvey Norman	–2.8
Toll Holdings	–2.9
AV Jennings Homes	–3.0
Rock Building Society	–3.1
K & S Corporation	–3.7
Programmed Maintenance Services	–4.5
Danks Holdings	–4.6
Santos	–4.6
Hills Industries	–5.1
McPherson's	–5.8
CSR	–6.4
Institute of Drug Technology	–7.7
Australian Gas Light	–8.4
Volante Group	–9.7
Central Equity	–10.0
Rebel Sport	–10.2
Flight Centre	–10.8
Australia & New Zealand Banking	–11.8
Australand	–12.9
Pacific Hydro	–13.9
Corporate Express Australia	–15.2
Westpac Banking	–17.8
ION	–19.7
Foster's Group	–21.0
Leighton Holdings	–24.0
Rio Tinto	–24.0
Crane Group	–24.4
Integrated Group	–24.5
AJ Lucas	–26.0
Woodside Petroleum	–26.0
Iluka Resources	–30.8
OrotonGroup	–31.0
Miller's Retail	–33.4
Incitec Pivot	–35.6
Wadepack	–39.2
Schaffer Corporation	–50.4
Cochlear	–52.4
STW Communications	–88.5

Table J

Debt-to-equity ratio

A company's borrowings as a percentage of its shareholder's equity is one of the most common measures of corporate debt. Many investors will be wary of a company with a ratio that is too high. However, a company with a steady business and a regular income flow — such as an electric power company or a large supermarket chain — is generally considered relatively safe with a high level of debt, whereas a small company in a new business field might be thought at risk with even moderate debt levels. Much depends on surrounding circumstances, including the prevailing interest rates. Of course, it is often from borrowing that a company grows, and some investors are not happy buying shares in a company with little or no debt.

There are various ways to calculate the ratio, but for this book the net debt position is used. That is, a company's cash has been deducted from its borrowings. For inclusion in this book no company was allowed a debt-to-equity ratio of more than 75%. Some of the companies had no net debt — their cash position was greater than the amount of their borrowings — and so have a zero figure in this table. The ratio has no relevance for banks, so they have been excluded.

	%
Adcorp Australia	0.0
AJ Lucas	0.0
Australian Stock Exchange	0.0
AXA Asia Pacific	0.0
Brazin	0.0
Cabcharge Australia	0.0
Cochlear	0.0
Colorado Group	0.0
Corporate Express Australia	0.0
Equigold	0.0
Fantastic Holdings	0.0
Flight Centre	0.0
Great Southern Plantations	0.0
HGL	0.0
Institute of Drug Technology	0.0
Leighton Holdings	0.0
Monadelphous Group	0.0
OAMPS	0.0
Perpetual Trustees	0.0
Portman	0.0
Rebel Sport	0.0
Reece Australia	0.0
Tasmanian Perpetual Trustees	0.0
Technology One	0.0
Troy Resources	0.0
Volante Group	0.0
Candle Australia	0.5
Alesco	2.0
Coles Myer	3.1
Sims Group	4.0
Coventry Group	7.4
ARB	7.9
Woolworths	8.0
STW Communications	8.5
Danks Holdings	8.6
National Foods	8.7
QBE Insurance	8.8
Select Harvests	9.6
Washington H Soul Pattinson	11.5
GUD	12.3
Woodside Petroleum	13.3
Angus & Coote	14.3
CSR	14.3
Integrated Group	17.9
Coffey International	18.7
Central Equity	21.3
Blackmores	21.8
Rural Press	22.2
United Group	22.5
Incitec Pivot	22.7
Publishing & Broadcasting	25.3
Fleetwood	26.3
OrotonGroup	26.7
Hills Industries	26.9
Auspine	28.7
Toll Holdings	29.0
Brickworks	30.1
BHP Billiton	33.0
SDI	34.1
Foodland	36.1
Foster's Group	36.1
Harvey Norman	36.3
Gazal	36.5
Computershare	36.6
GWA International	37.2
Cellnet	38.0
Pacific Hydro	39.5
Iluka Resources	39.7
Boral	39.8
Housewares International	39.8
Wadepack	39.8
Coates Hire	40.0
Santos	40.3
AV Jennings Homes	40.4
Programmed Maintenance Services	40.7
Downer EDI	40.9
Rio Tinto	42.0
Schaffer Corporation	42.2
Origin Energy	44.4
McGuigan Simeon Wines	44.7
Wesfarmers	45.3
Sydney Aquarium	46.0
Sigma	46.5
Primary Health Care	46.6
Cedar Woods Properties	48.4
Miller's Retail	49.2
Amcor	50.4
Pacifica	50.5
Macquarie Goodman Management	51.3
FKP	51.4
Fairfax (John) Holdings	52.7
K & S Corporation	52.7
Timbercorp	53.1
Plaspak Group	63.0
Gunns	64.5
ION	66.1
Australand	66.7
Orica	67.1
West Australian Newspapers	68.2
Australian Gas Light	68.8
Campbell Brothers	69.3
Crane Group	70.3
McPherson's	74.1

TABLE K

CURRENT RATIO

The current ratio is simply the company's current assets divided by its current liabilities. Current assets are cash or assets that can, in theory, be converted quickly into cash. Current liabilities are normally those payable within a year. The current ratio measures the ability of a company to repay in a hurry its short-term debt, should the need arise. Banks are not included.

Troy Resources	6.8
STW Communications	6.5
Macquarie Goodman Management	5.7
Pacific Hydro	3.8
Tasmanian Perpetual Trustees	3.8
HGL	3.6
Technology One	3.4
Cabcharge Australia	3.3
Coventry Group	3.3
Institute of Drug Technology	3.2
SDI	3.2
GWA International	3.1
Housewares International	3.1
Programmed Maintenance Services	3.1
Schaffer Corporation	3.1
Australand	3.0
AV Jennings Homes	2.6
Australian Stock Exchange	2.5
Perpetual Trustees	2.5
Colorado Group	2.4
Campbell Brothers	2.3
Woodside Petroleum	2.3
McGuigan Simeon Wines	2.2
Rebel Sport	2.2
Alesco	2.1
Fantastic Holdings	2.1
OrotonGroup	2.1
AJ Lucas	2.0
FKP	2.0
Gazal	2.0
Hills Industries	2.0
McPherson's	2.0
Central Equity	1.9
Cochlear	1.9
Portman	1.9
Reece Australia	1.9
Angus & Coote	1.8
Danks Holdings	1.8
Fleetwood	1.8
West Australian Newspapers	1.8
Auspine	1.7
BHP Billiton	1.7
Cellnet	1.7
Crane Group	1.7
GUD	1.7
Harvey Norman	1.7
Pacifica	1.7
Select Harvests	1.7
ARB	1.6
Blackmores	1.6
Brazin	1.6
Iluka Resources	1.6
Miller's Retail	1.6
Plaspak Group	1.6
Sims Group	1.6
Foodland	1.5
Monadelphous Group	1.5
Publishing & Broadcasting	1.5
Washington H Soul Pattinson	1.5
Wesfarmers	1.5
Candle Australia	1.4
Corporate Express Australia	1.4
Downer EDI	1.4
Integrated Group	1.4
Primary Health Care	1.4
Rio Tinto	1.4
Wadepack	1.4
Boral	1.3
Coffey International	1.3
Equigold	1.3
Flight Centre	1.3
Incitec Pivot	1.3
Orica	1.3
United Group	1.3
Adcorp Australia	1.2
Cedar Woods Properties	1.2
Coles Myer	1.2
CSR	1.2
Foster's Group	1.2
OAMPS	1.2
Origin Energy	1.2
QBE Insurance	1.2
Rural Press	1.2
Santos	1.2
Sigma	1.2
Timbercorp	1.2
Volante Group	1.2
Brickworks	1.1
Coates Hire	1.1
Toll Holdings	1.1
Amcor	1.0
Computershare	1.0
Fairfax (John) Holdings	1.0
Great Southern Plantations	1.0
Gunns	1.0
ION	1.0
K & S Corporation	0.9
National Foods	0.9
Woolworths	0.9
Australian Gas Light	0.8
Sydney Aquarium	0.6

Table L
Price-earnings ratio

The PER — the current share price divided by the earnings-per-share figure — is one of the best-known of all sharemarket ratios. Essentially it expresses the amount of money investors are ready to pay for each cent or dollar of a company's profits, and it allows you to compare the share prices of different companies with widely different profits. A high PER suggests the market has a high regard for the company and its growth prospects; a low one may mean that investors are disdainful of the stock. The figures in this table are based on share prices as of 18 August, 2004.

Central Equity	5.3
AV Jennings Homes	5.5
ION	6.8
Auspine	7.0
Great Southern Plantations	7.0
Cellnet	7.3
AJ Lucas	7.4
Brickworks	8.7
HGL	9.0
Plaspak Group	9.2
Australand	9.3
FKP	9.3
Sims Group	9.7
Cedar Woods Properties	10.1
National Australia Bank	10.1
Troy Resources	10.2
Coffey International	10.3
Rural Press	10.3
Gunns	10.7
Downer EDI	10.8
Wadepack	10.8
Boral	10.9
Pacifica	10.9
Australia & New Zealand Banking	11.4
Adelaide Bank	11.7
Angus & Coote	11.7
Housewares International	11.7
Rebel Sport	12.0
Iluka Resources	12.2
Suncorp-Metway	12.2
AXA Asia Pacific	12.4
Integrated Group	12.4
Schaffer Corporation	12.4
Timbercorp	12.4
Brazin	12.5
K & S Corporation	12.7
OrotonGroup	12.7
McGuigan Simeon Wines	12.8
Equigold	12.9
Santos	13.0
Pacific Hydro	13.1
Amcor	13.4
CSR	13.5
OAMPS	13.6
Westpac Banking	13.6
Foodland	13.7
Coventry Group	13.9
GWA International	13.9
Macquarie Bank	13.9
QBE Insurance	14.0
Commonwealth Bank of Australia	14.1
Monadelphous Group	14.1
Programmed Maintenance Services	14.1
Wide Bay Australia	14.1
GUD	14.3
Adcorp Australia	14.4
Rock Building Society	14.4
Gazal	14.6
Crane Group	14.7
McPherson's	14.7
Bank of Queensland	14.8
Candle Australia	14.8
Reece Australia	14.8
Coates Hire	14.9
Danks Holdings	15.1
Volante Group	15.4
St George Bank	15.9
Miller's Retail	16.0
Fairfax (John) Holdings	16.2
Colorado Group	16.4
Woolworths	16.4
Australian Gas Light	16.5
Orica	16.5
Incitec Pivot	16.9
Sydney Aquarium	17.0
BHP Billiton	17.5
Coles Myer	17.5
Harvey Norman	17.5
Bendigo Bank	17.7
Blackmores	17.7
Alesco	17.8
Cabcharge Australia	17.8
Select Harvests	17.8
Hills Industries	18.0
Australian Stock Exchange	18.2
ARB	18.4
Tasmanian Perpetual Trustees	18.5
Fleetwood	18.7
Publishing & Broadcasting	18.7
Campbell Brothers	19.0
Origin Energy	19.1
Wesfarmers	19.1
STW Communications	19.3
United Group	19.3
West Australian Newspapers	19.5
Toll Holdings	19.6
Perpetual Trustees	19.8
Technology One	19.8
National Foods	20.1
Portman	20.1
Foster's Group	20.3
Washington H Soul Pattinson	20.9
Corporate Express Australia	21.6
Fantastic Holdings	21.9
Leighton Holdings	21.9
Computershare	22.7
Flight Centre	22.7
Institute of Drug Technology	23.2
Woodside Petroleum	23.3
Rio Tinto	23.4
Macquarie Goodman Management	24.0
SDI	24.5
Sigma	24.7
Cochlear	27.5
Primary Health Care	33.5

Table M
Price to NTA-per-share ratio

The NTA-per-share figure expresses the worth of a company's net tangible assets — that is, its assets minus its liabilities and intangible assets — for each share of the company. Intangible assets, such as goodwill or the value of newspaper mastheads, are excluded because it is deemed difficult to place a value on them (though this proposition is debatable), and also because they might not have much worth if separated from the company. The price-to-NTA-per-share ratio relates this figure to the share price.

A ratio of one means that the company is valued exactly according to the value of its assets. A ratio below one suggests that the shares are a bargain, though usually there is a good reason for this. Profits are more important than assets.

In some respects this is an 'old economy' ratio. For many high-tech companies in the 'new economy' the most important assets are human ones whose worth does not appear on the balance sheet.

Auspine	0.8
Central Equity	0.9
Australand	1.2
Iluka Resources	1.2
AV Jennings Homes	1.4
Cellnet	1.4
Coventry Group	1.4
Santos	1.4
Danks Holdings	1.5
ION	1.5
Plaspak Group	1.5
Rural Press	1.5
Adelaide Bank	1.6
Bank of Queensland	1.6
FKP	1.6
AJ Lucas	1.7
Angus & Coote	1.7
Great Southern Plantations	1.7
HGL	1.7
National Australia Bank	1.7
Pacific Hydro	1.7
Wide Bay Australia	1.7
Downer EDI	1.8
Timbercorp	1.8
Wadepack	1.8
AXA Asia Pacific	1.9
Boral	1.9
McGuigan Simeon Wines	1.9
CSR	2.0
Brickworks	2.1
Commonwealth Bank of Australia	2.1
Crane Group	2.1
Pacifica	2.1
Portman	2.1
Rock Building Society	2.1
Bendigo Bank	2.2
Amcor	2.3
Cedar Woods Properties	2.3
Coates Hire	2.3
Programmed Maintenance Services	2.3
Publishing & Broadcasting	2.3
Australia & New Zealand Banking	2.4
Macquarie Bank	2.5
Suncorp-Metway	2.5
Westpac Banking	2.5
Gunns	2.6
Washington H Soul Pattinson	2.6
Harvey Norman	2.7
Incitec Pivot	2.7
K & S Corporation	2.7
Rebel Sport	2.8
Equigold	2.9
Leighton Holdings	2.9
Sims Group	2.9
STW Communications	2.9
Hills Industries	3.1
Monadelphous Group	3.1
QBE Insurance	3.2
Reece Australia	3.2
Housewares International	3.3
Gazal	3.4
Miller's Retail	3.4
Cabcharge Australia	3.5
Origin Energy	3.5
Toll Holdings	3.5
Rio Tinto	3.6
St George Bank	3.6
Alesco	3.7
Schaffer Corporation	3.7
Brazin	3.8
Coles Myer	3.8
Institute of Drug Technology	3.8
OrotonGroup	3.9
Troy Resources	3.9
Australian Gas Light	4.0
Foster's Group	4.1
Woodside Petroleum	4.1
Campbell Brothers	4.6
BHP Billiton	4.7
Integrated Group	4.8
National Foods	4.8
Volante Group	4.8
Colorado Group	5.0
Orica	5.1
Coffey International	5.3
Select Harvests	5.3
ARB	5.5
Sydney Aquarium	5.5
Candle Australia	5.6
Fleetwood	5.7
Tasmanian Perpetual Trustees	5.7
Wesfarmers	5.9
United Group	6.0
Blackmores	6.1
Foodland	6.7
Perpetual Trustees	6.8
Technology One	6.9
Australian Stock Exchange	7.0
GUD	7.1
Flight Centre	7.3
Cochlear	7.7
Adcorp Australia	7.8
Woolworths	8.1
OAMPS	9.7
Corporate Express Australia	9.8
Sigma	9.8
SDI	10.1
Fantastic Holdings	11.8
GWA International	12.3
West Australian Newspapers	18.1
Macquarie Goodman Management	26.0
Primary Health Care	30.4

Table N
Dividend yield

Many investors buy shares for income, rather than for capital growth. They look for companies that offer a high dividend yield (the dividend expressed as a percentage of the share price). Table N ranks the companies in this book according to their historic dividend yields. Note that the franking credits available from some companies can make the dividend yield substantially higher if you are in an appropriate tax bracket. The figures in this table are based on share prices as of 18 August, 2004.

	%
Cellnet	8.6
Australand	8.0
ION	7.4
Coffey International	7.1
Schaffer Corporation	6.8
Miller's Retail	6.7
Plaspak Group	6.6
AV Jennings Homes	6.3
Central Equity	6.3
Commonwealth Bank of Australia	6.3
Volante Group	6.3
Crane Group	6.2
National Australia Bank	6.2
Coventry Group	5.8
GWA International	5.8
Pacifica	5.8
Foodland	5.7
OrotonGroup	5.7
Adcorp Australia	5.6
Rock Building Society	5.6
Sims Group	5.6
Auspine	5.5
Hills Industries	5.5
Sydney Aquarium	5.5
Australia & New Zealand Banking	5.4
AJ Lucas	5.2
FKP	5.2
Adelaide Bank	5.1
Candle Australia	5.1
Gazal	5.1
Leighton Holdings	5.1
West Australian Newspapers	5.1
Angus & Coote	5.0
Suncorp-Metway	5.0
Cedar Woods Properties	4.9
Iluka Resources	4.9
OAMPS	4.9
Wide Bay Australia	4.9
CSR	4.8
Equigold	4.8
Integrated Group	4.8
McGuigan Simeon Wines	4.8
Monadelphous Group	4.8
Rural Press	4.8
Wesfarmers	4.8
Westpac Banking	4.8
Amcor	4.7
Australian Gas Light	4.7
Campbell Brothers	4.7
National Foods	4.7
Alesco	4.6
Housewares International	4.6
St George Bank	4.6
HGL	4.5
Technology One	4.5
Blackmores	4.4
Danks Holdings	4.4
Fairfax (John) Holdings	4.4
Tasmanian Perpetual Trustees	4.4
Boral	4.3
K & S Corporation	4.3
McPherson's	4.3
Cochlear	4.2
Downer EDI	4.2
Foster's Group	4.2
Bendigo Bank	4.1
GUD	4.1
Portman	4.1
Santos	4.1
STW Communications	4.1
Wadepack	4.1
Bank of Queensland	3.9
Australian Stock Exchange	3.8
Macquarie Bank	3.8
Woolworths	3.8
Cabcharge Australia	3.7
Gunns	3.7
Select Harvests	3.7
Programmed Maintenance Services	3.6
Rebel Sport	3.5
Brazin	3.4
Coates Hire	3.4
QBE Insurance	3.4
Coles Myer	3.3
Great Southern Plantations	3.2
Orica	3.2
Perpetual Trustees	3.2
Publishing & Broadcasting	3.2
United Group	3.2
Flight Centre	3.1
Reece Australia	3.1
Colorado Group	3.0
Institute of Drug Technology	3.0
Primary Health Care	3.0
BHP Billiton	2.8
ARB	2.7
AXA Asia Pacific	2.6
Harvey Norman	2.6
Sigma	2.6
Computershare	2.5
Corporate Express Australia	2.5
Rio Tinto	2.5
Woodside Petroleum	2.5
Brickworks	2.3
Troy Resources	2.3
Fantastic Holdings	2.2
Origin Energy	2.2
Washington H Soul Pattinson	2.2
Timbercorp	2.2
Fleetwood	2.1
Macquarie Goodman Management	2.1
Toll Holdings	2.0
Pacific Hydro	1.7
SDI	1.0

Table O

Year-on-year dividend growth

Most investors hope for a rising dividend, and this table tells how much each company raised (or lowered) its dividend in its latest financial year.

	%
Publishing & Broadcasting	72.0
Rebel Sport	66.7
BHP Billiton	66.6
Rural Press	65.3
Cellnet	64.3
Coffey International	63.0
Corporate Express Australia	62.5
Computershare	60.0
GUD	53.8
Candle Australia	50.0
Harvey Norman	50.0
Wadepack	50.0
Fantastic Holdings	47.1
Tasmanian Perpetual Trustees	44.4
Australian Stock Exchange	42.9
Cedar Woods Properties	42.9
Great Southern Plantations	42.9
Toll Holdings	41.4
Select Harvests	40.5
Flight Centre	40.2
Equigold	40.0
Macquarie Goodman Management	40.0
Primary Health Care	40.0
Timbercorp	40.0
K & S Corporation	37.5
Colorado Group	33.3
Programmed Maintenance Services	33.3
Reece Australia	33.3
Blackmores	31.4
Macquarie Bank	31.2
Boral	30.4
OrotonGroup	30.4
Origin Energy	30.0
Sigma	29.0
Fleetwood	28.6
United Group	28.6
Bank of Queensland	27.6
Alesco	26.9
Fairfax (John) Holdings	26.9
McPherson's	26.7
West Australian Newspapers	26.7
FKP	25.0
Gunns	25.0
Suncorp-Metway	25.0
Sims Group	22.2
Washington H Soul Pattinson	21.4
Auspine	20.6
Brickworks	20.0
Monadelphous Group	20.0
QBE Insurance	20.0
Bendigo Bank	19.4
Adelaide Bank	18.9
ARB	18.8
Commonwealth Bank of Australia	18.8
St George Bank	18.8
Coates Hire	18.2
Orica	18.2
Woodside Petroleum	17.9
OAMPS	17.6
McGuigan Simeon Wines	17.5
Downer EDI	17.2
Institute of Drug Technology	16.7
GWA International	16.1
Perpetual Trustees	15.4
Woolworths	15.4
Cabcharge Australia	14.6
Technology One	14.0
Coventry Group	13.3
SDI	13.3
Foodland	12.9
National Foods	12.8
Australia & New Zealand Banking	11.8
Coles Myer	11.5
Westpac Banking	11.4
Australand	11.3
Angus & Coote	11.1
Integrated Group	11.1
National Australia Bank	10.9
Rock Building Society	10.8
Wesfarmers	10.2
AV Jennings Homes	10.0
Campbell Brothers	10.0
Australian Gas Light	9.1
Troy Resources	9.1
Adcorp Australia	8.3
Plaspak Group	8.3
Pacifica	7.5
STW Communications	7.2
Hills Industries	7.1
Amcor	6.7
ION	6.7
Volante Group	6.3
Wide Bay Australia	6.3
AXA Asia Pacific	5.1
Housewares International	5.0
Sydney Aquarium	3.7
Foster's Group	2.7
Cochlear	2.6
Leighton Holdings	2.3
AJ Lucas	0.0
Central Equity	0.0
Crane Group	0.0
CSR	0.0
Danks Holdings	0.0
Gazal	0.0
Iluka Resources	0.0
Incitec Pivot	0.0
Miller's Retail	0.0
Pacific Hydro	0.0
Portman	0.0
Santos	0.0
Schaffer Corporation	0.0
Rio Tinto	–15.3
HGL	–28.3
Brazin	–40.0

TABLE P

FIVE-YEAR SHARE PRICE RETURN

This table ranks the return to investors from a five-year investment in each of the companies in the book. It is the accumulated return, which means it incorporates not only capital gain but also reinvested dividends, bonus stock and rights issues.

	% pa				
SDI	97.3	Woolworths	24.4	Santos	15.7
Macquarie Goodman Management	72.3	Sims Group	24.1	Rock Building Society	15.6
Gunns	71.4	OrotonGroup	24.0	Macquarie Bank	15.6
Fantastic Holdings	65.4	STW Communications	23.9	Adcorp Australia	15.5
Troy Resources	61.7	Cellnet	23.3	Tasmanian Perpetual Trustees	15.2
OAMPS	60.8	Angus & Coote	23.0	Volante Group	*15.1
Select Harvests	57.7	Auspine	22.7	Woodside Petroleum	14.7
Toll Holdings	57.4	Washington H Soul Pattinson	22.5	Primary Health Care	14.6
GUD	54.6	Alesco	22.4	Australian Stock Exchange	13.9
Colorado Group	*54.3	Coates Hire	21.9	Australian Gas Light	13.9
Schaffer Corporation	52.3	QBE Insurance	21.7	BHP Billiton	13.4
Sigma	*49.7	St George Bank	21.3	Miller's Retail	13.3
Fleetwood	48.2	Orica	20.6	Danks Holdings	13.0
ION	48.0	Perpetual Trustees	20.1	West Australian Newspapers	12.7
Coffey International	48.0	Wide Bay Australia	20.1	Flight Centre	12.2
McPherson's	47.1	AJ Lucas	20.0	GWA International	10.3
AV Jennings Homes	42.6	Gazal	19.6	Rio Tinto	10.2
Equigold	40.7	Foodland	19.5	Publishing & Broadcasting	10.2
K & S Corporation	40.6	Hills Industries	19.5	Iluka Resources	9.9
Portman	35.4	Australia & New Zealand Banking	19.2	Commonwealth Bank of Australia	9.8
Rebel Sport	35.0	Suncorp-Metway	18.8	McGuigan Simeon Wines	9.7
Corporate Express Australia	34.3	Institute of Drug Technology	18.8	Amcor	9.3
Integrated Group	32.8	Downer EDI	18.7	Sydney Aquarium	9.1
ARB	32.6	Bank of Queensland	18.7	Cabcharge Australia	8.5
Housewares International	31.2	Australand	18.5	National Australia Bank	8.4
FKP	30.8	Adelaide Bank	17.8	Crane Group	8.3
Pacific Hydro	29.5	Westpac Banking	17.6	Coles Myer	7.4
Reece Australia	28.8	Great Southern Plantations	17.5	Central Equity	7.2
Origin Energy	*28.2	Coventry Group	17.3	Cochlear	6.9
Cedar Woods Properties	27.6	Campbell Brothers	17.3	Foster's Group	5.1
Brickworks	27.3	National Foods	17.0	Fairfax (John) Holdings	2.3
Wadepack	26.8	AXA Asia Pacific	16.8	Timbercorp	1.8
Blackmores	26.7	Leighton Holdings	16.6	Adcorp Australia	1.15
United Group	26.0	Rural Press	16.3	Harvey Norman	1.1
Wesfarmers	25.8	Programmed Maintenance Services	16.3	Computershare	–2.7
Plaspak Group	25.1	HGL	16.3	Technology One	*–4.1
CSR	24.7	Bendigo Bank	16.1	Pacifica	–6.1
Boral	24.7			Brazin	–6.6
Monadelphous Group	24.5			Candle Australia	–6.7

*3-year share price return

TABLE Q

NON-INTEREST INCOME TO TOTAL INCOME

The final three tables rank the banks only. Most of the banks are working to diversify away from their traditional lending business into other operations, such as insurance and funds management. This table ranks them according to their success, showing how much of their income derives from non-interest sources.

	%
Macquarie Bank	89.0
Suncorp-Metway	85.7
Rock Building Society	67.2
Commonwealth Bank of Australia	48.4
National Australia Bank	42.4
Westpac Banking	40.7
Australia & New Zealand Banking	38.5
St George Bank	38.5
Bendigo Bank	38.3
Bank of Queensland	38.1
Wide Bay Australia	28.1
Adelaide Bank	7.9

TABLE R

COST-TO-INCOME RATIO

All the banks are working to reduce their high costs. The cost-to-income ratio — expressing costs as a percentage of operating income — is one of the measures commonly used by analysts to ascertain their success

	%
Australia & New Zealand Banking	46.0
St George Bank	49.6
National Australia Bank	51.4
Westpac Banking	53.6
Adelaide Bank	56.6
Commonwealth Bank of Australia	59.6
Wide Bay Australia	62.7
Bank of Queensland	64.9
Rock Building Society	68.4
Bendigo Bank	68.6
Macquarie Bank	72.2
Suncorp-Metway	76.5

Table S

Return on assets

Banks have large assets, and the return on assets ratio — profits as a percentage of total assets — is another popular measure of their efficiency.

	%
Suncorp-Metway	1.5
Macquarie Bank	1.3
Australia & New Zealand Banking	1.2
Wide Bay Australia	1.2
St George Bank	1.1
Westpac Banking	1.1
National Australia Bank	1.0
Commonwealth Bank of Australia	0.9
Rock Building Society	0.9
Adelaide Bank	0.7
Bank of Queensland	0.7
Bendigo Bank	0.7

APPENDIX: TOP OF THE STOCKS

One of the main aims of this book has always been to make stock selection more manageable for investors. Despite this being the biggest *Top Stocks* edition over the 11 editions of its lifetime in print, it still manages to focus the readers' attention on approximately 7.5% of the companies listed on the Australian Stock Exchange. Even such a small percentage equates to 115 stocks — too many for an efficient portfolio.

One way to distill the selection further would be to consider the 37 companies that have been in the book for five consecutive years. But let's narrow the list down further. Which are the real top stocks, those superior companies that keep boosting shareholder value with strongly-growing profits, year after year?

One of the best measures of a company's success is its return on equity (ROE) figure. This ratio — the after-tax profit as a percentage of shareholders' equity — is in effect the amount that the company made for you, the shareholder, on your money. And though actual profit growth is important, for the shareholder it is often earnings-per-share (EPS) expansion that is more important.

Thus, find a company with a high ROE figure, and with fast-growing EPS, and you have possibly found a growth stock, one whose share price has probably enjoyed excellent appreciation.

Few companies manage to achieve a ROE of 20% and annual EPS growth of 20%. Fewer still do it over five years.

Here are those select few, from companies listed in *Top Stocks* for five years or longer:

	Five-year average ROE (%)	Five-year compounded annual average EPS growth rate (%)
ARB Corporation	27.1	22.0
Flight Centre	32.7	20.0
Perpetual Trustees	22.9	24.1
Reece Australia	21.8	25.4
Woolworths	32.1	21.4

Looking at the Top Five many market myths are dispelled. The Woolworths' powerhouse only marginally out-performed the small Melbourne automotive accessories company, ARB, proving that size isn't everything. Who would have thought that Flight Centre's results would be so strong at a time when terrorism has so badly affected tourism worldwide?

Even regular 15% growth is highly commendable. Here are five more companies from *Top Stocks 2005*, those that have achieved an average ROE of more than 15% over five years, and average EPS growth during that period of at least 15%.

	Five-year average ROE (%)	Five-year compounded annual average EPS growth rate (%)
ANZ	18.5	15.0
Blackmores	30.3	17.7
Cochlear	55.6	16.1
Select Harvests	19.0	24.6
Wesfarmers	16.5	17.0

Most investors know that the big banks have been among the strongest performers in the market over the past decade, so it is little surprise to find one of them among the 'Second Five' top stocks of the past five year. But how many investors would have expected it to be out-performed by a company such as Select Harvests, Australia's largest almond grower?

Cochlear and Wesfarmers are widely acknowledged among investors for their superior stock market achievements, and are regularly written up in the financial media. But not nearly as many people are aware that the natural health care products manufacturer Blackmores has also performed extremely strongly. Its success has had far less coverage in the financial media.

Top Stocks is a book for investors wishing to do their own research into the markets, and not be reliant on the mainstream media. And one of its features is the way in which it regularly places a spotlight not only on the well-known stocks that are consistently featured in the press but also on strongly growing, but lesser known, companies. Often these are companies that have either just expanded sufficiently to be among the 500 largest, or which have been publicly listed only for the minimum five years required for inclusion in the book.

Thus, Perpetual Trustees and Blackmores have been in every edition of the book since *Top Stocks '97*, ARB has been in every edition since *Top Stocks '99* and Select Harvests has been in every edition since *Top Stocks 2000*. A reminder, though: past performance is no indication of future earnings or growth. Stock selection should be based on an investor's individual circumstances.